ECODEFENSE:

A Field Guide to

Monkeywrenching

Second Edition

**Edited by Dave Foreman
and Bill Haywood**

Forward! by Edward Abbey

A NED LUDD BOOK
Tucson, Arizona
1987

Published by Ned Ludd Books
POB 5871, Tucson, AZ 85703
Printed by Ed's Printing, Chico, California
Typesetting by Typografx, Chico, California
Printed on recycled paper

ISBN 0-933285-03-5

STANDARD DISCLAIMER

ECODEFENSE: A Field Guide To Monkeywrenching is for entertainment purposes only. No one involved with the production of this book — the editors, contributors, artists, printers, or anyone — encourages anyone to do any of the stupid, illegal things contained herein.

*This book is dedicated to the Fox,
the Tucson Ecoraiders,
the Bolt Weevils,
the Hardesty Mountain Avengers,
the Bonnie Abbzug Feminist Garden Club,
Barmaids for Howie,
and all of their ilk.*

*Special dedication to
"Mr. Goodwrench"
John Zaelit
1954 - 1986*

RAID AT COMB WASH
by Roger Candee

Wilderness needs no defense,
only more defenders.

CONTENTS

ECODEFENSE:
A Field Guide to
Monkeywrenching

Second Edition

INTRODUCTION TO THE FIRST EDITION

Many people have helped with the production of **ECODEFENSE: A Field Guide to Monkeywrenching.** For obvious reasons, however, their contributions can not be individually acknowledged. Nevertheless, they deserve the thanks and appreciation of all lovers of the wild. To the authors, artists, reviewers and others who have helped in the production of this book, let me offer my thanks, admiration, and comradeship. I particularly appreciate the help and support in this project from Leon Czolgosz, Mike Roselle, and Nancy Morton. I also owe a deep debt to Edward Abbey who inspired this book.

ECODEFENSE is an ongoing project. We hope to publish an updated edition every twelve to eighteen months. Techniques will be refined and updated, new techniques will be included, additional Field Notes will be printed. Your help in this updating process is essential. It is through field experience that the techniques of monkeywrenching can be made safer and more effective. Because direct communication among monkeywrenchers is dangerous, this book and its future editions, as well as the *Earth First! Journal*, is probably the best medium for communication among ecodefenders. It is your book, your forum, to discuss the techniques and philosophy of wilderness self-defense.

Even communication through **ECODEFENSE** could be dangerous, though. In writing to us, do not use your real name or put a return address on your missive. We do not need to know who you are. After taking the information from your letter, we will burn both the letter and the envelope. Similarly, no record will be kept of orders for copies of **ECODEFENSE** in case a group of "plumbers" decides to take a midnight stroll through our file cabinet. By the way, two good friends — Mr. Smith and Mr. Wesson — are our security agents.

There is some redundancy in the following pages — primarily concerning matters of security and safety. This redundancy is deliberate. It is for your benefit. *Be careful.* Do not take chances with your safety or that of others, or with your security. Read and re-read the tips on safety and security. Be rigorous about following such precautions — even to the point of constipation.

Of course, this book is for entertainment purposes only. No one involved with this project in any form encourages anyone to do any of the things described herein. We are all fat and out-of-shape (and would rather drink beer and watch TV at home than go out in the nasty, old outdoors). We're just hoping to make a buck with this book.

— *Dave Foreman*
January, 1985
Canada del Oro, Arizona

INTRODUCTION TO THE SECOND EDITION

In the eighteen months since its publication, **ECODEFENSE: A Field Guide to Monkeywrenching** has made a bit of a splash. It has been reviewed or discussed in dozens of publications including *The Wall Street Journal* and *US News & World Report*, and was the focus of a five minute report on the NBC Nightly News. The terms "monkeywrenching," "ecodefense," and "ecotage" have been introduced into the general language. 5000 copies of the book have been sold in less than a year and a half. Sales have been made in all fifty states and in several dozen countries.

The United States Forest Service, other agencies, and corporations have unleashed a terrified outcry against both the book and the practice. Forest Service offices in Oregon have offered rewards of $5000 for information leading to the arrest and conviction of tree spikers. One member of Congress has lashed out against monkeywrenching and I have had the pleasure of debating him on NBC's Today Show. The Willamette National Forest in Oregon produced a twelve page "white paper" which quoted heavily from **ECODEFENSE** and denounced the practice of monkeywrenching. Former Secretary of the Interior Cecil Andrus accused me of "destroying the environmental movement to sell a few books and make money" at a debate in Jackson, Wyoming, and Jay Hair, head of the National Wildlife Federation, has been quoted in newspapers as calling me a "terrorist." I've even been denounced on the floor of Parliament in New South Wales.

Monkeywrenching has become a common, if not frequent, practice against the destruction of the wild and the spread of urban cancer. There have been tree spiking incidents in National Forests in all of the western states and in several eastern states. In some cases the Forest Service has gone to great expense to remove spikes from trees so timber sales could proceed; in other cases, timber sales have been quietly withdrawn. Tree spiking incidents have also occurred in Canada and Australia.

What all of this indicates is that monkeywrenching can be an effective means of protecting wild country from the depredations of industrialism gone berserk. But monkeywrenching must also be rigorously and strategically executed or it may be counterproductive, or dangerous to the perpetrator. Several examples should suffice as a warning to the wise:

Howie Wolke, a guide and outfitter from Jackson, Wyoming, received the maximum sentence, six months, for pulling up survey stakes along a proposed gas exploration road in an important roadless area and elk habitat on the Bridger-Teton National Forest. The sentencing Justice of the Peace admitted to having been under strong political pressure from the oil industry to throw the book at Wolke. Howie spent six months in a cramped cell in Pinedale, Wyoming, growing fat on prison hot dogs and white bread, cut off from fresh air and exercise because he was careless.

Two young men were talked into a poorly-considered billboarding caper in Corvallis, Oregon, by an attractive writer for a national magazine. They were caught. Both pulled several weeks apiece in the slammer and paid thousands of dollars in restitution. The reporter got her story, and her magazine's lawyers got her out of trouble with the law.

The United States Forest Service has received authorization and funds from Congress to hire 500 law enforcement specialists ostensibly to combat marijuana growing on the National Forests, but we can be sure that they will be on the lookout for monkeywrenchers, too. These Freddie coppers will be concentrated in the Pacific Northwest where tree spiking has been especially rife. They will doubtlessly be outfitted with sophisticated surveillance equipment including night vision devices, and will likely be in better physical condition and perhaps more woods-wise than the standard lardass Freddie law enforcement specialist.

Just last week, FBI agents appeared at my home in Tucson to question one of my housemates, Roger Featherstone, about last spring's sabotage of the high voltage lines leading from the Palo Verde Nuclear Power Plant in Arizona.

All of this, of course, means that the empire is striking back. Monkeywrenchers are effective. They are hitting the exploiters where it hurts — in the pocketbook. In an era when lobbyists for conservation groups can't even prevent Congress from *increasing* the already bloated Forest Service road-building budget (which is specially targeted at roadless areas), monkeywrenching may be the most effective tool at the disposal of wilderness lovers. But security, now more than ever, must be of prime importance. Carefully study the **Security** chapter of this book before you do anything — even something as seemingly innocuous as pulling up survey stakes. Remember Howie Wolke.

The Second Edition of ECODEFENSE represents a major revision and expansion of the first edition. Nearly every chapter of the book has been updated and expanded. Particular attention has been given to the tree spiking, overgrazing, surveying, trapping, and security sections. New material has been added for mining, computer, and urban ecotage. The greatest expansion, however, has been made in the chapter on heavy equipment. Even mechanical idiots should be able to take on a bulldozer with this new material. Many additional illustrations have been used to improve the value of the text. Good as the first edition was, we believe this second edition is a significant improvement.

Looking back over the practice of monkeywrenching, I would offer the following advice to make our defense of the wild even more effective:

1) More attention should be given to destroying roads and using "road spikes" to flatten tires.

2) In tree spiking, clipping the heads off spikes will make them considerably more difficult for the Forest Service to remove — even more so if they are the "helix" type of spike. (Several timber sales have been dropped because spike heads were clipped off and the Freddies couldn't remove them.)

3) Tree spiking is not the only tool to use against logging. Road spiking and destruction, and decommissioning of heavy equipment and trucks deserve to be more widely employed than heretofore.

4) Read, study, memorize and faithfully observe the section on **Security** in this book. It will keep you out of jail unless your luck is just plain bad.

5) Finally — go out and *do* something. Pay your rent for the privilege of living on this beautiful, blue-green, living Earth. Monkeywrenching will succeed as a strategic defense of the wild only if it is enthusiastically and joyously undertaken by many individuals in many places.

Again, many people have helped with the production of the second edition of **ECODEFENSE**. This book would not have been possible without the numerous Earth defenders who have experimented with the techniques described in the first edition and have sent in their suggestions for improvement. (We, of course, welcome suggestions for the third edition!) We are particularly indebted to T.O. Hellenbach who has done as much as anyone, including your editors, to contribute to this book.

Please note that Bill Haywood is listed as the co-editor of this second edition of **ECODEFENSE**. This book would simply not have been possible without his careful work in evaluating new ideas, editing and rewriting much of the text sent in, and generally helping to carry the entire project along. I am proud to share credit with Bill for this edition. Thanks to John Davis whose editorial skills straightened out some convoluted sentences in the draft, and whose conscientious love of the wilderness is a continuing inspiration to all of us who work with him. Finally, I owe a special thank-you to my wife, Nancy Morton, for her support and constructive criticism of all that I do, as well as for many fine days in the wilderness.

Of course, all the above highfalutin' strategy is merely in the abstract. This book is for entertainment purposes only. Cecil Andrus is entirely correct. I'm only trying to make a buck with this book and I don't care if I destroy the environmental movement in the process. I'm only in it for myself, and for the wine, women, and song that goes along with it. What's on the teevee tonight?

Happy Trails

— *Dave Foreman*
November, 1986
Sierra Tucson, Sonoran Desert

FORWARD!

by Edward Abbey

If a stranger batters your door down with an axe, threatens your family and yourself with deadly weapons, and proceeds to loot your home of whatever he wants, he is committing what is universally recognized — by law and morality — as a crime. In such a situation the householder has both the right and the obligation to defend himself, his family, and his property by whatever means are necessary. This right and this obligation is universally recognized, justified and even praised by all civilized human communities. Self-defense against attack is one of the basic laws not only of human society but of life itself, not only of human life but of all life.

The American wilderness, what little remains, is now undergoing exactly such an assault. Dave Foreman has summarized the character and scale of the assault in the first chapter of this excellent and essential book. With bulldozer, earth mover, chainsaw and dynamite the international timber, mining and beef industries are invading our public lands — property of all Americans — bashing their way into our forests, mountains and rangelands and looting them for everything they can get away with. This for the sake of short-term profits in the corporate sector and multi-million dollar annual salaries for the three-piece-suited gangsters (M.B.A., Harvard, Yale, University of Tokyo, *et alia*) who control and manage these bandit enterprises. Cheered on, naturally, by *Time, Newsweek* and the *Wall Street Journal*, actively encouraged by those jellyfish Government agencies which are supposed to protect the public lands, and as always aided and abetted in every way possible by the quisling politicians of our Western states (such as Babbitt, DeConcini, Goldwater, Hatch, Garn, Symms, Hansen, Wallop, Domenici — to name but a few) who would sell the graves of their own mothers if there's a quick buck in the deal, over or under the table, what do they care.

Representative democracy in the United States has broken down. Our legislators do not represent those who elected them but rather the minority who finance their political campaigns and who control the organs of communication — the Tee Vee, the newspapers, the billboards, the radio — that have made politics a game for the rich only. Representative government in the USA represents money not people and therefore has forfeited our allegiance and moral support. We owe it nothing but the taxation it extorts from us under threats of seizure of property, or prison, or in some cases already, when resisted, a sudden and violent death by gunfire.

Such is the nature and structure of the industrial megamachine (in Lewis Mumford's term) which is now attacking the American wilderness. That wilderness is our ancestral home, the primordial homeland of all living creatures including the human, and the present final dwelling place of such noble beings as the grizzly bear, the mountain lion, the eagle and the condor, the moose and the elk and the pronghorn antelope, the redwood tree, the yellowpine, the bristlecone pine, even the aspen, and yes, why not say it?, the streams, waterfalls, rivers, the very bedrock itself of our hills, canyons, deserts, mountains.

For many of us, perhaps for most of us, the wilderness is as much our home, or a lot more so, than the wretched little stucco boxes, plywood apartments, and wallboard condominiums in which we are mostly confined by the insatiable demands of an overcrowded and ever-expanding industrial culture. And if the wilderness is our true home, and if it is threatened with invasion, pillage and destruction — as it certainly is — then we have the right to defend that home, as we would our private rooms, by whatever means are necessary. (An Englishman's home is his castle; an American's home is his favorite fishing stream, his favorite mountain range, his favorite desert canyon, his favorite swamp or patch of woods or God-created lake.)

The majority of the American people have demonstrated on every possible occasion that they support the ideal of wilderness preservation; even our politicians are forced by popular opinion to *pretend* to support the idea; as they have learned, a vote against wilderness is a vote against their own re-election. We are justified in defending our homes — our private home and public home — not only by common law and common morality but also by common belief. We are the majority; they — the greedy and powerful — are the minority.

How best defend our wilderness home? Well, that is a matter of strategy, tactics and technique, which is what this little book is about. Dave Foreman explains the principles of ecological defense in the complete, compact, and conclusive pages of his chapter on strategy. I can think of nothing I could add nor of anything I would subtract; he says exactly what needs to be said, no more and no less.

I am happy to endorse the publication of **Ecodefense**. Never was such a book so needed, by so many, for such good reason, as here and now. Tomorrow might well be too late. This is a book that will fit handily in any saddlebag, in any creel, in any backpack, in any river runner's ammo can — and in any picnicker's picnic basket. No good American should ever go into the woods again without this book and, for example, a hammer and a few pounds of 60-penny nails. Spike a few trees now and then whenever you enter an area condemned to chainsaw massacre by Louisiana Pacific and its affiliated subsidiary the U.S. Forest Service. You won't hurt the trees; they'll be grateful for the protection; and you may save the forest. My Aunt Emma back in West Virginia has been enjoying this pleasant exercise for years. She swears by it. It's good for the trees, it's good for the woods, it's good for the earth, and it's good for the human soul. Spread the word — and **carry on!**

Edward Abbey
July 1984
Oracle, Arizona

CHAPTER 1

STRATEGIC
MONKEYWRENCHING

By Dave Foreman

In early summer of 1977, the United States Forest Service began an 18 month-long inventory and evaluation of the remaining roadless and undeveloped areas on the National Forests and Grasslands of the United States. During this second Roadless Area Review and Evaluation (RARE II), the Forest Service identified 2,686 roadless areas of 5,000 acres or more totaling 66 million acres out of the 187 million acres of National Forest lands. Approximately 15 million acres of roadless areas were not included in RARE II because of sloppy inventory procedures or because they had already gone through land use planning after the first RARE program in the early '70s. All in all, there were some 80 million acres on the National Forests in 1977 retaining a significant degree of natural diversity and wildness (a total area equivalent in size to the state of New Mexico or a square 350 x 350 miles).

About the same time as the Forest Service began RARE II, the Bureau of Land Management (BLM) initiated a wilderness inventory as required by the Federal Land Planning and Management Act of 1976 (FLPMA) on the 189 million acres of federal land that they manage in the lower 48 states. In their initial inventory, BLM identified 60 million acres of roadless areas of 5,000 acres or more (a total area approximately the size of Oregon or a square 300 x 300 miles).

Along with the National Parks & Monuments, National Wildlife Refuges, existing Wilderness Areas and some state lands, these Forest Service and BLM roadless areas represent the remaining natural wealth of the United States. They are the remnant of natural diversity after the industrial conquest of the most beautiful, diverse and productive of all the continents of the Earth: North America. Turtle Island.

Only one hundred and fifty years ago, the Great Plains were a vast, waving sea of grass stretching from the Chihuahuan Desert of Mexico to the boreal forest of Canada, from the oak-hickory forests of the Ozarks to the Rocky Mountains. Bison blanketed the plains — it has been estimated that 60 million of the huge, shaggy beasts moved across the grass. Great herds of pronghorn and elk also filled this Pleistocene landscape. Packs of wolves and numerous grizzly bears followed the immense herds.

One hundred and fifty years ago, John James Audubon estimated that there were several *billion* birds in a flock of passenger pigeons that flew past him for several days on the Ohio River. It has been said that a squirrel could travel from the Atlantic seaboard to the Mississippi River without touching the ground, so dense was the deciduous forest of the East.

At the time of the Lewis and Clark Expedition, an estimated 100,000 grizzlies roamed the western half of what is now the United States. The howl of the wolf was ubiquitous. The condor dominated the sky from the Pacific Coast to the Great Plains. Salmon and sturgeon filled the rivers. Ocelots, jaguars, margay cats and jaguarundis roamed the Texas brush and Southwestern deserts and mesas. Bighorn sheep in great numbers ranged the mountains of the Rockies, Great Basin, Southwest and Pacific Coast. Ivory-billed woodpeckers and Carolina parakeets filled the steamy forests of the Deep South. The land was alive.

East of the Mississippi, giant tulip poplars, chestnuts, oaks, hickories and other trees formed the most diverse temperate deciduous forest in the world. On the Pacific Coast, redwood, hemlock, Douglas fir, spruce, cedar, fir and pine formed the grandest forest on Earth.

In the space of a few generations we have laid waste to paradise. The tall grass prairie has been transformed into a corn factory where wildlife means the exotic pheasant. The short grass prairie is a grid of carefully fenced cow pastures and wheat fields. The passenger pigeon is no more. The last died in the Cincinnati Zoo in 1914. The endless forests of the East are tame woodlots. The only virgin deciduous forest there is in tiny museum pieces of hundreds of acres. Six hundred grizzlies remain and they are going fast. There are only three condors left in the wild and they are scheduled for capture and imprisonment in the Los Angeles Zoo. Except in northern Minnesota and Isle Royale, wolves are known merely as scattered individuals drifting across the Canadian and Mexican borders (a pack has recently formed in Glacier National Park). Four percent of the peerless Redwood Forest remains and the monumental old growth forest cathedrals of Oregon are all but gone. The tropical cats have been shot and poisoned from our southwestern borderlands. The subtropical Eden of Florida has been transformed into hotels and citrus orchards. Domestic cattle have grazed bare and radically altered the composition of the grassland communities of the West, displacing elk, moose, bighorn sheep and pronghorn and leading to the virtual extermination of grizzly, wolf, cougar, bobcat and other "varmints." Dams choke the rivers and streams of the land.

Nonetheless, wildness and natural diversity remain. There are a few scattered grasslands ungrazed, stretches of free-flowing river undammed and undiverted, thousand-year-old forests, Eastern woodlands growing back to forest and reclaiming past roads, grizzlies and wolves and lions and wolverines and bighorn and moose roaming the backcountry; hundreds of square miles that have never known the imprint of a tire, the bite of a drill, the rip of a 'dozer, the cut of a saw, the smell of gasoline.

These are the places that hold North America together, that contain the genetic information of life, that represent sanity in a whirlwind of madness.

In January of 1979, the Forest Service announced the results of RARE II: of the 80 million acres of undeveloped lands on the National Forests, only 15 million acres were recommended for protection against logging, road building and other "developments." In the big tree state of Oregon, for example, only 370,000 acres were proposed for Wilderness protection out of 4.5 million acres of roadless, uncut forest lands. Of the areas nationally slated for protection, most were too high, too dry, too cold, too steep to offer much in the way of "resources" to the loggers, miners and graziers. Those roadless areas with critical old growth forest values were allocated for the sawmill. Important grizzly habitat in the Northern Rockies was tossed to the oil industry and the loggers. Off-road-vehicle fanatics and the landed gentry of the livestock industry won out in the Southwest and Great Basin.

During the early 1980s, the Forest Service developed its DARN (Development Activities in Roadless Non-selected) list outlining specific projects in specific roadless areas. The implication of DARN is staggering. It is evidence that the leadership of the United States Forest Service consciously and deliberately sat down and asked themselves, "How can we keep from being plagued by conservationists and their damned wilderness proposals? How can we insure that we'll never have to do another RARE?" Their solution was simple and brilliant: get rid of the roadless areas. DARN outlines **nine thousand** miles of road, one and a half million acres of timber cuts, seven million acres of oil and gas leases in National Forest RARE II areas by 1987. In most cases, the damaged acreage will be far greater than the acreage stated because roads are designed to split areas in half and timber sales are engineered to take place in the center of roadless areas, thereby devastating the biological integrity of the entire area. The great roadless areas so critical to the maintenance of natural diversity will soon be gone. Species dependent upon old growth and large wild areas will be shoved to the brink of extinction.

But the situation on the National Forests is even worse than DARN indicated. After a careful review of Forest Service documents, Howie Wolke reported in the June 21, 1985, issue of *Earth First!* that more than 75,000 miles of road are proposed for construction in currently roadless areas on the National Forests over the next fifteen years. This immense road network (enough to encircle the planet three times) will cost the American taxpayer over 3 billion dollars to provide large timber corporations access to a mere 500 million dollars worth of timber.

The BLM wilderness review has been a similar process of attrition. It is unlikely that more than 9 million acres will be recommended for Wilderness out of the 60 million with which the review began. Again, it is the more spectacular but biologically less rich areas that will be proposed for protection.

During 1984, Congress passed legislation designating minimal National Forest Wilderness acreages for most states (generally only slightly larger than the pitiful RARE II recommendations and concentrating on "rocks and ice" instead of crucial forested lands). In the next few years, similar picayune legislation for National Forest Wilderness in the remaining states and for BLM Wilderness will probably be enacted. The other roadless areas will be eliminated from consideration. National Forest Management Plans emphasizing industrial logging, grazing, mineral and energy development, road building, and motorized recreation will be implemented. Conventional means of protecting these millions of acres of wild country will largely dissipate. Judicial and administrative appeals for their protection will be closed off. Congress will turn a deaf ear to requests for additional Wildernesses so soon after disposing of the thorny issue. The effectiveness of conventional political lobbying by conservation groups to protect endangered wild lands will evaporate. And in half a decade, the saw, 'dozer and drill will devastate most of what is unprotected. The battle for wilderness will be over. Perhaps 3% of the United States will be more or less protected and it will be open season on the rest. Unless . . . .

Many of the projects that will destroy roadless areas are economically marginal. It is costly for the Forest Service, BLM, timber companies, oil companies, mining companies and others to scratch out the "resources" in these last wild areas. It is expensive to maintain the necessary infrastructure of roads for the exploitation of wild lands. The cost of repairs, the hassle, the delay, the down-time may just be too much for the bureaucrats and exploiters to accept if there is a widely-dispersed, unorganized, *strategic* movement of resistance across the land.

It is time for women and men, individually and in small groups, to act heroically and admittedly illegally in defense of the wild, to put a monkeywrench into the gears of the machine destroying natural diversity. This strategic monkeywrenching can be safe, it can be easy, it can be fun, and — most importantly — it can be effective in stopping timber cutting, road building, overgrazing, oil & gas exploration, mining, dam building, powerline construction, off-road-vehicle use, trapping, ski area development and other forms of destruction of the wilderness, as well as cancerous suburban sprawl.

But it must be strategic, it must be thoughtful, it must be deliberate in order to succeed. Such a campaign of resistance would follow these principles:

* MONKEYWRENCHING IS NON-VIOLENT

Monkeywrenching is non-violent resistance to the destruction of natural diversity and wilderness. It is not directed toward harming human beings or other forms of life. It is aimed at inanimate machines and tools. Care is always taken to minimize any possible threat to other people (and to the monkeywrenchers themselves).

* MONKEYWRENCHING IS NOT ORGANIZED

There can be no central direction or organization to monkeywrenching. Any type of network would invite infiltration, *agents provocateurs* and repression. It is truly individual action. Because of this, communication among monkeywrenchers is difficult and dangerous. Anonymous discussion through this book and its future editions, and through the Dear Ned Ludd section of the *Earth First! Journal*, seems to be the safest avenue of communication to refine techniques, security procedures and strategy.

* MONKEYWRENCHING IS INDIVIDUAL

Monkeywrenching is done by individuals or very small groups of people who have known each other for years. There is trust and a good working relationship in such groups. The more people involved, the greater are the dangers of infiltration or a loose mouth. Earth defenders avoid working with people they haven't known for a long time, those who can't keep their mouths closed, and those with grandiose or violent ideas (they may be police agents or dangerous crackpots).

* MONKEYWRENCHING IS TARGETED

Ecodefenders pick their targets. Mindless, erratic vandalism is counterproductive. Monkeywrenchers know that they do not stop a specific logging sale by destroying any piece of logging equipment which they come across. They make sure it belongs to the proper culprit. They ask themselves what is the most vulnerable point of a wilderness-destroying project and strike there. Senseless vandalism leads to loss of popular sympathy.

* MONKEYWRENCHING IS TIMELY

There is a proper time and place for monkeywrenching. There are also times when monkeywrenching may be counterproductive. Monkeywrenchers generally should not act when there is a non-violent civil disobedience action (a blockade, etc.) taking place against the opposed project. Monkeywrenching may cloud the issue of direct action and the blockaders could be blamed for the ecotage and be put in danger from the work crew or police. Blockades and monkeywrenching usually do not mix. Monkeywrenching may also not be appropriate when delicate political negotiations are taking place for the protection of a certain area. There are, of course, exceptions to this rule. The Earth warrior always thinks: Will monkeywrenching help or hinder the protection of this place?

* MONKEYWRENCHING IS DISPERSED

Monkeywrenching is a wide-spread movement across the United States. Government agencies and wilderness despoilers from Maine to Hawaii know that their destruction of natural diversity may be met with resistance. Nation-wide monkeywrenching is what will hasten over-all industrial retreat from wild areas.

* MONKEYWRENCHING IS DIVERSE

All kinds of people in all kinds of situations can be monkeywrenchers. Some pick a large area of wild country, declare it wilderness in their own minds, and resist any intrusion against it. Others specialize against logging or ORV's in a variety of areas. Certain monkeywrenchers may target a specific project, such as a giant powerline, construction of a road, or an oil operation. Some operate in their backyards, others lie low at home and plan their ecotage a thousand miles away. Some are loners, others operate in small groups.

* MONKEYWRENCHING IS FUN

Although it is serious and potentially dangerous activity, monkey-wrenching is also fun. There is a rush of excitement, a sense of ac-complishment, and unparalleled camaraderie from creeping about in the night resisting those "alien forces from Houston, Tokyo, Washington, DC, and the Pentagon." As Ed Abbey says, "Enjoy, shipmates, enjoy."

* MONKEYWRENCHING IS NOT REVOLUTIONARY

It does *not* aim to overthrow any social, political or economic system. It is merely non-violent self-defense of the wild. It is aimed at keeping industrial "civilization" out of natural areas and causing its retreat from areas that should be wild. It is not major industrial sabotage. Explosives, firearms and other dangerous tools are usually avoided. They invite greater scrutiny from law enforcement agencies, repression and loss of public support. (The Direct Action group in Canada is a good example of what monkeywrenching is *not*.) Even Republicans monkeywrench.

* MONKEYWRENCHING IS SIMPLE

The simplest possible tool is used. The safest tactic is employed. Except when necessary, elaborate commando operations are avoided. The most effective means for stopping the destruction of the wild are generally the simplest: spiking trees and spiking roads. There are obvi-ously times when more detailed and complicated operations are called for. But the monkeywrencher thinks: What is the simplest way to do this?

* MONKEYWRENCHING IS DELIBERATE AND ETHICAL

Monkeywrenching is not something to do cavalierly. Monkeywrenchers are very conscious of the gravity of what they do. They are deliberate about taking such a serious step. They are thoughtful. Monkeywrenchers — although non-violent — are warriors. They are exposing themselves to possible arrest or injury. It is not a casual or flippant affair. They keep a pure heart and mind about it. They remember that they are engaged in the most moral of all actions: protecting life, defending the Earth.

A movement based on these principles could protect millions of acres of wilderness more stringently than any Congressional act, could insure the propagation of the grizzly and other threatened life forms better than an army of game wardens, and could lead to the retreat of industrial civilization from large areas of forest, mountain, desert, plain, seashore, swamp, tundra and woodland that are better suited to the maintenance of natural diversity than to the production of raw materials for overconsumptive technological human society.

If loggers know that a timber sale is spiked, they won't bid on the timber. If a Forest Supervisor knows that a road will be continually destroyed, he won't try to build it. If seismographers know that they will be constantly harassed in an area, they'll go elsewhere. If ORVers know that they'll get flat tires miles from nowhere, they won't drive in such areas.

John Muir said that if it ever came to a war between the races, he would side with the bears. That day has arrived.

CHAPTER 2

THE FUTURE OF MONKEYWRENCHING

By T.O. Hellenbach

In an era of international tensions over bombings, shootings and acts of mass destruction, the word "terrorism" is a guaranteed headline-grabber and a simplistic brand for anyone's political opposition. Recently, Democratic Representative Pat Williams of Montana used this number one media buzzword to condemn Earth First!, announcing his refusal to consider any EF! wilderness proposals while tree spiking continues.

His sense of moral outrage was shared by another public official, Thomas Hutchinson, governor of Massachusetts colony. The indignant governor refused to negotiate with radical colonists whom he associated with numerous attacks on public and private property. Rebels had attacked his home and trashed the offices of the vice-admiralty courts and the Comptroller of Customs, smashing windows and burning records. For turning a deaf ear, Hutchinson received a harbor full of tea in what came to be known as the "Boston Tea Party." No isolated incident, the destruction of what, in today's economy, would be over a hundred thousand dollars worth of private property was followed three months later by another successful nighttime raid on a tea ship at dock. Elsewhere in the area, citizens put the monkeywrench to the construction of British fortifications by sinking barges loaded with bricks, tipping over supply wagons and burning hay intended for use as soldier's bedding.

The Tories of yesteryear lacked only the word "terrorism" with which to brand the women and men who created the United States of America. One of those founding radicals, Thomas Jefferson, warned that "strict observance of the written law is doubtless one of the highest duties of a good citizen, but it is not the highest." He further wrote, "To lose our country by a scrupulous adherence to written law would be to lose the law itself."

Last century, the institution of slavery was only brought down by prolonged and determined protest that, at its core, was lawless and destructive of property. Slaves used work slowdowns and feigned illness to hurt cotton production. Costly supervision was necessary to prevent deliberate trampling of crops and breaking of tools. At night, cotton fields, barns and gins were burned. Runaway slaves formed guerrilla bands with poor whites and dispossessed Indians, staging swift raids against plantations.

Even the work of white abolitionists, encouraging runaways and funneling them to safety through the "underground railroad," was destructive of the private economic concerns of those who saw the slave as just another exploitable resource. As with the former British colonial government, the sluggish minds of men in government failed to acknowledge the changing times, and another war was needed to resolve the issues.

To the west, the invasion of sacred lands was rarely welcomed by the native tribes of America. Survey markers and telegraph poles were favorite, and vulnerable, targets of sabotage. The railroad was attacked by Indians who unbolted the rails, or constructed barriers of stacked ties secured to the rails with freshly cut telegraph wire.

Even the peaceful Hopi were not spared the meddling of industrial society. In 1891 came a plan to move them out of their clustered mesa-top villages and onto single-family plots of private land. After survey markers were destroyed, government troops were dispatched to arrest the leaders responsible. Faced with a roadblock of warriors armed with bows and arrows, the cavalry officer in charge lured out a Hopi delegation to talk terms. The Indians were seized and marched forward as a human shield. Soldiers occupied the village, and native religious leaders made the first of many trips into imprisonment.

Elsewhere in the West, the introduction of barbed wire in the 1880s saw cattlemen attempt to dominate the formerly public grasslands. Fence cutting wars resulted, with small ranchers and farmers forming secret societies with names like the "Owls," the "Javelinas," and the "Blue Devils." Their spies passed information about new fencing at nighttime meetings protected by the use of secret passwords. Sometimes a damaged fence was posted with signs warning against rebuilding. Estimates of fence cutting damage in Texas alone ranged from 20 to 30 million dollars. Typical of government response, it became a more serious crime to cut an illegal fence, than to build one.

Similarly, in New Mexico, small groups of raiders from Hispanic communities calling themselves "Gorras Blancas" ("whitecaps") used fence cutting to resist the takeover of their communal land grants by large Anglo cattle corporations.

Even wild animals resisted the destruction of their homelands under the hooves of invading livestock. Many of the so-called "renegade" Wolves, who undertook seemingly wanton attacks on cattle and sheep, were the last surviving members of their packs and had watched their fellow pack members trapped and killed. Arizona's "Aguila Wolf" ('aguila' is Spanish for 'eagle') killed up to 65 sheep in one night. Near Meeker, Colorado, "Rags the Digger" would ruin traplines by digging up traps without tripping them. Many of these avenging Wolves were trap victims themselves, bearing names like "Crip," "Two Toes," "Three Toes," "Peg Leg" and "Old Lefty."

Whole communities would marshal their resources to kill the last of the Wolves. "Three Toes of Harding County" eluded over 150 men in 13 years of attacking livestock in South Dakota. As recently as 1920, a trapper worked for eight months to kill the famous "Custer Wolf." East of Trinidad, Colorado, ran a renegade Wolf called "Old Three Toes," the last of 32 Wolves killed in Butler Pasture. This lonely Wolf befriended a rancher's collie, who was penned into a chicken run to keep him away from the Wolf. One night they found freedom together by digging from opposite sides of the fence. The collie never returned home, and was killed weeks later by poison bait. Old Three Toes and her litter of Wolf-collie whelps were discovered shortly thereafter and all were killed.

Throughout most of the land, the Wolf has vanished, barbed wire rules, the natives have lost their sacred soil, and we are largely slaves to the industrial culture born in the coal-fired furnaces of Europe. Resistance, both lawful and lawless, has come and gone, won and lost, and remains more "American" than apple pie. And somewhere, beyond the edge of the ever-spreading pavement, are tales of solitary Wolves and Grizzlies, "traditionals" who shun the missionaries, wild lands that know only freedom, and small bands of monkeywrenchers, wild-eyed and unbending. Is there a future for any of them? Or more to the point, can acts of sabotage really influence events? History has proven that resistance can be effective, so let's briefly examine how this is possible.

Most businesses, both large and small, operate to produce a relatively small margin of profit, frequently a single digit percentage of overall gross sales. This small net profit is vulnerable to outside tampering, such as a successful consumer boycott which reduces sales. A determined campaign of monkeywrenching affects the other end, by increasing operating costs to the point that they cut into profits. The random act of sabotage accomplishes little, but when cautiously repeated, striking weak points again and again, an exploitative corporation is forced to expand their security efforts and related expenses. Repairs of damages, such as abrasives in lubricating oil, result in several costs, including down-time. Since many businesses run on tight budgets or borrowed money, loss of production, even on a temporary basis, becomes costly. Interest payments on borrowed funds increase, payrolls for idled workers must be met, and buyers of finished products become impatient with missed deadlines. Since reputation, as much as other factors, influences credit, imagine the chilling effect on banks, finance companies, equipment manufacturers (who often extend credit to buyers), and insurance companies (who finance anything these days) when they realize that a few operators, working in critical wild lands, are more susceptible to delays in repayment.

Production scheduling is so critical to financial planning that most businesses have various contingencies to minimize the impact of mechanical failure, inclement weather and other factors. They may anticipate losing an average of two weeks to weather when logging in a certain season. Or there may be plans to rent extra equipment in the event of serious breakdowns. Repeated hits by ecoteurs exhaust the contingencies and cut into the eventual profit.

Some ecotage damage is repaired by funds from insurance companies. If the damage is recurrent, the insuror will increase the deductible, thereby forcing higher out-of-pocket expenses upon the operator. The insurer will also often increase premiums, insist on higher security expenditures and may even cancel coverage. Also, of course, the operator's standing with his insurance company is of critical importance to his lenders.

Increases in security costs include pay for guards, guard dog services, security fencing and lighting, and mundane security measures, like driving all heavy equipment to a single secure location (resulting in higher operating costs and lost work time). Heavy equipment is especially vulnerable to sabotage, with down-time often exceeding $50 an hour. Security expenditures can be increased by including urban targets like warehouses, mills and offices as ecotage targets.

In addition, if smaller supporting businesses fear the impact of monkeywrenching against a business to which they sub-contract, they may hesitate to do business, or increase their charges to compensate themselves for also becoming targets.

Ultimately, the entire industry and its financial backers must be made aware that operations in de facto wilderness areas face higher risks and higher costs. Press coverage of monkeywrenching can drive this point home and alert the public in a manner that hurts the corporate image. The charge that monkeywrenching alienates public opinion stems from an incomplete understanding of propaganda and history. Scientific studies of propaganda and the press show that the vast majority of the public remembers the news only in vaguest outline. Details rapidly fade from memory. Basic concepts like "opposition to logging" are all that are retained. History informs us that direct action engenders as much support as opposition. The American Revolution saw as many colonists enter the Tory ranks as enlisted in the Continental Army. During World War II, as many Frenchmen joined Nazi forces as participated in the famous French Underground. The majority of the public floats noncommittally between the conflicting forces.

Finally, the actions of monkeywrenchers invariably enhance the status and bargaining position of more "reasonable" opponents. Industry considers mainline environmentalists to be radical until they get a taste of real radical activism. Suddenly the soft-sell of the Sierra Club and other white-shirt-and-tie eco-bureaucrats becomes much more attractive and worthy of serious negotiation. These moderate environmentalists must condemn monkeywrenching so as to preserve their own image, but they should take full advantage of the credence it lends to their approach.

As for other types of activism, picketing and sit-ins quickly lose their newsworthiness. Boycotts can't touch primary industries because they lack a consumer market. Even letter-writing campaigns and lobbyists are losing ground as the high cost of television advertising places election financing in the hands of well-heeled industrial and labor union PACs (Political Action Committees set up to undermine campaign "reform" laws).

In these desperate times, it is difficult to be both close to Earth and optimistic about her future. The hope that remains is found in the minds of those who care, and the hearts of those few who dare to act.

CHAPTER 3

DEVELOPMENTS

Clearcuts springing up in every nook and cranny of the National Forests; high-voltage powerlines marching arrogantly across desert valleys and Midwest farms; seismograph crews scarring roadless areas with their bulldozers, thumper trucks and explosives; survey stakes and their day-glo orange flagging warning of who-knows-what awful scheme; and the ubiquitous signs of overgrazing on the public lands are the hallmarks of the industrial siege on the wild and open space areas of America. As Ed Abbey has said, it looks like an invasion, an invasion from Mars.

As good patriots, lovers of our native land, it is our duty to resist invasion and to defend our planet. The following chapter describes some of the tools for that defense. A hammer and nails to save the forests, a pair of gloves to pull up survey stakes, a socket wrench for power towers . . . and so on.

The assault on wild nature is on marginal financial ground. By making it cost even more, a few monkeywrenchers can stop the destruction in many places and slow it in others. As evidence of how effective even a few actions can be, look at the hue and cry being raised by the timber industry, their flunkies in the Forest Service, and their hired politicians over a small number of tree-spiking operations. If these efforts multiply, significant blocks of wild country can be preserved by wilderness patriots.

TREE SPIKING

Tree spiking is an extremely effective method of deterring timber sales, which seems to becoming more and more popular. Mill operators are quite wary of accepting timber which has a likelihood of contamination with hidden metal objects — saws are expensive, and a "spiked" log can literally bring operations to a screeching halt, at least until a new blade can be put into service. The Forest Service and timber industry are very nervous about spiking — when the subject of monkeywrenching is brought up, this is the form most commonly discussed. On the one hand, the Forest Service often fails to publicize incidents of spiking, on the theory that the less the practice is publicized, the less it is likely to spread. But when the Freddies *do* publicly acknowledge that a spiking has occurred, they often make a considerable effort to find the perpetrators, even to the point of offering substantial cash rewards.

There are two basic philosophies of tree-spiking. Some people like to spike the base of of each tree, so that the sawyer, in felling the tree, will almost certainly encounter one of the spikes with the chainsaw. This would at the very least require the sawyer to stop and sharpen the saw, and might require the replacement of the chain. If this happens with enough trees, the amount of "down time" caused to the sawyers would pose a serious hindrance to operations. In this type of spiking, the spiker drives several nails (or non-metallic spikes, about which more later) at a downward angle into the first two or three feet of each tree above the ground. The nails are spaced so that a sawyer, in felling the tree, is likely to hit at least one of them.

There is an objection to this type of spiking — the possibility, however remote, that the sawyer might be injured, either by the kickback of the saw striking the nail, or by the chain, should it break when striking the spike. A friend of ours who worked for many years as a logger in Colorado says that in numerous incidents of striking metal objects with his saw — including one time when the impact was great enough to cause him to swallow his chaw of tobacco — he never once had a broken chain or was otherwise hurt. Yet the possibility is there. Because of this possibility, we do not recommend this type of spiking.

The second philosophy of tree spiking favors placing the spikes in the trees well above the area where the fellers will cut — as many feet up the trunk as one can conveniently work. The object of the spiking in this case is to destroy the blades in the sawmill. Since in large mills the blades are either operated from a control booth some distance from the actual cutting, or are protected by a plexiglas shield, this method is unlikely to cause anyone physical injury even should a blade shatter upon striking a spike, which is an unlikely event. It is true that in small, "backyard" sawmills the operator might be standing close to the blade, but we would assume that anyone contemplating spiking would never consider doing it on other than the largest timber sales, where the trees are destined for a corporate, rather than a small, family-operated mill. Locally owned and operated sawmills are seldom a major threat to wilderness. It is usually the big, multi-national corporations whose "cut-and-run" philosophy devastates the land and leaves the local economy in shambles when all the big trees are cut and the main office decides to pull out and move to greener pastures.

I anticipate an objection at this point. "Wait a minute," someone says, "if the purpose of spiking trees is to save them from being cut, then what good does it do if the tree wrecks a blade in the mill? It's too late to save the tree, isn't it?" The answer is that the value of spiking is in its long-term deterrent effect. If enough trees are spiked in roadless areas, eventually the corporate thugs in the timber company boardrooms, along with their corrupt lackeys who wear the uniform of the Forest Service, will realize that timber sales in our few remaining wild areas are going to be prohibitively expensive. And since profits are the name of the game, they will begin to think twice before violating the wilderness.

In many cases, people have spiked timber in a given area, and then have sent (anonymous!) warning to the authorities. If this is done before the timber has actually been sold (the Forest Service plans timber sales years in advance, but actual sale of the timber to a logging company is one of the last steps in the process) the effect on competitive bidding can be considerable. In fact the sale may be quietly dropped. In cases where the timber has already been sold prior to spiking, the Freddies (upon receiving a warning) have sent crews into the woods to locate and remove the spikes — at substantial expense in overtime to the agency. If this happened often enough, it could not fail to reduce the total number of timber sales substantially, particularly in this era of concern over the federal budget.

We will describe several methods of spiking trees, will go into the "when" and the "where" of spiking, and will deal with the sensitive matter of when and how to announce a spiking. First, we stress some basic security considerations.

Spiking trees is a potentially dangerous activity. The Forest Service has increased its law-enforcement budget considerably in the last couple of years, and one reason has been the increased incidence of monkey-wrenching. Another reason for increased law-enforcement has been the stepped-up campaign by the Feds to eliminate marijuana growing from the public lands, but it should be obvious that a cop who's in the woods looking for dope is going to try to arrest any monkeywrenchers he might encounter by chance as well.

The Freddies (and other Federal land-use agencies as well) are becoming increasingly sophisticated in law-enforcement, and it would be unfortunate to underestimate them. According to a recent column by Jack Anderson, these agencies employ such methods as surveillance (of suspicious persons), and mail interception (presumably again involving those who have for some reason attracted their suspicions). They may have agents in the woods in plain clothes, posing as hikers, campers or fishermen, and it is even possible that agents might be in the woods at night on stakeouts, equipped with night-vision devices.

Obviously, if a monkeywrencher is contemplating spiking trees in a remote roadless area long in advance of a timber sale, the chances of encountering cops are relatively slim. Conversely, if a highly controversial timber sale is involved, especially one in which there already has been monkeywrenching committed or at least threatened, the danger to the monkeywrencher is very real. For this reason alone, it is preferable to spike trees preventively, rather than as a last-ditch effort to save a seemingly doomed grove.

Tree spiking should *never* be done alone. In addition to the person or persons who are doing the actual spiking, at least one person should have the sole duty of acting as lookout. At the first sign of *any* other people in the vicinity, spiking should cease and the team should quietly withdraw. The team should use the drop-off and pick-up method of access, and should follow all recommended precautions as to clothing, footwear and tools (see chapter on **Security**).

Spiking is much easier done in broad daylight than in the dark. Not only can a team work much faster in full light, but in darkness it is all too easy to be sloppy and fail to cover up the signs of one's activities. If a team is spiking in a remote roadless area and takes full security precautions, there is no reason why they cannot operate securely in daytime. While it is true that in daylight one is more likely to encounter other humans in the woods, it is conversely true that almost *any* activity in the woods at night, if detected, will be automatically deemed suspicious and investigated.

Assuming that spikers are working in a remote roadless area, and

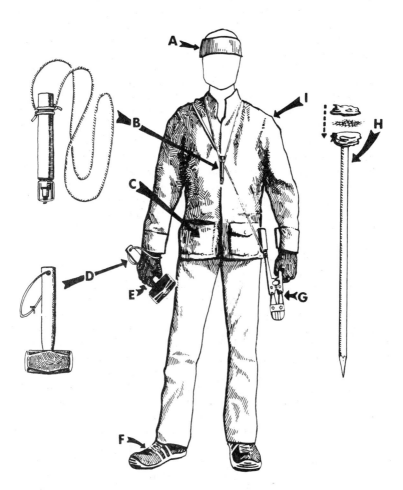

THE WELL DRESSED TREE SPIKER

A: Concealing headgear (cold weather watch cap shown); B: Felt-tip pen; C: Pockets with flaps: D: Hammer with lanyard to free hand for using cutters; E: Cheap cloth gloves; F: Running shoes; G: 14 to 18 inch bolt cutters (carried from cord sling); H: Spike nail with reinforced silicon silencer; I: Lightweight jacket in forest colors.

are not working during the hunting season (a dangerous time to be out in the woods, since on much of the public lands the highest period of use occurs at this time), the greatest danger will be from casual encounters with Forest Service field personnel — timber markers, survey crews and the like — who might be working in or near your area. It is best if you know where these crews are working at all times. If you have a source within the agency, fine, but you can more safely get this information from continued observation and from knowing your area well. These crews tend to work in the same area for weeks at a time, and often will live in temporary field quarters (trailers or even tents) rather than commute every day from the District Ranger Station or Supervisor's Office. Another type of people you might encounter in the woods, especially if you are working in the area of a timber sale which has already been announced for public bidding, is representatives of logging companies who might be checking out the timber before deciding their bids. Needless to say, the last thing you want to happen to you is to fall into the hands of these people.

When to Spike Trees

A general rule on when to spike might be, "the earlier the better." If one waits until just before the timber is sold, not only are security problems greater, but it will be easier for the authorities to locate the spikes. On the other hand, if one is able to spike several *years* in advance of a sale, nature has had time to disguise the work of the monkeywrencher by covering the spikes with bark. Of course, if the Freddies have already marked the boundaries of the sale area or perhaps even the individual trees which are to be cut, the spiker knows exactly where to work without any guessing. Nevertheless, with proper intelligence monkeywrenchers can have a good idea of where future timber sales will be long before the marking stage.

Not only does the Forest Service earmark specific timber sales five years in advance, but in their 50-year Forest Plans, the Freddies conveniently identify all of the concentrations of "commercial" timber in each National Forest — and all too often, they openly acknowledge that they intend to cut almost all of it, sooner or later. See the section on **Security** (the part on intelligence gathering) for secure means of keeping posted on what an agency is up to. Study the data and identify areas of critical interest to you which appear to be threatened. With plenty of advance warning, you can act deliberately and precisely.

Since a lot of monkeywrenching is nevertheless going to occur at the last possible minute, it is helpful to have a basic knowledge of timber marking practices. Unfortunately, there is really no uniform system, and practices may change from time to time. Timber markers generally use spray paint, although sometimes flagging (or flagging *and* paint) is used to mark the boundaries of the area (the "unit" within which cutting will take place). One color will be used to mark the perimeter, while another color will be used to mark individual trees to be cut within the unit. *In a clearcut, only the perimeter is marked, since everything within is to be removed.* A given timber sale will usually have several units within it, and they may be widely scattered or close together. You may see numbers painted on some of the trees — these are the unit numbers. At the present time in the Northern Rockies, the Freddies are using red or orange paint to mark unit boundaries, and yellow or blue paint to mark the trees within the units which are to be cut. Trees to be cut are sometimes marked with an "X," although sometimes only a horizontal slash of paint is used. But beware — in timber sales in which *most but not all* of the trees are to be cut, the trees which are to be *left* may be painted. Because of the many differences in marking practices, it is advisable to know the system being used in your area.

Basic Spiking Techniques

Basic spiking involves the use of a large hammer and a number of large nails. The hammer should be fairly large — it is difficult to drive large nails into a tree with an ordinary carpenter's hammer. The best type of hammer to use is one of the "single-jack" variety (a one-handed sledgehammer) with a head weighing 2-1/2 or 3 pounds. As for the nails, they should be reasonably large, but one should bear in mind that the larger the nails, the more time and energy are required to drive them. Perhaps the ideal size would be a 60 penny (60d) nail. This nail is about 6-1/4 inches long and is the largest "common" nail readily available in most building supply stores. Larger nails (called spikes) are sold by their size in inches. Spikes should not be needed in most cases, although they would be useful in special cases, such as where extremely large trees are involved.

Another tool should probably be added to the basic spiking kit. This is a small pair of bolt-cutters. It need only be powerful enough to cut the heads off the nails. The reason to add this tool is that in several cases, the Freddies have sent crews into the woods to locate (with metal detectors) and remove (with crowbars) as many spikes as possible. Cutting the heads off the nails (after driving them nearly all the way into the tree) should make the Freddies' task all the more fun. *Note:*

31

Drive the nail almost all the way into the tree. Cut the head off with the bolt-cutters. Then, drive the now-headless nail the remainder of the way into the tree. Remember, the more time and money the Freddies expend on this sort of thing, the fewer trees are going to be cut and the more wilderness saved. We cannot overestimate the value of removing the heads from the nails. We have heard of at least one case in which the Forest Service has located trees with spikes so treated — and has been *unable* to remove the nails. Although the Freddies publicly announced that they had removed all the spikes, the sale was quietly scuttled.

Since the more trees that are spiked, the greater the deterrent factor, one nail per tree ought to be sufficient. To deter a major timber sale, the spiking of several hundred trees might be a worthy goal, but even a few dozen spiked trees will be of some deterrent value. It might be noted that on Meares Island in British Columbia, opponents of logging,

Spiking at an angle at a low level to prevent felling of the tree.

A bridge timber spike and single jack hammer for use with very large trees. Smaller spikes are fine for general use and can be driven in with a heavy standard hammer.

working systematically and in teams, have spiked literally *thousands* of trees to great effect. But spiking does not have to be on this scale to be effective. It need only be repeated in enough roadless areas to slow down the logging of old growth trees.

Trees should be spiked at various intervals above the ground. While it would be acceptable to drive some of the nails in at the height of a standing person, since this is the most convenient location, an effort ought to be made to place them higher. There are a couple of reasons for this. First, nails placed above head height will be more difficult to spot by investigators, and second, if all the nails are driven in at the same height it will render the searchers' task all the more easy. There are a number of ways in which nails can be placed high. If it is possible to obtain climbing spikes (metal spurs which attach to boots, used in conjunction with a waist belt) these can be employed. Climbing spikes are fairly expensive when purchased from forestry supply houses, but it might be possible to locate an old pair (they are used by smokejumpers and others in forestry work) or to improvise a pair. Or, a spiker can fabricate a light, portable ladder which can be carried from tree to tree. Another method would be for the spiker to stand on a partner's shoulders while driving the nails. In regions which get considerable snowfall, a good solution would be to spike in the winter, using skis or snowshoes when there is several feet of snow on the ground.

Some effort should be made to cover the signs of one's work in a spiking operation. The ideal spiking would take place several years before a timber sale, indeed even a couple of years or so before marking crews or survey crews are likely to be in the area. This gives nature a chance to cover the signs of the spiking by growing bark over the nails. When a sale is imminent, it may be necessary to issue a warning to the effect that the trees have been spiked, but if this was done several years in the past the task of the authorities in locating (and especially in removing) all the spikes will be difficult, if not impossible. Perhaps the greatest deterrent effect to a timber sale would be in a situation in which the authorities actually find a few spikes in an area but realize that there are probably many more unlocated ones out there.

However, in many cases a spiker will not have the luxury of knowing that there will be time for nature to cover the signs of the work. After driving the nail in flush, the head of the nail should be covered so as to camouflage all signs of the work. Ideally, a piece of bark should be fixed (perhaps with glue or cement) over the nail. But pitch might be used, or in a pinch, paint which blends in with the natural bark. A brown felt marker can also be used to disguise the shiny head of the nail after it is driven into the tree.

FIELD NOTES

*Be cautious when buying large quantities of nails. Although nails are common items and their possession (in the absence of other evidence) would constitute only the barest of circumstantial evidence, it would be wise never to buy them where you are known or might be remembered.

*Be careful about leaving fingerprints on spikes. After purchasing them, carefully wipe them clean and place them in a cloth bag or wrap them up to be carried in your pack for field use. Wear gloves while spiking trees (see below) and do not touch the spikes unless your hands are gloved.

*In addition to the security reasons for wearing gloves, they will protect your hands. A hard day of pounding spikes can blister the hands of the toughest. Besides being painful, blisters might well be considered evidence against someone suspected of spiking.

*It has been suggested that a non-ferrous hammer be used for spiking, as such a hammer would be less noisy than one with a steel head. (Such hammers, made of brass or other soft alloys, are used for specialized purposes, such as in working around flammable gases or liquids where a spark struck from a steel hammer might be disastrous.) However, drawbacks associated with this type of hammer might be its cost and uncommon nature (though such hammers might be available from an electrical parts store). The softer metal would also probably tend to mar easily.

*For large old-growth trees, "bridge timber spikes" (about one foot long) can be particularly effective. These spikes cost about 70 cents each and require a stout arm to drive. A heavy hammer (small sledge) that can be gripped with both hands may be the most effective tool. Suburban building supply stores sometimes have these large spikes in bins with the rest of the nails.

*Helix (spiral) nails are the ultimate in metallic spikes — these are the type of nails which were used in large quantities on Meares Island. The spiral makes the nail extremely difficult to remove, and removal is virtually impossible when the head of the nail is clipped off. These nails come in three sizes suitable for tree spiking: 8″, 10″ and 12″. While the 8″ size is adequate for most jobs, the 10″ and 12″ sizes can be driven even when the head has been removed in advance — a great advantage. *Note: Driving these spikes is not easy. You will need to be in shape. You may want to use a heavier hammer, with a longer (18″) handle.*

A disadvantage of helix nails is that they may not be available in just any building supply store — you may have to look around to find them. They are also expensive, although they are much cheaper if bought in quantity (by the box). Call around (use a pay phone) to check on availability and price (prices may vary widely). If you need an excuse for buying them, say you are building a bridge to a piece of remote property owned by your uncle. Use the same precautions to protect your identity in buying helix nails that you would use with any unusual item — *never* buy such nails in your own community (unless it is a large city), never go back to the same store twice, and never leave such things lying around your house or car.

*A good quality, US-made 20″-24″ bolt-cutter (cost about $80) is adequate for 60d spikes or helix spikes 8″ and smaller. This size bolt-cutter can easily be carried in the woods with you to de-head your spikes after you drive them most of the way into the tree. You can then drive them in the rest of the way without their heads. Be sure to use eye protection when using bolt-cutters to de-head spikes (goggles or something comparable). The heads of nails can really fly.

For 10″ and larger helix spikes, 30″-36″ bolt cutters are necessary. De-head these spikes at home (large bolt-cutters are cumbersome and heavy to carry in the woods). These larger spikes can be easily driven in without their heads. You may prefer to rent one of these larger bolt-cutters for a day or two and de-head an entire box of spikes at home. If you do rent one (to save the cost of purchase), do not leave your ID as security. Instead, leave a cash deposit ($150 generally required) which will be refunded when you return the bolt-cutter.

*Most large (8″ to 12″) spikes are either 5/16 or 3/8-inch in diameter. Choose a bolt cutter with a slightly larger capacity than your spikes, i.e., 1/2-inch or larger. (Spike metal falls into the "soft" or "medium" category on the "capacity chart," which is a small metal tag usually affixed to each set of bolt-cutters.) Getting cutters with greater capacity allows for easier, faster clipping and prolongs the bolt-cutter's life.

*The distinctive marks left by your particular bolt cutter will be destroyed by pounding in the spikes. The marks on the jaws of the bolt cutter can be removed by simply filing the jaws.

*A flat-faced, 3 pound sledge with a long handle (18″) is ideal for driving large helix spikes.

*It has been suggested that "power-actuated fastening systems" might be used for spiking trees. These are simply "nail guns" which are used in construction. They fire a special cartridge (generally .22 caliber) to drive masonry nails into concrete. The longest nails which these guns fire are usually only 3″, but since the gun is designed to put them into concrete it is likely that they would bury themselves completely in wood. An obvious advantage to using one of these would be that a spiker could drive many nails without tiring. Disadvantages include noise, the necessity to retrieve all expended cartridge cases (which would certainly constitute traceable, "ballistics" evidence), cost, and possible difficulties in purchasing the guns, nails and cartridges. Under OSHA regulations, these tools can only be used by trained workers. The distributors will provide training, but it is obvious that prospective purchasers should keep their real identity secret. Manufacturers of these "fastening systems" include UNISET, San Diego Powder Tool, Red Head, and Gunnebo. *Editor's note: this method has not yet been field tested, to our knowledge.*

*Spikes have actually been shot into trees using a bow and arrow. A 55 lb. bow was used to shoot aluminum-shafted arrows with a special adapter on the head into which 20d or 30d nails had been inserted. Penetration of up to 3½ inches was reported. The shaft was removed after shooting.

*It has been suggested that spikes (perhaps short sections of rebar or nails encased in sabots) might be shot high into trees from a muzzle-loading rifle of large caliber. This idea has yet to be field tested, to our knowledge. It is not recommended that anyone try this unless they have great knowledge of firearms, and then it should be done *very carefully.*

*Since the Freddies have been known to search for spikes by sending crews into the woods with metal detectors, some means of confusing and complicating their operations would be useful. One method would be for a team to drive numerous small nails into trees as part of a large spiking operation. The small nails can be driven much more quickly and quietly than large ones, but if they are well concealed only an experienced operator with a good metal detector would be able to differentiate them from the large nails.

*It has also been suggested that steel shot might be sufficient to trigger a positive response in a metal detector. This needs to be field tested. If it works, an ecoteur need only to walk through the woods, firing into trees with a shotgun, to cause the timber beasts endless confusion.

*In places where spiking is rampant, the authorities may go so far as to "dust" trees with dyes in powder form. These powders are almost invisible to the naked eye, but will show up under an ultraviolet or "black" light. To avoid compromising oneself in such a situation, minimize contact with the tree (resist the temptation to hug it!), put your gloves in a plastic bag when you are done (if you're not disposing of them immediately), and launder your clothes after you get home. You might also purchase an ultraviolet light (available from scientific supply houses, novelty and "head" shops). *Editor's note: in this age of budgetary restraints, the Freddies are not likely to go to this extreme except in special cases, such as ones in which timber already sold has been spiked en route to the mill.*

*In spiking a large timber sale, concentrate on the closest part of the sale to the main road as this will tend to disinterest the contractor in continuing with the rest of the sale.

*For extra effect, combine large and small nails. Use only one large spike per tree, but pound in several smaller nails as well. This gives people who cannot drive in large spikes something to do and it further protects the tree. The metal detector can't tell the difference between large and small spikes.

*A hand-operated bit and brace can be used to drill holes into trees for the insertion of "super spikes." After drilling the hole, a section of sharpened rebar can be driven into the tree. Be sure to cover the hole with bark (liquid wood or some other adhesive can be used to secure the bark). While this method of spiking is very labor-intensive, it shouldn't take many such spikes to have a deterrent effect.

*For a major spiking operation, you may wish to stash a box of spikes in the woods in the summer (when access is easier), and then ski in during the winter and do the spiking. Be sure to hide the spikes where you can find them even if they are buried under several feet of snow.

*A military surplus green canvas ammo bag is perfect for transporting spikes in the woods.

*Avoid imported (Korean, Taiwanese, etc.) spikes and stick to U.S. or Canadian brands. Cheap imports may be softer and bend easier when driving.

*The type of tree may determine the size of your spikes and whether or not you de-head them before driving. Pines and cedars are relatively soft, allowing even de-headed 60d nails to be driven in without bending (a de-headed 60d nail would likely bend in harder wood). Douglas Fir is a bit harder; spikes smaller than 5/16-inch diameter should not be de-headed prior to driving. Old growth Hemlock is *extremely* hard. Experiment with the various types of trees in your area.

*Resist the temptation to use your spiking nails around the house.

Examination of spikes can determine their manufacturer, and it's best not to have similar nails where you live.

*"Traditional" spiking, as described above, is relatively simple and quite effective. However, the serious eco-raider might do well to consider some of the alternative methods of spiking, as described by T. O. Hellenbach. These methods do require more specialized equipment, and are therefore more costly in monetary terms to the spiker, but they offer distinct advantages, both in added security and in effectiveness.

BACKCOUNTRY SPIKING CAN BE FUN FOR THE WHOLE FAMILY

TREE PINNING

Tree Pinning: The Art of Silent Spiking

Just as spiking is named for the spike-like quality of the fifty and sixty-penny nails used, so "pinning" is named for a lowly steel pin which, buried in the tissue of a living tree, is designed to wreak havoc with the butchering blade of the sawmill. As levels of protective security increase to stem the swelling tide of tree spiking, silent new methods will become necessary for those courageous enough to infiltrate the guarded stands of doomed trees. The loud ring of hammer on spike is replaced by the gentle hum of the cordless electric drill as it creates a small cavity for the secreting of a steel pin.

Equipment
Because the basic equipment for tree pinning is more expensive than that required for spiking, it is essential to "shop by phone" and get the best price possible. Drill prices, for example, can vary as much as $50 from one store to the next.

DRILLS — Many models and types of cordless electric drills are currently available, but the best, in terms of torque and price, are probably those manufactured by Black & Decker. Their basic model 9020 sells for $25 to $40. Its slow speed and limited battery storage capacity allow for drilling only 15 to 25 holes, depending on the toughness of the wood. Still, you can buy three or four of this model for the price you'll pay for the vastly superior model 1940 ($80 to $100). The model 1940 will drill twice as many holes as the 9020, and will do it more quickly due to its higher RPM rate. It also has a detachable power pack that allows you to plug in a fresh set of batteries as needed. The battery packs range in price from $25 to $50, but you may have to check with a considerable number of retailers to find someone who stocks them on the shelf. Do not order them from the manufacturer unless you can have them shipped to a trusted friend who lives a thousand miles away. Also, never return the warranty registration cards to the manufacturers since this creates a paper trail that is of great assistance to Officer Dogooder and his trusty bloodhounds.

Finally, read the instructions that come with your drill and follow them to the letter. This is your best insurance against equipment failure.

DRILL BITS — Use only high speed "twist" drill bits of a type normally used to drill through metal. The flutes and grooves in this type of bit force the sawdust debris out of the hole unlike the wood bit. On the first try, a twist bit can drill a 4 to 4-1/2 inch deep hole. A second effort in the same hole (after clearing out the sawdust) can extend the depth to double this. Usually, however, it is not necessary to drill in more than 4 inches to accommodate a pin of up to three inches.

APRON — A simple cloth apron makes a handy holder for pins of at least two sizes. It also allows you to wipe your gloves clean (of silicon — more on this later).

PINS — At a welder's supply, buy one-quarter inch steel welding rod. It comes in thirty-six inch lengths, two rods per pound, at $1 to $1.50 a pound. For the sake of variety on different jobs, substitute either the threaded or zinc-coated steel rod found in the hardware section of most lumber yards.

Use a hacksaw to cut the steel rods into three and four inch lengths. This allows you to fit the pin to different hole depths.

SAFETY GLASSES — Buy and wear the simple plastic safety glasses that do not block your side vision.

RAGS — Always have plenty of clean rags available to keep your equipment wiped free of fingerprints.

CAULK — Buy a standard caulk gun and tubes of clear silicon caulk (like GE's Silicon II). This keeps it quick, clean and cheap.

Pinning

Pinning is best accomplished by a two-person team using the following five steps:

1) Drill a hole at a slight downward angle in the tree. Your drill bit should be slightly larger in diameter than that of your steel pins.

2) Use the caulk gun to squeeze some clear silicon into the hole.

3) Insert the steel pin. If the hole is more than four inches deep, use a four inch pin. If the wood in a particular spot is too tough, don't force it. Use a three or even two inch pin in a shallower hole. Another piece of steel rod, from 6 to 12 inches long, is used to push the pin to the bottom of the hole. The silicon glues it in place (otherwise a powerful magnet could pull it out).

4) Place another dab of clear silicon at the mouth of the hole. This seals the hole against invasion by bugs or disease.

5) Use a chip of bark stuck onto the silicon to camouflage the opening.

Targets

Because of the relative silence of this technique, it can be used in patrolling sections of timber slated for felling. You should not limit yourself to standing trees alone, however. Effective monkeywrenching involves examining every step in the processing of old-growth timber, from mountainside to mill door. Since metal detectors are often used to locate nails, old fence wire and other scrap metal in logs before milling, observe this process from a safe distance to see if you can infiltrate the work area at night and insert your pins after the metal detection phase. If additional silence is necessary, switch to a brace and bit (a cranklike hand drill available at all hardware stores). This entails more manual labor, but you're not going to need to pin fifty logs. Six to a dozen will do quite well. Make sure you remove any telltale shavings or sawdust that can reveal your activities.

— *T.O. Hellenbach*

FIELD NOTES

*Jam a branch in a drilled hole after it is pinned. When the tree is de-barked in the mill, it will not appear as suspicious as a plastic-filled hole would, and will merely appear to be a knot.

CERAMIC SPIKES

Foiling the Detectors: Non-Metallic Tree Spikes

Tree spiking has forced the development of a number of counter-measures, the most significant of which include the use of metal detectors to locate metallic spikes embedded in tree trunks. Many sawmills routinely screen all fallen logs at the mill to remove commonplace metallic objects like nails and old barbed wire. There is an increasing likelihood that conventional metal spikes will be detected before reaching their intended target — the costly sawmill blade. *Editor's note: this does not mean that metallic spikes are not still useful — the reaction to their use thus far indicates that they are having an impact. But non-metallic spikes have obvious advantages.*

Ongoing research has developed several non-metallic spikes, or pins, that promise to defeat the metal detector and wreak havoc inside the sawmill. The first of these is a high-fired ceramic pin made of the same type of stoneware used by potters who hand-throw (on a potter's wheel) the usual line of cups, bowls, plates, etc. The primary ingredient is stoneware clay, produced in a wide range of formulations by clay companies and ceramic supply outfits scattered across the nation. Most such manufacturers and suppliers are located in large metropolitan areas where monkeywrenchers can purchase their clay over the counter for cash — leaving no paper trail like name and address for the curious police investigator. The clay usually comes in twenty-five pound bags, two such bags making up a fifty-pound box. Be sure that the clay type (known as the "clay body") that you purchase contains no iron oxide, an ingredient that is commonly added to stoneware clays. If sufficiently concentrated, this iron oxide may be picked up by metal detectors. To find a clay that is suitable, make your first inquiry by phone, obtaining the name or number of the stoneware clay that contains no iron oxide. At a later date, send the most inconspicuous-looking member of your spiking team in to purchase a bag or box. If necessary, they can be "picking it up for a friend," or can be college art students purchasing materials for a project.

As an additional measure, these clay bodies can be stiffened and made even more durable by the addition of "grog," a gritty, sand-like material usually made of a high-fired refractory material (ground stoneware) or simply a pure quartz sand. This can also be purchased from clay suppliers, and you should specify an 80 or coarser screening. Do not buy fine powder grog, or "soft" grog made of weaker lower-fired materials. The grog is blended into the clay body through a process called "wedging" which consists of simply kneading the material in by hand until it is thoroughly and evenly distributed throughout the clay. Since clay formulas vary from one type to another and from one company to the next, we cannot specify the amount of grog to add to your clay. Just add a little at a time until the clay feels a little coarser and stiffer. If you add too much, the clay will be hard to roll out and will not stick together well. Keep in mind that the clay must remain "plastic" to allow you to readily shape it.

When handling the clay directly, always wear plastic gloves. The best types are the disposable examination gloves used by doctors and available at medical supply houses. More expensive, but more readily available, are the plastic gloves sold at all grocery stores in the kitchenware section. These types are more durable and will survive repeated use. Whichever type you use, try to obtain gloves with a skin-tight fit.

The pins are made simply by rolling the clay out to the desired thickness, and cutting them to the appropriate length. As with the metallic pins described above, you will have to use a drill to make a hole in the tree for inserting the pin. Decide what type of drill (cordless battery-type or old fashioned brace and bit) you will use and find the largest bit you can readily use, up to one inch in diameter. Experiment on a recently fallen tree to insure that your drill and bit combination allows you to drill a hole up to four or five inches deep. The thicker your ceramic pin is, the more likely it is to either dull or break a sawmill blade. Therefore, if you can drill one-inch diameter holes, roll out the clay to a one-inch thickness. It will shrink some in drying and firing and will fit easily in a one-inch hole. As to pin length, four inches is about the maximum necessary, but be sure to cut some shorter lengths, like two and three inches. In this way, if your drilling should encounter a hard spot like a knot in the wood preventing you from drilling to the desired depth, you have a shorter pin available for the shallow hole.

Once your pins are rolled and cut, set them aside for a couple of weeks to thoroughly dry. They must be completely dry before firing or they will break apart in firing. Also, make sure the clay is well-compressed during the rolling-out, as even tiny air pockets left inside the clay will blow up during firing.

Finally, your ceramic pins will be ready for the final stage in preparation — the firing. High temperature firing brings about chemical changes in the clay, causing the particles to bond together through vitrification. The end product is a material so hard it will easily scratch glass. In hardness, it ranks with some types of steel, although it will shatter under a heavy blow (making it unsuitable for spiking with hammers). Still, it is high enough on Moh's scale of hardness to cause damage to sawmill blades.

High-temperature firing can be achieved only in a gas-fired kiln. The pins must be fired to "cone 10," which generally ranges from 2350 to 2400 degrees Fahrenheit. Firing to lower temperatures will not produce the same hardness. Following are some of the sources of gas firing:

SCHOOLS — Various college classes, adult education courses, and private instructors maintain gas kilns for student use.

DO-IT-YOURSELF — This approach entails purchasing a gas kiln and making the necessary hookups to a source of bottled LP gas. This entails several hundred dollars in expenses. Be sure to take a college course or private course through a competent potter to learn the principles and mechanics of gas firing before undertaking this step yourself.

CERAMIC SHOPS — Most ceramic shops sell mold-cast pieces for the public to "finish." Their clays are unsuitable for pins and they usually fire only electric kilns up to a cone 5 maximum. Still, if you call around, you might luck onto one that will have a gas kiln and custom fire up to a cone 10.

PRIVATE INDIVIDUALS — Across the nation, there are thousands of professional potters selling their hand-thrown wares through art and craft shows attended by the public. Some of them will be amenable to letting you pay for custom firing in their kilns. This allows you to have the job done professionally. As a way of developing this contact, you might buy several pieces from them at a show, and ask if you can come to their studio in a few weeks to buy more of their wares. If you appear to be a good customer, the potter might agree to firing a few dozen pins for you. To make sure your contact is a competent professional, check out their product line. They should carry a wide range of practical goods (cups, bowls, planters, etc.) and should stock large numbers of items. Avoid those who don't seem to have much to choose from. Check the quality of their firing by breaking one of the inexpensive items you bought from them. The broken edge, revealing the inside of the fired clay, should be a medium to dark brown. If it appears very dark, almost blackish, the work is poorly fired (over-vitrification) and is too brittle. Do not let such a potter do your firing. Make sure you check the broken edge, as an external examination will not reveal this type of sloppy firing. Of course, make sure their goods are stoneware fired to a cone 10.

Security is of primary consideration when firing in someone else's kiln, or when having a custom firing done. If possible, do not use your real name. Never reveal the intended use of the ceramic pins unless the person handling the firing is also a member of your spiking team. Do not attempt to recruit for your spiking team the person doing your firing unless they are a trusted friend of many years' acquaintance, or a trusted relative. If possible have a trusted confidant handle the manufacture and firing of the pins at a location far distant from the forest where they will be used. Try at least for the next state.

When necessary, make up an air-tight reason for your intended use of the pins. Make up a convincing story about how you are going to assemble them into an abstract sculpture. Use your imagination. The possibilities are limitless.

As a further means of obscuring their intended use, fire the pins in twelve inch lengths. These can later be cut-down to suitable lengths using a diamond wire hand saw available for $15 to $25 through a jeweler or lapidary supply house (found in most large cities).

In pursuing the use of the ceramic pin for spiking, it's a good idea to have a member of your team take a college-type course in pottery to familiarize them with the materials, techniques and terminology. This can help in manufacturing a convincing cover story for the firing of your peculiar pins. Competent private instructors, although not as widely available, can be a good source of schooling and kiln access.

Inserting Ceramic Tree Spikes

A hand-powered brace and bit type of drill is both inexpensive and very effective for drilling large diameter holes in trees. It is also laborious and time-consuming, so you should plan to work on only six to a dozen trees per hit. This small number will be very effective if using non-metallic and undetectable pins since most will make it to the sawmill to attack the blades.

When a team is working in an area currently being logged, it is necessary to take additional security precautions that might not be necessary when working in a remote roadless area. Night work may be essential, and this creates additional problems. One of the most critical elements is the ability to conceal all signs of your work. First and foremost, you *must* practice this operation during daylight hours in a safe and secluded location. Only by polishing your technique beforehand can you be sure that you will leave no evidence at the scene. When the chips of bark are glued back into place, there must not be any telltale seams, cracks or excess glue. All wood shavings must be carefully swept onto the towel and carried away a short distance for shallow burial. A dark terrycloth towel is recommended since the shavings will stick better to the rough surface.

When working at night, use a flashlight to carefully double-check your work when finished. The best flashlight is the current-issue GI flashlight available at most army surplus stores. It is made of green high-impact plastic, has an angled head (the light shines at a right angle to the body) and takes two "D" cell batteries. Unscrew the base cap and inside you'll find a red plastic lens that fits under the "O" ring screwed onto the standard lens. This red light is sufficient for close work and will not ruin your night vision. If you insist on using a penlight type of flashlight, be sure to close one eye to protect at least half of your night vision. As with all tools, make sure all surfaces inside and out (including batteries) are wiped clean of fingerprints.

Your brace should be lightly oiled to insure silence, and you should carry a spare bit so that you can always work with a sharp bit. Since you have to lean into the brace to get maximum effectiveness, this tool is particularly effective on felled trees that have been limbed and bucked (cut into shorter lengths). These can be found either scattered about the logging site, or piled near skid trails or "landings" where they are stockpiled for loading onto trucks.

When working in an area currently being logged, even in the dark, one must remain concealed by working low to the ground, hidden by shadows, or in areas where the terrain prevents viewing from any distance. As in *any* spiking operation, it is essential to have an alert lookout well posted to guard the approaches. Working low will protect you from Forest Service enforcers using night vision devices. The lookout and pinner(s) must have a signaling system of bird calls or short range radios. Always use a nondescript code on the radio.

It takes a brave monkeywrencher to work a logging site in the night, but remember that you have the choice of time and place. This advantage, when coupled with basic security precautions, will guarantee your success.

— *T.O. Hellenbach*

FIELD NOTES

*A simple way to test ceramic pins for metallic content is to run a magnet over them. If you detect any significant magnetic attraction, the pins probably contain ferrous metals, and *may* be susceptible to metal detectors.

AND WE THOUGHT THINGS WERE BAD IN THE EIGHTIES...

THROUGH THE TEEMING MASSES AND FOUL SULFUROUS AIR OF THE PACIFIC MEGALOPOLIS, MOVES AN UNOBTRUSIVE FIGURE—THE UNDERGROUND HERO KNOWN ONLY AS...

BLADE RUINER

EPISODE 2: FOILING THE DETECTORS

AT THE STUDIO OF A MASTER POTTER...

UP 'N AT 'EM, COMPADRE..YOU GOT MY CUSTOM ORDER?

HUH?

MOMENTS LATER, IN THE CERAMIC STUDIO, IN FRONT OF A GAS KILN STILL VERY WARM

WHADUYA THINK?

YOU FIRED THESE TO A "CONE TEN"?

OH YEAH... 2400°F, JUST LIKE YOU SAID.

DON'T SUPPOSE I SHOULD EVEN ASK WHAT THEY'RE FOR?

DON'T S'POSE

THE BLADE RUINER MAKES HIS WAY ACROSS TOWN TO THE FOURTH SECTOR TO MEET WITH HIS PARTNER IN MAYHEM...

PURPLE PUSSYCAT CLUB

...A DANCER NAMED 'LEILA'.

MONTHS EARLIER, LEILA RODE THE TUBE TRAIN TO DOWNTOWN L.A. WHERE SHE BOUGHT A BOX OF STONEWARE CLAY, CAREFULLY SELECTING A TYPE THAT CONTAINS NO IRON OXIDE.

HER DISGUISE WAS DESIGNED TO INSURE THAT THE SALES CLERK WOULD NOT REMEMBER HER FACE.

CLAY WAREHOUSE INC.
50 LB.

DONNING THROWAWAY PLASTIC SURGICAL GLOVES, THE CLAY IS CAREFULLY ROLLED OUT TO A ONE-INCH THICKNESS...

THEN CUT TO VARIOUS LENGTHS UP TO FOUR INCHES. AFTER DRYING-OUT, THEY'RE KILN-FIRED...

PRODUCING AN UNDETECTABLE NON-METALLIC "PIN" CAPABLE OF DULLING A CARBIDE-STEEL DRILL BIT...

OR A SAWMILL BLADE!

BACK IN LEILA'S "DRESSING" ROOM

A WEEKEND IN THE WOODS? SURE... I'D LOVE TO...

STOP
LOGGING PERSONNEL ONLY

CAN'T WE EVER JUST GO CAMPING LIKE NORMAL PEOPLE?

ARRIVING AT THE "SCENE OF THE CRIME"...

GASP!

NEXT EPISODE: A CLEARCUT CASE

49

EPISODE THREE: A CLEARCUT CASE

BLADE RUINER

T.O. KELLENBACH

UPON REACHING THE "SCENE OF THE CRIME", THE BLADE RUINER AND LEILA CAREFULLY SET ABOUT THEIR "WORK".

LEILA SETS UP AN OBSERVATION POST TO WATCH ALL OF THE LOGGING ROAD APPROACHES.

THE BLADE RUINER LOCATES A PILE OF FELLED TREES AND REACHES INTO HIS TOOL BAG.

WITH A SHARP KNIFE HE EXPERTLY REMOVES A CHIP OF BARK...

FIRST HE PLACES A DARK TOWEL SO THAT IT WILL CATCH ALL OF THE TELL-TALE WOODSHAVING'S

ON THE FRESHLY EXPOSED INNER WOOD, A WELL-OILED BRACE & BIT STARTS TO DRILL.

WHEN THE HOLE IS FINISHED A CERAMIC PIN IS DROPPED IN.

FOLLOWED BY A GENEROUS AMOUNT OF WHITE GLUE TO HOLD IT IN PLACE.

THE BARK CHIP IS THEN CAREFULLY GLUED BACK IN PLACE-CONCEALING THE HOLE!

ALL OF THE WOOD SHAVINGS ARE SWEPT ONTO THE TOWEL AND CARRIED AWAY TO BE BURIED IN A SHALLOW HOLE.

SPREADING THE TOWEL ON THE GROUND, THE BLADE RUINER GOES TO WORK ON THE STANDING TREES,

THEN SUDDENLY...

THE CHICKENS ARE COMIN' HOME TA ROOST!

PULLING OUT A HANDFUL OF CALTROPS, LEILA PREPARES TO DROP THEM ON THE ROAD BELOW TO STOP THE ADVANCE OF THE GUARD PATROL

SHOULD I FEED THE CHICKENS?

KNOWING THAT ABSOLUTE SECRECY IS ESSENTIAL, THE BLADE RUINER RESPONDS—

NEGATIVE... LET'S GO HOME!

AN HOUR LATER, THEY RENDEZVOUS WITH THEIR DRIVER

AT THIS POINT, MOST MONKEY-WRENCHERS WOULD TAKE A BREAK AND CONGRATULATE THEMSELVES,

BUT NOT THE BLADE RUINER...

GOLDEN GATE LAPIDARY SUPPLY

OPEN

NEXT: HARD ROCK vs. HEAVY METAL!

50

ROCK SPIKES

Hard Rock vs. Heavy Metal: Quartz Tree Pins

Certain types of rock could well be the ideal type of anti-sawblade "pin" for planting in condemned trees. As with other types of monkey-wrenching, proper materials and technique are essential.

Equipment

Begin by obtaining copies of lapidary magazines at a quality newsstand. Among these are *Gems and Minerals* and *Lapidary Journal*. Scan the ads for lapidary supply houses and supplies in large cities. For security reasons, select a business in a distant city. For example, if you live in Oregon, plan a trip to the Los Angeles area to make your equipment purchases in cash. Never leave your name or address.

In the magazine ads, you are looking for either manufacturers or retailers of lapidary saws, particularly a type called a "trim" saw, used to cut small stones into precise sizes and shapes. This power tool handles a circular saw blade made of high grade steel core with a cutting edge impregnated with chips of industrial or human-made diamond. The smallest size, a six-inch blade, should be more than adequate. These circular sawblades are far better than band or wire saws for our purposes, as they will handle greater pressures. Make sure your trim saw has a vise for holding the stone during cutting. You will also want to purchase the recommended coolant, as it is essential that the saw blade's bottom edge is immersed in this oil-based protective material. An extra blade or two can save you a return trip should you damage your first one while learning proper cutting technique. Trim saws vary in price from about $160 to $350, with good quality models averaging around $300. Diamond blades range in price from $20 to $45. The more costly types are thin blades for fine cutting with a minimum of material loss (important only for work with precious and semi-precious stones), so the lower priced general-purpose blades are what you will need. Dulled or damaged blades can be repaired and re-surfaced by manufacturers, but be sure you don't leave a name and address for investigators to trace to you.

Information on proper use of the trim saw can be found at a large public library in lapidary and jewelry-making books, but make sure you read and/or photocopy the information at the library. If you check out a book, you will leave a paper trail betraying your interest in this subject.

Following are some of the most important rules for correct operation of a trim saw:

1) Always put safety first. Wear safety glasses. Be patient while learning to use the saw.

2) Don't use long extension cords to power the saw as this will cause a loss of power through voltage drop.

3) Check the coolant level to insure proper levels. Otherwise you will quickly destroy an expensive blade.

4) Make sure the surface of the rock you are cutting into is at right angles to the blade. Cutting into an angled surface can create side pressures that bring about a wobble and rapid wear-out of the blade.

5) Slow down at the end of every cut to keep the rock from breaking and leaving a jagged spur protruding from the cut surface.

Stones can be cut into any elongated shape that will fit into the holes drilled into trees, generally not exceeding one inch in diameter. After cutting, clean the stone "pins" in warm water and a little dish soap. When finished, they must be free of fingerprints and stored in a container to prevent accidental handling with bare hands.

Rock Types

The large majority of rock types are not suitable for modification into "pins" simply because they are not hard enough to damage a sawmill blade. For a number of reasons, quartz and related minerals are perhaps best. On the Moh's scale of hardness (from one to ten), quartz rates a seven, making it harder than steel which ranks from 5.5 to 6.5. Furthermore, virtually anyone with outdoor experience will recognize quartz in the field. Quartz is found throughout most of the U.S.

Quartz comes in a variety of colors, from clear or milky white, to rose or reddish, yellowish, and even blue grey in some gold-bearing regions. A good field test for rocks you think are quartz can be carried out with a small piece of glass. If the rock is quartz, it will scratch the glass. If it will not scratch glass, it is simply a quartz look-alike. Start with small quartz rocks until you know what your trim saw can handle. Proper use of the saw will permit a single diamond blade to cut thousands of square inches of quartz.

Lower Cost Alternatives

If the cost of procuring a trim saw is prohibitive, one can scour the area of quartz deposits for small fragments or river-worn pieces small enough to insert into a one-inch hole. On the negative side, they can be difficult to load into the drilled hole and are less likely to come into proper contact with a sawblade.

Smaller quartz gravel can be combined with cement to make a round pin of some value. First, roll-up heavy paper and glue it into tubes one-inch in diameter or a little less. Mix three parts gravel with one part cement and one and one-half parts sand. Add water, a little at a time, until the mix is wet but still very stiff. Next, load it into the tube a little at a time and use a dowel to tamp it into place, eliminating air bubbles. Wearing plastic gloves will protect your hands from the lime in the cement. Set your pins in a cool but moist place to cure. Ideal conditions are 70 degrees fahrenheit and 80 percent relative humidity. Allow them to cure from three to six months for maximum strength. Finally, peel off the paper tube exterior and paint the pins with a coat of exterior latex paint. The paint will protect the concrete from deterioration both inside and outside the tree. Make sure the concrete is never exposed to freezing temperatures while curing. Use as large pieces of quartz gravel as is feasible.

Still another low cost pin involves using large quartz gravel or cobbles in a matrix of a good quality resin epoxy available at hardware stores and lumber yards. Form it into pins in the same way you would the concrete method. This can allow you to use larger quartz rock fragments with a better chance of impacting a blade properly. The paper can be soaked in water and gently scrubbed off once the epoxy has set-up properly.

Rock and concrete pins require the drilling of large-diameter holes in trees which are best done with a brace-and-bit. Use the techniques described earlier for drilling and disguising the presence of the pins. As with ceramic pins, setting rock and concrete pins is time consuming and you should not expect to set a great many in one working session. However, properly placed and disguised, such non-detectable pins should be a highly effective deterrent. *Note: As always, avoid placing the pins in the lower three feet of the tree, where they can cause chainsaw kickback, with the possibility of injury to the feller. After all, we're in it to save trees, not hurt people.*

— *T.O. Hellenbach*

FIELD NOTES

*You may be able to find granite cores from old mining operations in rock shops. These circular cores from drilling are ideal non-metallic spikes.

EPISODE FOUR: HARD ROCK vs. HEAVY METAL

BLADE RUINER

R.T.D.

INTENT UPON STAYING ONE STEP AHEAD OF THE FOREST (DIS-)SERVICE, THE BLADE RUINER HAS BEGUN TO PREPARE HIS NEXT SURPRISE — THE HARDEST "SPIKE" EVER ENCOUNTERED!

FROM HIS LOCAL NEWSTAND HE BOUGHT SEVERAL GEM AND LAPIDARY MAGAZINES.

ROCK & MINERAL JOURNAL

STUDY OF THE MAGAZINE ADS REVEALED A LARGE LAPIDARY SUPPLY HOUSE LESS THAN A DAY'S DRIVE DOWN THE CONGESTED COASTAL FREEWAY.

THERE HE PURCHASED A TRIM SAW WITH DIAMOND SAW BLADES DESIGNED TO CUT ROCKS!

HE DIDN'T KNOW WHICH HURT WORST: THE THREE HUNDRED BUCKS...

SHEEEIIIT!

...OR THE DAMN ROCK HAMMER!

SOON HE FOUND THAT THE SMALL FRAGMENTS OF QUARTZ LAYING AROUND AT THE BASE OF LARGE OUTCROPS

WERE JUST THE SIZE HE NEEDED.

WITH A LITTLE PRACTICE, HE WAS SOON ABLE

BZZZZ

TO TRIM THE QUARTZ ROCKS DOWN...

TO AN ASSORTMENT OF PIECES SUITABLE FOR INSERTING INTO HOLES...

DRILLED AT NIGHT INTO ANCIENT TREES MARKED FOR DEATH!

SOON EVERY SAWMILL WAS PLAGUED WITH DAMAGED AND BROKEN BLADES. THE CHAINSAW SLAUGHTER OF THOUSAND YEAR-OLD TREES BEGAN TO SLOW DOWN.

FRUSTRATED AT EVERY TURN...

DAILY FEE
REWARD
$10,000

THE FOREST SERVICE OFFERED REWARDS...

...DISPATCHED STAKE-OUT TEAMS WITH NIGHT VISION SCOPES.

KILLER MILLS INC.

FOREST RANGER

BUT THERE WERE TOO MANY NIGHTS AND TOO MUCH FOREST... AND THE BLADE RUINER WAS A CAUTIOUS MAN!

COMPLICATING MATTERS WERE "TREE SITTERS"...

DON'T CUT US DOWN

PROTESTERS...

HANDS OFF STOP THE
EARTH FIRST
SAVE OUR WOODS

ATTACKS ON CORPORATE OFFICES.

STOP ME BEFORE I KILL AGAIN!!!

FINALLY, RELUCTANT OFFICIALS WERE FORCED TO PROTECT WILDERNESS FOREST THAT NO CORPORATE TIMBER BARONS WOULD BID ON.

THE BLADE RUINER AND LEILA HIT THE ROAD FOR THE GREAT SOUTHWEST. THEY HAD HEARD OF NEW DAMS, URANIUM MINES IN THE GRAND CANYON, AERIAL GUNNING OF COYOTES AND A HOST OF OTHER OBSCENITIES!

ECO-RAIDERS are a LOST ART

SURVEY STAKES

"Always pull up survey stakes!" This was the advice of a well-known writer to all outdoor visitors. Certainly, it seems as if a great many people are following his advice. Wherever the long arm of the machine has been spreading its destruction, be it in the city suburbs or in the remote backcountry, a near-epidemic of stake-pulling has the land rapers –be they Freddie bureaucrats or corporate developers—on the defensive. Interestingly enough, it is not just wild-eyed eco-freaks who are pulling stakes. Redneck hunters of the old school, the sort who pack in to get their elk and who well know what development is going to do to their favorite hunting grounds — these folks are doing it, too. We've even heard of *miners* pulling up stakes from Freddie logging roads up in Idaho — although we doubt they were motivated by lofty ideals — they just wanted to be left to their destructive activities in peace, undisturbed by rival rapists.

Unfortunately, a great deal of stake-pulling is haphazard. In fact, most stake-pulling is probably unplanned and done on impulse by someone just out for a hike. This is unfortunate on two counts. First of all, to pull a few survey stakes here and there, while leaving the bulk of them untouched, will merely have a nuisance effect on the developers. The surveyors will come to work, notice the damage done, curse a bit, and replace the missing stakes with a day or two of extra work.

Not much has been done here to halt the machine, beyond making a simple gesture of defiance (not that there aren't times when a gesture of defiance is better than nothing). The second reason why casual, spur of the moment stake-pulling is unfortunate is because it exposes the monkeywrencher to possible arrest. And to pull up survey stakes *is* a crime. It is considered destruction of property, and it is not inconceivable that someone taken in the act of removing survey stakes could be charged with a felony. At the very least, she/he will be charged with a mis- demeanor. Howie Wolke in Wyoming received six months in the county jail and a $750 fine combined with $2500 of restitution to Chevron for pulling survey stakes on a proposed oil & gas exploration road in a roadless area — this was after he had plea-bargained a guilty plea to a misdemeanor in exchange for dropping felony charges which could have sent him to the state penitentiary for several years.

Yet stake-pulling, well-planned and systematically done, can be one of the most effective means of monkeywrenching. It requires no esoteric technical know-how and no specialized tools. It can be done with the absolute minimum number of people — one monkeywrencher and one alert lookout. And it *can* be effective — very effective. While it is certainly possible to trash the wilderness without the benefit of scientific surveying — the crude roads bulldozed by half-assed small-time miners are the classic example — accurate surveying is essential for even the most mildly sophisticated construction projects. Logging haul roads, for instance, require precise gradients and curves — the faster the trucks can get the logs out, the greater the profit margin for the operators. Even more precise surveying is needed for the construction of buildings (corner locations and elevations are critical), the layout of water and sewer lines and the like. If the work of the surveyors is obliterated before such a project is completed, it is necessary that their work be repeated before the project can proceed. A day's work of systematic monkeywrenching can — and in numerous known cases *has* — resulted in many *weeks* of extra work for the survey crews. In those parts of the country where winter stops construction activities, a day or two of well-planned stake removal could easily postpone a project until the next year . . . and the next year. Done often enough and well enough, the trashing of the work of the surveyors can increase the costs of environmentally destructive projects to the point where there will be less of them carried to completion. After all, profits are the name of the game in the land rape business.

As we have said, surveying may precede a wide variety of develop- ment projects, whether it is a shopping mall gobbling up open space on the edge of a city, a new ski resort or hotel replacing grizzly bear habitat in a mountain meadow, or a new road gutting the heart of a previously roadless area just to make things easier for the loggers and the big oil corporations. The first tangible signs of all of these things will most likely be the surveyors in their bright orange vests, leaving behind them a trail of confusing wooden stakes and multi-colored ribbons.

Roads

The most ubiquitous form of development, at least in previously unviolated areas, is the road. Roads are of necessity a precursor of any large-scale development in the wilderness, whether it is for logging, mining, oil and gas exploration, or simply modern, "industrial" tourism.

Roads range from paved, high-speed highways which may involve measurements down to the hundredths of a foot, through unpaved but still relatively sophisticated "all-weather" roads (the major trunk roads on the National Forests are of this variety) down to fairly crude logging "feeder" roads, which are measured, during the surveying phase, merely to the nearest foot. But what all these roads do have in common is that they require surveying.

For the sake of explanation, we will discuss the surveying of a typical low-grade logging road of the sort which are constructed on the public lands. *Thousands of miles* of these roads are built each year, generally at taxpayers' expense, to the benefit of a few big logging companies and to the detriment of a healthy forest. The basic principles used in this example would apply, with only minor differences, to the surveying of any road.

Our hypothetical road will be built into the "Last Stand Grove" on the Timber Sale National Forest. In the beginning, timber cruisers indicated the presence of "commercial" timber in the Last Stand Grove area. This may have originally happened many years ago, when even the Freddies didn't think that the trees in Last Stand Grove were economically feasible to cut. But the bureaucracy has a long memory, and finally the day arrives when even remote and marginal stands of trees are sought. So the "timber beasts" schedule a sale in Last Stand Grove — no matter that only five million board feet of timber will be cut in return for the construction of ten or twelve miles of new road — since their job is to meet the Forest's annual projected "cut," they don't worry about economics.

Since each National Forest maintains a "Five-Year Timber Plan," updated annually, the Last Stand Grove Timber Sale is planned five years ahead of the projected date. Sometimes due to fluctuations in the timber industry, the projected date may not be met, but as a rule about a year or two prior to the scheduled date of the sale, depending on available personnel and other work priorities, the actual surveying of the road network into the sale area begins. In the meantime, timber marking crews have probably already been sent into the sale area to mark trees for cutting (although sometimes this is not done until after the survey crews have begun laying out the roads).

Just as the timber cruising, "stand exams" and marking are done by the Timber Branch of the service, the design and surveying of the road network fall under the jurisdiction of the Engineering Branch. The engineers study topographical maps and get a rough idea of the most likely route a road might follow to get into the Last Stand Grove. This being done, the next step is to send a couple of people out into the woods to see if this route is practical. This crew flags the route as they go, by tying brightly-colored ribbon to the trees, while trying to keep within a certain grade. Sometimes the route roughly charted on the maps proves infeasible in the field due to the topography, and the engineers are forced to take a different approach. But usually they will manage to find a workable route. The biggest difficulty is usually in keeping within the required grade. While short stretches of logging road may exceed 8 or 9 percent, it is common to try to keep from exceeding 6 percent on most stretches. The steeper the road, the slower the haul traffic.

If you happen across a line of flagging in the woods, it is possible that you have encountered a road in the earliest stages of survey. Should you remove the flagging, you have probably cost the developers a couple of days' work at the most. It would be better to wait until the surveying has progressed further, when monkeywrenching would have a greater effect. Incidentally, "flagging" is what surveyors call the brightly colored plastic tape which they use to mark their work and make it easy to locate. Red and orange are the colors most favored by surveyors, although they may well use others. *Others* besides surveyors may use flagging; timber crews frequently use it to mark sale boundaries, although they usually favor blue, yellow or striped flagging.

After the engineers have roughly flagged-in the route of the road, a more proper survey is done. This employs a crew of from three to five people. On large road projects, several crews may be working simultaneously on different sections of the road. Sometimes the crews live in temporary housing (usually trailers; rarely tent camps) near the work area. However, this is the exception. Often survey crews spend nearly as much time driving over forest roads as they do working in the woods.

The survey crew performs a two-fold function as it surveys the road. On the one hand, the survey crew will precisely mark the location of the road on the ground, a route that will be later followed by the construction workers when the road is actually built. But at the same time, the crew will be gathering and recording data which will be later used in the actual design of the road. This data will enable the designers to estimate such things as the amount of cut and fill, necessity for blasting (if any), need for culverts or bridges, and the like. Since this information will be used to estimate construction costs, the data-gathering function of the survey crew is of considerable importance. At the present time, actual road design is generally done by computer, after all the pertinent data has been collected and processed.

The survey crew follows the line of preliminary flagging, laying out the route. Distances are measured from the beginning of the road, and are measured from point to point along the "centerline" of the route. Each point on the centerline is numbered, and is called a "station." Each station is marked (usually with a stake and also sometimes in other ways, which will be described later). On low grade logging roads, where precision measurements are not essential, measurements are usually done by "chaining," which involves the use of an engineer's tape. These tapes are usually made of reinforced cloth, and are 50 or 100 feet long. Where more precise measurements are needed it was formerly the practice to use a "steel chain," which is a thin, flexible steel measuring tape up to 200 feet long. However, where sophisticated surveys are needed now it is common to employ various forms of "electronic distance meters," or EDM's, which use a laser beam to take instantaneous and accurate measurements between the instrument and a "rodman" holding a reflector. Whatever the means used, the purpose is the same, the measurement of distances between stations along the centerline of the road.

On a low-grade logging road such as the one to the Last Stand Grove, stations may be placed at pre-set intervals of 50 feet or so. Stations are also placed wherever there is a "break" in the terrain. A "break" is a significant change in the terrain — it might be a slight hollow or it might be a major rock outcrop. In complex terrain, stations are more closely spaced. At a stream crossing, for instance, stations might be placed at the top of the banks, at the actual edge of the stream, and one will probably be placed in the center of the stream. Stations are also placed at any point where the centerline of the road changes direction.

The survey crew makes a note of anything of significance in the terrain at each station, and also generally runs a "cross-section." In a cross-section, an imaginary line is plotted at right angles to the centerline of the road. The crew takes a chain out 50 or 100 feet above and below the centerline and records differences in elevation at various distances from the centerline. In low-grade roads this is done by simply recording angles from the centerline with a clinometer or hand level. In more sophisticated surveys a tripod-mounted level is set up over the centerline station to record exact elevation differences along the cross-section. *Sometimes* stakes are placed above and below the centerline along the line of each cross-section ("cross-section stakes"), but this is usually not done.

When the crew "puts in" each station, they place a stake with the numerical designation of that station in the ground. On a low-grade road, like the one into Last Stand Grove, the survey stake itself is the only indicator of the station. However, in more elaborate surveys, where precise distances are required, the actual station is marked by a nail or a "hub and tack." A hub is a fat (usually 2"x2") stake which is pounded flush into the ground — a small tack is then placed in the top at the precise location of the station. This is of importance to the monkeywrencher, since when you see a line of survey stakes you may not immediately notice a hub flush with the ground and almost certainly will not notice something as small as a nail, unless you know to look for such things around survey stakes. But if you want to do a thorough job of monkeywrenching a survey project, you will want to remove *everything* you find — every bit that you leave will make the job of re-surveying easier.

Sometimes, especially in areas in which there is heavy cattle grazing, small colored flags attached to long wires are fastened to the point of a stake or hub before it is driven into the ground. These flags make the stakes easier to locate, but their real purpose is this: survey stakes are frequently pulled out of the ground or broken off due to the activities of cows or other large herbivores (cows as monkeywrenchers?). Often the stake will be totally absent but the flag remains. Monkeywrenchers should pull up such flags. Be sure to look for a hub — it may be covered with a layer of dirt, pine needles, or the like.

Stakes are numbered beginning with the starting point of the road. The numbering system used is fairly standard, and a brief explanation may be of some use to the serious monkeywrencher. Theoretically, the starting station on a road would be "zero," which would be written as "00 + 00." The first digit represents thousands, the second hundreds, the third tens (of feet) and the last digit represents feet. Thus, a station 50 feet from the starting point would be written as "00 + 50." But in practice, it is common to start out at 1000′ ("10 + 00") to allow for later adjustments in the design. So if "10 + 00" is the beginning station in a road, a station 250 feet further down the centerline would be written as "12 + 50," and one 1000 feet from the starting point would be written as "20 + 00." You can therefore determine by the station numbers where you are in relation to the starting point of a line of survey stakes — if you cross a survey line in the woods at station "62 + 00 " for example, you can assume that you are about a mile from the starting point (assuming the first station was "10 + 00"). Of course, only exploration will tell you how far the stakes go in the opposite direction — unless you happen to have some "inside" information on the project.

In addition to a number, each stake will probably have a letter or series of letters written on it. These may be "PT" or "POT," which stand for "point on tangent," or "PC" or "POC," which stand for "point of curve." A point on tangent is simply a station along a straight section of the centerline, while the point of curve is a station where the centerline either begins or ends a curve. On low-grade logging roads such as our hypothetical one into the Last Stand Grove, the Freddies usually employ a simpler designation: stations on a straight line are designated with a "P," for "point," while stations at the beginning or ending of a turn are designated "PI," for "point of intersection." The importance of this to the monkeywrencher lies in the fact that "PC" or "PI" stations, where the road will change direction, are more critical than the stations which merely lie in a straight line. At "PC," "POC," and "PI" stations, the survey crews, in addition to their usual cross-section, also record the angle and direction of the turn. For low-grade roads this is done with a hand or staff compass; on more sophisticated roads this is done more accurately with a theodolite or its electronic equivalent. Because the "loss" of a PC or PI station can cause a lot of additional work in its replacement, these stations often receive special attention from the surveyors — "reference points," which are additional means of locating the station should the original hub and/or stake be removed or otherwise effaced.

Reference points (or "RP's," as they are usually termed) are *not* inspired by monkeywrenchers, although their use has certainly become more common in areas where the deliberate removal of survey stakes has become a popular pastime. Survey stakes, hubs, and the other markings of survey crews are often obliterated in perfectly "innocent" ways. If a road is not immediately built, for example, the ravages of nature begin to take their toll. Stakes weather fast, flagging fades and eventually disintegrates, and some forest creatures speed the process up by gnawing on the stakes. An additional reason for the use of RP's is that when the construction workers arrive on the scene, they frequently accidentally knock over stakes before their usefulness is finished.

There are several ways in which RP's may be placed. Perhaps the simplest and most common is to set a hub and tack a given distance from the station (remember,it will probably be a "PC," "POC," or "PI" station). The hub and tack (in extremely hard ground a nail will probably be used instead of a hub and tack) will be placed to the *side* of the roadway. The distance will vary, but it might be as far as 25′ or even 50′ away, although the distance has a lot to do with visibility. Then a *second* hub and tack (or nail) will be placed a number of feet beyond the first one, on a tangent (straight line) leading to the station that is being RP'd. Thus, if the original station is obliterated, by lining up the two RP's and measuring the distance it is possible to re-set the station. It is important for the prospective monkeywrencher to check carefully for RP's when removing survey stakes. If you don't find any on your first couple of "PC" or "PI" stations, it is probably safe to assume that there aren't any, but if they are present a thorough job of monkeywrenching requires their removal. Fortunately, RP's are also usually marked by stakes and flagging, so that the surveyors can find them again.

Another way in which RP's are sometimes done is to place a hub and tack, nail or whatever a given distance off the centerline, measure the distance, and take a compass bearing from the RP to the centerline station. This method is not as accurate as the previous method, and is not likely to be employed on sophisticated surveys. On simple surveys in wooded terrain, RP's usually consist of no more than a couple of stakes nailed to widely-separated trees away from the centerline. By simultaneously measuring known distances from those two stakes, the surveyors can relocate the original station. (No bearings are taken).

Just before actual construction of a road begins, a final survey is done. Any changes in the centerline suggested in the final design are made. More importantly (for the monkeywrencher, at least) additional staking is done. "Slope stakes" are placed above and below the centerline. These stakes indicate such things as the top of the cut and the bottom of the fill. At stream crossings they indicate such things as the position of culverts. Slope stakes usually bear written information regarding the width of the roadway, depth of cut and so on. Slope stakes are more for the benefit of the inspectors than the bulldozer operators, who rarely read them and knock them out with their 'dozers as soon as work commences. The best time to monkeywrench a road survey is after the main survey has been completed but *before* slope staking begins. Not only does a monkeywrencher have far more stakes to remove if he/she waits until this final phase, but it is also frequently too late to effectively stop the road. Although the Forest Service prefers to slope-stake roads a full season before construction is to take place, in actual practice slope-staking crews have been known to work only a few days ahead of the 'dozers.

FLAGGING. Survey crews leave lots of bright-colored flagging to mark their path. While this flagging may be offensive to the aesthetic sense, it certainly makes it easier for a monkeywrencher to locate all the stakes, hubs and nails. Usually flagging is placed on the stakes themselves (although there is a trend to use pre-painted stakes instead — red or orange are the most common colors). Hubs are not flagged, since they are generally pounded flush into the ground, but nails have a strip of flagging tied around the head before they are driven into the ground. In addition, flagging is usually hung on a branch above the stake (in wooded country). Thus the centerline of the road is usually well-marked with flagging. When slope-staking is done, two additional lines of flagging (one above and one below the centerline) are usually placed. This flagging delineates the zone which will be cleared of trees ahead of the bulldozers. In addition to pulling out all stakes, nails and hubs, the thorough monkeywrencher should remove *all* flagging. The harder it is for the surveyors to re-locate the route of a road, the more costly and time-consuming a re-survey will be.

A monkeywrencher removing stakes and flagging from a road project will quickly accumulate more stakes and flagging than can be conveniently carried. A good idea is to carry a pack in which to place stakes and flagging. Periodically, the monkeywrencher should detour some distance away from the route of the road, and dispose of this material in such a way that it is not likely to be seen. Burning has been suggested, but this is time-consuming and might jeopardize security, and in any event is not recommended for flagging, which is plastic. A better method would be to bury the material. At the very least, stakes should be broken and all stakes and flagging hidden under logs or rocks. Resist the temptation to carry any of the material out with you once you've finished monkeywrenching a project. Stakes and flagging would constitute incriminating evidence should you be stopped and searched. (See **Field Notes** for additional and important security considerations.)

Construction Sites

Any development involving structures is extensively surveyed prior to construction. Not only are the locations of corners, water and sewer lines and such important, but it is necessary to have precise elevations for foundations and to provide proper drainage for sewer lines. For these reasons the surveying done on construction sites is more precise than that done for most roads. Monkeywrenching can seriously retard major construction projects.

The basic principles of surveying are the same as for roads, and you will find a profusion of hubs and tacks, nails and stakes around any major construction site. The main thing to keep in mind around a construction site is that reference points, or RP's, are almost certainly used for all major points of significance. This is because as soon as actual construction starts, all of the hubs, nails, and the like marking important locations get ripped out during excavation for the buildings, even though it is absolutely necessary to relocate all of these points. Therefore, well away from the building site you will find numerous RP's. A proper job of monkeywrenching will require removal of all of these, in addition to the hubs, stakes and such on the actual building site.

On a construction site, the stakes will often carry a description of what they represent, as "water line," "corner of building," "edge of sidewalk," and such. Frequently, longer-than-usual stakes are employed. These are called "laths," and may be 2' or 3' long. Laths are also frequently used in the slope-staking of roads.

Miscellaneous

*OFFSET STAKES — Survey stakes may be *offset* from the actual location of the station. This may be for several reasons. If the station falls on a rock where a stake cannot be driven, a masonry nail may be driven into the rock to mark the station, and the stake offset several feet. Sometimes the ground is simply too hard to admit a stake (but usually not a nail). On road *reconstruction* projects, where stations may fall in an existing roadway, stakes or laths are offset to the side of the road. You have probably seen these frequently while driving down a highway which is about to be improved. If the existing road is unpaved, nails with flagging or shiners on them (a shiner is a small, bright metal disk through which a nail is driven) are driven into the actual station, while the stake bearing the station number is offset to the side of the road. If the existing road is a paved highway a masonry nail is driven into the pavement at the station, and the station number is spray-painted on the surface of the pavement. This is also something you have probably seen frequently while driving, although you may not have paid any attention to it.

When a stake is offset, the distance of the offset is written at the top of the stake, enclosed in a circle or oval. The writing on the stake faces the direction of the station. If you find such a stake, you can usually find the actual station by roughly measuring the distance written on the stake and searching for a nail. Sometimes a stake may be offset several feet from a hub, particularly in hard ground. A hub can sometimes be successfully driven into ground which is hard enough to shatter the thinner identifying stakes.

*BENCH MARKS — A "bench mark" is a point of known elevation. The classic example is the USGS markers (usually a brass cap) which one finds frequently on mountain tops or other prominent locations. In many survey projects (including some road projects) it is necessary to know exact elevations. Working from a permanent bench mark, like a USGS bench mark, the surveyors establish the elevation of a number of "temporary bench marks" (or "TBM's") in the project area. Large, stable rocks which have a small protuberance on them are favorite subjects for temporary bench marks. The rock will frequently be spray-painted and the elevation of the protuberance written on the rock. Another frequently used method is to drive a large nail most of the way into a tree. The head of the nail is the TBM, and its elevation is usually written on a stake nailed to the tree. The tree will also probably be prominently flagged or spray-painted. While TBM's painted on rocks would be difficult to efface, nails in trees can either be driven all the way in and disguised or removed with a claw hammer.

Sometimes for major construction projects survey crews establish permanent bench marks at the construction site. These usually consist of small copper caps or larger (4″ - 5″ dia.) aluminum ones set in concrete. The cap is attached to a metal rod (sometimes up to 2′ long) which is driven to within a few inches of the ground surface, after which a few inches of concrete are poured around the metal cap. These are called "monuments." Removing one is certainly feasible, but it would probably require a shovel and/or prybar. Needless to say, removal of a monument is illegal; in fact it usually says so right on the metal cap.

*PHOTO PANELS — You have probably seen these in the woods. They consist of sheets of plastic, a foot or two wide and ten or more feet long, usually arranged in a "cross" or "X." The plastic is usually white, although black plastic is sometimes used on a light-colored surface. The purpose of these is to aid in mapping by aerial photography. If you look at the center of the "X," you will find a hub, or a nail or maybe a piece of rebar. This marks a point with known coordinates (i.e., it has been set after the surveyors have run a traverse out to it). Several of these panels will be laid out in advance of a photo session. While this may sound innocent, such mapping is frequently done in connection with major construction projects. Unfortunately, photo panels are frequently left to rot in the woods after the job is done; effective monkeywrenching would have to be done during the short interval between the time they are laid out and the time the photos are taken — this sometimes is a matter of days, though it may be several weeks.

FIELD NOTES

*TOOLS — While little specialized equipment is necessary for the saboteur of survey stakes, there are a few items which are helpful. As mentioned earlier, a pack to carry stakes, flagging and other trash one might pick up would be helpful. *Don't carry out anything that might be incriminating. Bury or otherwise conceal it away from the road or construction site.*

A claw hammer is perhaps the only recommended tool. Not only is it useful for pulling nails out of trees and out of pavement, but it makes it simpler even to remove nails from soft ground. It also can prove useful in removing hubs from hard ground. Give the head of the hub a few good whacks to one side or another. That will probably loosen the hub enough so that it can be pulled out by hand.

*SECURITY —Removing survey stakes may seem like a relatively innocuous occupation, but rest assured that the authorities and the corporate minions do not consider it trivial. Always use a lookout. If you see anyone else in the vicinity, stop what you are doing, get rid of anything incriminating, and get out of the area. Always have an escape route planned. Treat this activity as seriously as you would any other form of monkeywrenching.

If you are working in an area in which there has been considerable monkeywrenching, the authorities may well be on the lookout for saboteurs. Do not discount the possibility that a survey project may be staked out (no pun intended) or that someone may have followed you into the woods. It has even been reported that on some highly-contro-versial timber sales the Freddies have resorted to putting invisible dyes on survey stakes. The idea apparently is that anyone touching these stakes will get some of the dye on their hands, but not be aware of it, and that should they be apprehended, the dye would show up under ultraviolet light. While it is not likely that this tactic will be widely used, since it will obviously complicate the task of the surveyors and construction workers themselves, prospective monkeywrenchers should be aware of the lengths to which the authorities may be prepared to go.

The use of invisible dyes is really nothing new in law enforcement, and has long been used to mark money. If you suspect that the authorities might be using this technique in your area, you can take a few simple precautions. Wear cheap cotton gloves while monkeywrenching. Place the stakes, as they are removed, in a plastic trash bag. Avoid touching clothing with either gloves or stakes. Before leaving the area, dispose of gloves, stakes, and trash bag(s), preferably where they will never be found. Be sure that you have left no fingerprints on anything — be especially careful with the trash bags. At the earliest opportunity, wash the clothes you were wearing on your mission.

*Do not neglect other tactics discussed in this book (road spiking, sand in the oil, etc.) to harass surveyors.

MINING

There are few of us who haven't encountered the ubiquitous mining claim markers while out for a stroll in the wilds — even in designated Wilderness Areas such claims are legal if they were filed before December 31, 1984. A brief rundown on mining claims will help the prospective monkeywrencher deal with these disgusting intrusions.

On public land (i.e., Federal land not specifically withdrawn from mineral location) any U.S. citizen (or corporation) may "locate" (i.e., stake) one or more claims entitling the claimant to extract any minerals that might be found there. Foreign corporations subvert the citizenship requirement by forming a U.S.-based subsidiary to do the claim-staking.

Two types of mining claims may be located: placer and lode. "Placer" claims involve mineral extraction from water-borne deposits, usually in or around streams, whereas "lode" mining involves the original source of the mineralization: the vein or "lode." Each claim measures 600' by 1500' and must be posted at all four corners. In some states "side-centers," "discovery posts" and/or flagged or blazed perimeters are also required. Each post must be 4' high and at least 4" in diameter. Where trees are not legally acceptable as "posts" or in open country, wooden 4 x 4's, 4" PVC pipe or rock cairns may be utilized.

Claims may be staked individually, or in blocks that commonly include as many as 5,000 claims (10,000 acres). To be valid, a "Location Notice" specifying exact geographical location, who staked the claim and when it was staked must be filed (for each claim) with the Regional BLM office (assuming the claim is on Federal land) and the County Recorder's office. In addition, a location notice must be posted somewhere on the claim itself. Jars, cans or fold-up aluminum tags are commonly used to hold location notices, and these will be attached to one of the four corner posts or to the "discovery post" if one is required.

Let's assume that you find a claim marker on your next trip into the backcountry. The amount of time and energy you are willing to expend to trash the claim markers will determine your next move. If you're in a hurry, simply remove post, tag, flagging and any other assorted materials, and bury them or otherwise dispose of them where they are unlikely to be found. But first, look around for more corner posts — there should be at least three additional ones, even if you have discovered a single, isolated claim.

If you can't find all of the corner posts, or if you think the claim you have encountered may be only one of many filed by the same individual or corporation in that area, *and* you have the time and inclination to do a thorough trashing, *don't* do anything to the marker yet, except to copy down any information on the notice or tag attached to the marker, for further research.

Most corporate or large-scale claims will use aluminum tags which will have the required information scribed into them. Some sample tags will be described here:

Illustration "A." From this tag (a corner tag) you can tell that "Greed, Inc." staked the "Dig and Dash" claims on 8/7/85, that four claims in the grid share this point as a common corner, that this is point P47 on the claim block grid, and that there are *at least* 217 claims in this block. The "location notice" *may* also be attached to this post.

Illustration "B." This is the discovery post for the "Dig & Dash #137." The location notice *will* be attached to this post. (Remember, not all states require separate discovery posts like this.)

Illustration "C." Such a tag may be found midway between two corners (the "Discovery Line") and gives directions and distances to the discovery posts for D & D claims numbers 217 and 137, to wit: Number 137 (tag in illus. "B," above) can be found by walking 158' to the east (set your compass with zero on north, taking into account the declination for your area, then set your course at 90 degrees to the east and begin walking). Similarly, go 50' to the west to find the discovery post for #217. If your claim block does not have this sort of tag, distances to the discovery posts are recorded on the copy of the location notice filed with the BLM. *Note: the copy of the location notice attached to the discovery or corner post may give adequate information to find the remaining posts of a claim; then again, it may not.*

Once you've copied down the information on the tag, figure out your exact township and range. Record this information. It will help greatly if you have a map, but even if you don't you may be able to figure this out later if you sketch nearby landforms. Once you've done this, you're ready for the next step — a visit to the mining section of the BLM regional office for your area. Remember, BLM administers mining claims for Forest Service lands as well as other public lands.

At the BLM office, information on mining claims is filed by township. What you are after is the map showing the layout of the claim blocks and specific information on the particular staking requirements for your state — this last so you know what you need to look for when you return to the field ("discovery posts," "side centers," etc.). The maps will be filed on microfilm along with the location notices, and you

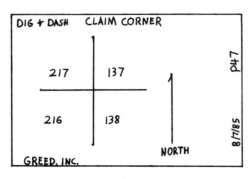

A

B

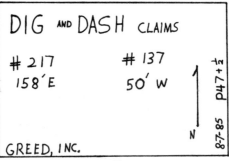

C

Corner Posts ●

Side Centers (in applicable states) ✗

Discovery Posts (in applicable states) ⊕

Discovery Line — usually not marked on ground. Discovery Post may be anywhere along this imaginary line. — — — —

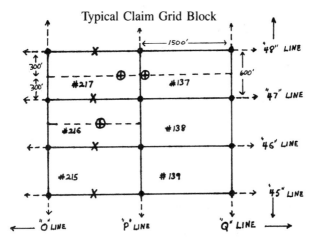

Typical Claim Grid Block

should be able to obtain copies for a small charge.

There is generally no problem in asking a clerk for specific information — just say you are interested in staking a claim in a particular area and want to know what land is open. Act naive. Few BLMers are likely to consider such an inquiry to be suspicious or unusual, whereas someone at the County Recorder's Office just might.

With map in hand, you can plot your strategy for systematically removing the claim markers in a large block. When you return to the site, do a proper reconnaissance, then remove *everything* for maximum effectiveness. Flagging, notices and tags can be buried; wooden or plastic posts can be stashed in the nearest thicket or ravine. One way to deal with PVC pipes in bare or rocky country is to shatter them against rocks in a dry wash, where the next flash flood will bury the debris. Whatever you do, *don't* carry wooden corner posts or PVC pipes out! A pickup full of posts or pipes 4′ long is a dead giveaway. Backwoods miners are a suspicious lot, given to carrying guns and infected with exaggerated ideas about the "wild west." To be taken for a "claim jumper," let alone an environmentalist monkeywrencher, migh† result in an unenviable fate. Once in an area, work quickly, finish as soon as possible, and leave before anyone catches on. Disguise yourself as a camper or hunter, and have a good story ready should you be questioned by anyone.

Your action will at the very least provide a costly hassle, particularly to the small miner (a type whose depredations in the backcountry are perhaps the least defensible of all). As for the big corporations, while you may not stop their operations, you may delay them and make them more costly. There is always the chance that after claim markers are removed, a competitor may restake the area, causing no end of time consuming legal hassles to determine which claims are valid.

Much mining in the American west is a fraud. Elaborate mining corporations are set up with the real purpose of "mining" the gullible investor. Once enough investors have been "milked," the company announces that the mine is a financial failure and declares bankruptcy. The sleaziest operators don't even go through this formality, but just slip away in the dead of the night leaving an empty office, a mine site stripped of all but worthless equipment, and a pile of debts with local merchants. Unfortunately, even these scam mining operations (which are more common these days than the average citizen might suspect) do a great deal of environmental destruction. During the phase when the phony company is still looking for more investors, they may actually initiate mining and milling operations so they have something tangible to show prospective suckers. (In one such scam mining venture in Idaho a couple of years ago the operators even put in an airstrip so they could fly in the prospective investors to show them the "progress" that was being made.)

Serious ecotage of such marginal operators can be effective. With large staking projects costing tens, even hundreds of thousands of dollars, it is entirely possible that such an operation might be shut down before it really gets started.

FIELD NOTES

In going after a mining operation in a wild area, do not limit yourself merely to removing the claim markers. Because so many of these "mines" are on a shaky financial footing, spiking roads to cause flat tires, plugging culverts to wash out newly bulldozed roads, and midnight maintenance on heavy equipment and trucks can cause crippling financial losses to a small or medium-sized operator, and even act as a serious discouragement to a major company, which can in turn cause the abandonment of the project. (The major asset many "small miners" have is their bulldozer which they use with wild abandon to scrape up the earth to look for the "mother lode." These fellows are among the most destructive characters loose on our public lands. If you can cripple their bulldozer with the techniques described elsewhere in **ECODEFENSE,** you might put them out of business, or at least run them out of the area you are trying to defend.) Security is of prime importance in any monkeywrenching activity around a mine site because of the forty-niner mentality still prevalent amongst such "get rich quick" cretins. Do not take unnecessary chances here — you are not simply courting jail, but possible death.

POWERLINES

Powerlines are highly vulnerable to monkeywrenching from individuals or small groups. The best techniques are 1) removing bolts from steel towers; 2) cutting steel towers with hacksaws, torches (be careful not to breathe the vapors of galvanized metal — see **Cutting Torch** article), or cutting wheels in the event that tower bolts are welded to the nuts; and 3) shooting out insulators (with a shotgun), and shooting the electrical conductor itself (a high-powered rifle is best) which frays it and reduces its ability to transmit electricity. Chain saws, or crosscuts where noise is a problem, are appropriate for the large wooden towers. Techniques that connect the conductors directly to each other (cable lifted by balloons or shot by harpoon guns) are also effective Used creatively, these techniques can completely baffle the opposition.

* Most powerline towers are attached to a concrete base(s) by a number of large bolts and nuts (with or without the addition of guy wires). (See illustration.) Check the size of the nuts, get a socket set for that size nut, a cheater pipe for better torque, and remove the nuts. (See illustration.) You may also want to tap out the bolts with a hammer. Wind will do the rest after you are safely away from the area.

* The more vulnerable towers are those spanning a canyon, at corners, on long spans, going up or down mountains — anywhere there is added stress or powerful wind. The "domino effect" can be achieved by monkeywrenching a series of towers leading up to a corner, or an otherwise stressed tower, and then monkeywrenching the stressed tower. *Do not expect to monkeywrench a stressed tower and then allow the wind to finish the job for you after you are safely away from the area — it will probably come down in your presence. Be prepared.*

* If the nuts are welded to the bolts to prevent removal, use a hacksaw to cut through the bolts or even through the supports. This is more difficult, but a night's work can still prepare a good number of towers for toppling in the next storm.

* A cutting torch could also be used for cutting through tower supports (see **Cutting Torch** article).

* Another effective method, where noise is not too much of a problem, is to shoot out the insulators holding the power cables themselves. A twelve-gauge shotgun loaded with double-ought shot is the best tool. Walk under the line until you are directly beneath the insulators on a tower. With your back to the wind, take two large steps backwards,

aim at the insulators and commence firing. Be prepared to dodge large chunks of falling glass. Large powerlines are suspended from strings of 20 or more insulators. Breaking 70 - 90% of them in one string is usually enough to ground out the conductor. This may take several rounds (the record is two), and will cause bright sparks. A team of three shotgunners, each taking the string of insulators for one conductor (or conductor bundle), is best for a typical AC line. The lines themselves seldom are shot through and fall, but be alert for this possibility.

* When insulators are shot out, the line quits carrying power and has to be shut down until the point of disruption is found and repaired. A helicopter may have to fly several hundred miles of powerline to find where it has been monkeywrenched. Monkeywrenching at a number of locations on the same night compounds the effectiveness.

* Because of the noise from the use of the shotguns, extreme security measures are necessary and several escape routes should be planned. Furthermore, the use of a firearm makes this a potentially more dangerous activity. *Do not leave any empty shotgun shells at the scene, since they can be positively traced to the gun that fired them.*

* Smaller powerlines are vulnerable to having their insulators shot out by a .22 rifle from a car driving along backroads, or by a hiker. "Powerline? What powerline? I'm just hunting rabbits." This is an effective method to discourage power companies from spraying powerline rights-of-way with toxic herbicides. Be sure to let the power company know that the damage is being done because of herbicide spraying (techniques for safe communication of this sort are in the section on **Security**) and that it will stop when they stop poisoning the area.

These nuts and bolts hold the powertower support to its concrete base. They are removable with a ratchet wrench and cheater pipe.

Shotgunner's view of powertower and powerlines. Note the glass or ceramic insulators.

75

SEISMOGRAPHIC LINES

SEISMIC SURVEY CREWS: HOW THEY WORK

One of the biggest potential threats to wilderness is the amount of land under lease for mineral exploration. According to the Utah Wilderness Association, for example, over ninety percent of BLM land in Utah is covered by oil and gas leases. The holder of the lease has the right to explore for mineral wealth with helicopters, trucks and sometimes earthmoving equipment; roads have been bulldozed for drilling rigs in several Wilderness Study Areas, even though this violates BLM regulations for WSA's. Clearly, mineral exploration, drilling and mining continue to be regarded in Washington as priority uses for public lands in the West.

Permits to explore for oil and gas are regularly granted by the BLM and Forest Service with little or no fuss. Environmental damage is supposed to be kept to a minimum, but some is inevitable and nobody watches seismic crews to prevent needless tearing up of the land, with the exception of archaeological sites which must be surveyed and marked by an expert before the seismic work can begin. I heard a story which typifies this kind of situation. A crew was doing a line in Montezuma Canyon in Utah, where they were preceded by a bulldozer to make a road through the rocks. Because this canyon is a very rich archeological area full of Basketmaker and later Cliff Dweller sites, an archeologist marked these sites off limits with blue flagging. Human nature being what it is, the surveyors and the "juggies" raided every blue-flagged area for pot sherds and arrowheads!

Exploration on private land often crosses fields, where compaction of the soil by the heavy trucks can cost a farmer money. So a permit agent calls on the landowner with cash in return for granting a permit. Often, this includes restrictions such as "one set of tracks" or "no vehicles" (so the cable must be packed in on foot); and these are often adhered to, although mistakes are made.

After the permit agent has done his work, the next step is to send in the surveyors. Working with a "chain," the line is laid out cross country or along a road using colored flags at regular intervals of 110, 220, 440 feet or whatever for the pattern being used. Later (sometimes not until after the line is "shot") the surveyors sight in the whole line with a theodolite or its electronic equivalent, leaving survey stakes to mark instrument positions. Survey work is easy, although tedious, to undo. As an ecodefender, the biggest problem is finding a seismic line in the first place; unless you have talked to somebody on the crew over a beer, a glimpse of colored flags along the road or trail is the only clue. Walk along the line and pull them all up. Be sure to bring a pack because seismic lines often run thirty miles or more, and that's a lot of flags.

Wilderness areas commonly have a lot of rugged terrain, or they would have been explored and drilled years ago. The advent of "portable" crews has overcome terrain problems, however, and created problems for wilderness defenders instead. Portable crews arrive by helicopter and use lightweight cable and geophones, and a portable seismograph or "recorder" unit which puts the data on magnetic tape. To create echoes for the geophones to pick up, holes are drilled for dynamite charges or else surface charges which are set off on command from the senior observer at the recorder. These explosive charges do little damage to the landscape, but they play hob with any wild animals that may live in the area. In some cases where an area has been repeatedly explored (oil companies don't share information with one another, so redundant work is commissioned) deer and other living things have reacted by moving out to a quieter neighborhood.

A "shot-hole" crew is much worse than a portable crew. I talked to a Park Service ranger at Hovenweep National Monument, where some very large Anasazi ruins are perched precariously atop sandstone boulders. He had had a visit from a shot-hole operation that ran a line just outside the monument boundary at Square Tower Ruins, less than a mile from monument headquarters. Their artificial earthquakes did not cause any harm to the ruins, but I think that ranger was very glad to see them go. Shot-hole operations use a truck-mounted drilling rig and leave a lot more physical evidence than a portable crew. There are restrictions in the use of this kind of equipment near human habitation, naturally, but most oil and gas exploration is on back country roads and trails. The major threat to wilderness here is when seismic crews, needing a road to work, get a bulldozer and make one.

"Vibroseis" crews are a relatively new development in geophysical work. Instead of dynamite charges, vibrator trucks are used. Each "vibe" lowers a plate into contact with the ground, and shakes it hydraulically. There are usually four vibes on a crew, most often trucks, but tracked vibes are used by some companies that work off the roads a lot.

A typical crew has about three or four miles of cable and geophones on the ground at any one time. During the work day, the recorder truck is plugged into the cable, "reading" off about two miles of line as the vibes shake at intervals along it. The "jug crew" is picking up the geophones and cable behind the vibes and laying it all out again ahead. At night, the vehicles are usually parked in town but the cable is left in place on the line. Very often the cable heads are disconnected at intervals or where the line crosses a road, since people have been known to use a pickup truck or whatever to drag cables away. This has allegedly happened on the Ute Mountain Indian Reservation. Cable and geophones are very expensive, and often hard to replace if lost or damaged.

Vibes and jug trucks come in threes and fours on a seismic crew, and the crew can usually operate well enough despite the loss of one of these vehicles. However, each crew possesses one and only one recorder. If it goes down, no work can be done until it is fixed. Recorders are expensive, complex electronic equipment, and too costly to replace with a spare. If the recorder is down, the crew has to shut down. "Juggie" lore tells of the time one crew was tired of working seven days a week, 12 hours a day and they created a vacation by putting a ping pong ball in the diesel fuel of the recorder truck.

If you come across seismic equipment in the mountains or desert, there are a couple of cheap, easy ways to cause them untold grief and expense. It's the thick cables paralleling the strings of geophones that you should concentrate on. Only two cheap, obtainable-anywhere items are necessary: A box of straight pins and a few tubes of super glue or similar product. Push two or three straight pins completely into as many cables as you have time for, then bend the pins until the heads break off, so they can't be seen or easily removed. This will short out all wiring in the cable, rendering it useless. Next find the cableheads (where the cable hooks to the next one: 100-300 feet apart). Open the heads by unscrewing or opening the latches—depending on the type of cable. Inside, you will see male and female plugs—2 each—containing 48 or 96 "pins." Cover these with super glue, as well as the joining edges of the cable heads, and put them back together. Most crews only have a few replacement cables, so if you can "fix" 10-20 heads you will certainly shut them down.

If you come across the "doghouse" (computer center of the crew), you probably won't be able to get inside it to do any real damage, unless you're carrying bolt cutters or a hacksaw, but these things run off generators sitting right next to them so any usual monkeywrench tricks will work there.

In themselves, seismic survey crews do little damage to the environment when compared to strip mines, power plants and dam projects. However, our remaining de facto wilderness areas (which are not protected by legislation) lie open to road making for seismic operations. and when the results from this type of survey are positive we get drilling rigs. This type of work should be restricted to land already dominated by the works of man. In wilderness areas, seismic crews are the vanguard of the "rape, ruin and run boys" and should be stopped.

The "doghouse" or computer center truck.

Truck with seismic cable.

Vibe truck.

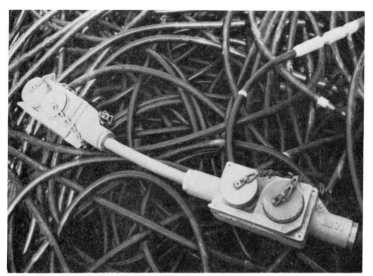

Seismic cable. Note cableheads.

Geophones.

OVERGRAZING

The livestock industry has probably done more basic ecological damage to the western United States than has any other single agent. The wolf and grizzly have been exterminated throughout most of the West for stockmen (and grizzlies are still being killed around Yellowstone National Park and the Rocky Mountain Front for sheep ranchers). The mountain lion, bobcat, black bear and coyote have been relentlessly shot, trapped and poisoned for and by ranchers until lion and bobcat populations are shadows of their former numbers. Elk, bighorn, pronghorn and bison have had their numbers tragically reduced through the impacts of livestock grazing. Streams and riparian vegetation have been degraded almost to the point of no return throughout much of the West. The grazing of cattle and sheep has drastically altered natural vegetative communities and has led to the introduction of non-native grasses palatable only to domestic livestock. Sheet and gully erosion from overgrazing have swept away most of the topsoil in the West. In non-timbered areas, most "developments" on public lands — roads, fences, juniper chainings, windmills, pipelines, stock tanks, and the like — are for the benefit of only a few welfare ranchers. Vast areas of the Great Basin and Southwest could be designated as Wilderness if it were not for the livestock industry. And throughout the West, public lands ranchers are the most vocal and militant lobby against environmental protection or Wilderness designation.

Nonetheless, conservationists have been slow to face the challenge from the livestock industry. So afraid have we been of their loud talk and pointy-toed boots, that environmental groups have acquiesced in allowing ranchers motorized access in Wilderness Areas to "manage" their cows and sheep. Monkeywrenchers and others have shied away from fighting the ranchers because of the Marlboro Man mystique.

Great care must be taken in selecting targets for this kind of ecotage. Despite the negative aspects of the livestock industry, many ranchers are decent folks. They are trapped in a hopeless situation and are trying to do the best they can. In Montana and Wyoming, particularly, there are ranchers who support Wilderness, oppose predator control, and have a deep and abiding respect for the land. Some of the best conservationists in the Northern Rockies are ranchers. Unfortunately, they are the exception. But the monkeywrencher must make *absolutely certain* that the intended target of grazing ecotage fully deserves it. Suitable targets may include:

1) Vocal leaders of the Sagebrush Ripoff and other anti-public lands schemes;

2) Vocal opponents of Wilderness designation and other environmental protection measures;

3) Notorious killers of grizzlies, wolves, mountain lions, bobcats, coyotes, etc.

4) Poor land managers and egregious overgrazers;

5) Overgrazers who operate in particularly sensitive areas (Wilderness Areas, National Parks & Monuments, National Wildlife Refuges, etc.).

Selective monkeywrenching against the *worst* ranchers will not only help eliminate the negative impacts of grazing from sensitive areas but will encourage all ranchers to do a better job.

Security must be highly stressed for any anti-grazing activity. Although the actual numbers of welfare ranchers in the West are small, they generally control the politics of rural areas, most counties and many states. Legal penalties are severe and date from the old days of the cattle/sheep wars and widespread rustling. A monkeywrencher caught in the act by livestockmen may well wish he had never been born. Be careful. *Damn careful!*

Overgrazing is vulnerable to monkeywrenching for two reasons: 1) places most suitable for this activity are generally remote, rugged, and seldom visited; and 2) some of the most damaging livestock operations are on a precarious financial basis where enough losses from ecotage can eliminate the grazing problem.

Operations by monkeywrenchers against overgrazing include the following:

1) Cutting fences;

2) Damaging water developments;

3) Moving salt blocks; and

4) Spiking roads.

Spiking roads and additional techniques discussed elsewhere in this book may have applications against overgrazers. Today's welfare rancher is soft and prefers a pickup truck to a horse. Take away his wheels and you remove his access to the range you wish to protect. Be creative.

Salt Blocks

Salt blocks are used to disperse livestock grazing. In arid areas, salt blocks are supposed to be placed several miles away from riparian areas and water sources in order to prevent the livestock from congregating and doing excessive damage in watered areas. Often, though, a hiker may discover salt blocks placed in canyon bottoms or near streams.

Such placement of salt blocks leads to concentrated cattle use which causes extensive damage to the stream banks, the vegetation and the aquatic ecosystem. (After cattle have been fenced out of dry, barren, former streams in Nevada, the streams have begun to flow year-round again; cottonwoods, willows, and other vegetation have sprung up, and fish have returned.) If you chance upon salt blocks in riparian areas, tote them away and deposit them miles from water. Expect to sweat a little. The damn things are heavy.

If one is feeling especially energetic, and is carrying a shovel, it would also be possible to bury salt blocks.

Water Developments

In arid areas of the West, grazing is water-based. This means that the amount of overgrazing possible in an area is determined by the availability of water. There may not be natural, dependable water for miles in any direction. In such a case, the area cannot be grazed. To remedy this problem, pipelines are constructed from water sources and carry water to various types of drinking troughs for cattle. Windmills may also be drilled. Such developments are vulnerable to minor ecotage.

PIPELINES — These are of a variety of types, ranging from simple ones consisting of the ubiquituous black flexible PVC pipe, to more elaborate systems using steel or aluminum pipe. Sometimes rigid PVC pipe is used as well, though this highly breakable pipe is uncommon in "range improvements." Pipelines may lead from springs, wells or small dams to distant stock tanks. In some areas pipelines several miles long have been constructed (frequently at taxpayers' expense) to enable cows to graze in areas that would be livestock-free otherwise. While sometimes these pipelines are buried, it is more common for large segments of them to be above ground, especially in rocky country, a fact which renders them vulnerable to monkeywrenching. The black PVC pipe can be easily cut with a pocketknife, although it would probably be more practical to carry a small hatchet for this purpose. Cutting a pipeline once may render it temporarily useless, but for effective monkeywrenching it would be far better to walk along it cutting it repeatedly. Rigid PVC pipe can easily be shattered with a large rock. Aluminum pipe can be punctured with a hammer and large nail, although a hammer and cold chisel would probably work better. The latter may also suffice for small steel pipelines, although it may be necessary to disassemble the pipe with a couple of pipe wrenches.

STOCK TANKS AND WATER TROUGHS — Small metal stock tanks may be punctured with a hammer and large nail or chisel. The larger ones may not be so easy to puncture. You may think that shooting them full of holes during hunting season is a good idea. *This is not recommended. Ballistics tests may trace your spent bullets to your gun.*

Sometimes small drinking troughs will be fed from a large stock tank by means of a float valve, like the one in your toilet (See illustration.) Find the float valve. It will usually be between the tank and the drinking trough, and will probably be covered by a removable hatch. Wire the float valve in the "up" position. When the water level in the drinking trough drops, the float will remain up and no more water will flow into the trough.

WINDMILLS — Windmills can be damaged in a number of ways. The towers for most windmills are now made of steel members which are assembled on the spot using simple nuts and bolts. With enough time and the proper tools (a couple of crescent wrenches or maybe a socket set) a monkeywrencher could completely disassemble a tower. However, there are less-laborious ways of putting windmills out of business.

Windmills generally have a mechanism (it may look like a small crank attached to a chain or cable) which will stop the vanes from turning, which in turn will cause the "sucker rods" to stop their up-and-down motion *(This motion is what pumps the water out of the well).* The sucker rods are usually made from a number of sections of steel pipe, or solid steel rods, threaded together.

An effective way to render a windmill inoperative is as follows:

*Stop the motion of the windmill.

*Using a couple of pipe wrenches, disassemble the sucker rods at a joint.

*Draw the sucker rod out of the well casing until you come to another joint. *The weight of the rod will depend on the depth of the well, but unless the well is deep, one or two people should be able do this.*

*Using the wrenches, remove the next section(s) of rod.

*Let the remaining sucker rod fall down into the well casing, where it will be difficult to retrieve. *Note: it might be possible to cut the sucker rods with a hacksaw, if they are not too thick. This would probably be simpler.*

Cutting Fence

Fences are what tamed the West for the livestock barons. They impede the movement of elk, pronghorn, deer and other wildlife, as well as that of hikers and other recreationists. They destroy the open-space feeling of the land and give it a cow-pasture, private property look.

Windmill. Note windlass (arrow).

Typical stock tank.

Float-valve regulates water level in stock tank.

Fences also are expensive and the key management tool in making the range available to overgrazing abuse. Simply cutting fence will cause great disruption to our landed gentry.

The best tool for fence cutting is a "fencing tool." It looks like a weird, overgrown pair of pliers and can be purchased for about $10 at most hardware stores. It can be used for hammering, twisting wire, pulling staples and cutting wire. Most fences are constructed of barbed wire or netwire. A fencing tool will cut either with great ease.

You should not just go out and cavalierly start cutting fence. In some cases, a fence is the land's friend. You do not want to cut a fence and allow cattle from overgrazed areas to enter an ungrazed area or one in relatively good condition. It is dangerous to cut fence along highways. People die every year in the West from hitting cows in "open range" areas with their cars. Leave highway fences up. Think about the results of your fence cutting before you cut.

When you have selected suitable fencing to cut, pick your time carefully. Avoid hunting season. There are more people out in the field then (hunters and game wardens, of course, and ranchers to make sure that cows aren't shot, etc.). If possible, pick a season when the cattle or sheep have been removed to another pasture. A quarter moon night is good. So is bad weather. (Beware of lightning — barbed wire fences can attract it.)

After you have selected the fence you want to cut, walk along it in one direction, cutting as you go. *Do not double back. You might find someone looking for you.* Check behind yourself frequently. You are, after all, leaving a perfect trail. Binoculars may be useful for watching your backtrail. When you leave your fencing work, do not leave a trail that someone can follow back to your home, camp, or vehicle. Beforehand you should select several possible escape routes if necessary. Do not loiter. Do your work and leave.

You can cut a mile of fence in an hour once you get moving. Snip each strand of wire between posts but do not damage the posts. They will be needed for reconstruction of the fence later and will prevent other trees from being cut for fence posts. Give special attention to corner posts since they are an integral part of supporting the entire line of fence. Instead of cutting between each post, you also can randomly cut wire along a greater length of fence and probably still necessitate the complete restringing of the fence.

Caution - barbed wire is usually strung under tension, so be careful when cutting it. When cutting, both sides of the wire should be held securely to prevent it springing back. If working alone, you can minimize this effect by cutting at a fencepost; you need only worry about one end of the wire. Fortunately, many public-lands ranchers are too lazy to keep their fences in good repair, so the wire is apt to be loose.

Miscellaneous

Public lands ranchers, being no doubt well aware of the indefensible nature of many of their practices, are hypersensitive about the slightest hint of public criticism. For this reason any means of bringing their depredations to the attention of the public will have a twofold benefit — it will both educate the public and give the ranchers high blood pressure.

Recently in the Southwest the press reported an outbreak of sign alteration. Someone was using a stencil to modify those ubiquitous highway signs that warn the motorist of open range — the ones that show a big cow on a yellow background. (see section on **Stencils**.) They were adding to the signs messages like "Stop Overgrazing," "Get cows off the public lands," and the like. Needless to say, the outrage expressed by the ranching community was substantial. *Editor's note: $500 rewards were offered for information leading to the arrest of the perpetrators and serious penalties were threatened should they be apprehended.*

If you live in a rural area and decide to try to rectify the abuses of overgrazing through monkeywrenching, it would probably be best to keep a low profile on other conservation issues and to go out of your way to not publicly criticize the livestock industry. Indeed, it may be wise *not* to engage in anti-grazing monkeywrenching in your home area at all.

FIELD NOTES

*There has recently been a trend in some parts of the West for ranchers to install submersible electric pumps in wells, even in wells in remote areas without electric lines. Evidently the ranchers are using portable electric generators to run the pumps — the pump will be run long enough to fill a large stock tank; then the generator will be removed.

It may be difficult to remove the submersible pump from the well casing without special equipment (although if this can be done, it certainly would be effective). However, such wells do have vulnerable electrical wiring and circuit boxes on the surface. The circuit boxes can be smashed with a sledge or large rock; the wiring can be repeatedly cut with a fencing tool or bolt-cutters.

CHAPTER 4

ROADS AND TIRES

Napoleon's army may have traveled on its stomach, but the army of wilderness destruction travels by road and vehicle. Indeed, one of the most commonly used criteria for "wilderness" is "roadlessness." Roads are used for logging, for mineral exploration and development, for oil & gas activity, for overgrazing "management," for powerline construction, for dam building, for ski area, recreational and subdivision development. Trappers, poachers, slob hunters, archaeological site vandals, prospectors, seismographic crews, and other vanguards of the industrial destruction of the wild use four-wheel-drive vehicles on dirt roads, jeep trails and cross-country. Then there are the mindless masturbators on their 4x4s, ATVs, ORVs, dune buggies, muscle wagons, dirt bikes, tricycles, and nature knows what else — ripping up the land, leaving their macho tracks as their imbecilic calling cards, running down wildlife, and disrupting non-motorized recreation.

The road network on public lands, however, cannot be effectively protected from a serious campaign to close it. The money is not available to both build and constantly repair roads in rough, remote country. And vehicles — whether on the roads or off — are highly vulnerable to having their tires flattened if they enter areas where they don't belong.

With the simple tools and techniques discussed in this chapter, an Earth defender can essentially declare her or his own wilderness boundary and safeguard an area from penetration by vehicle-borne destruction. Are there two roadless areas separated by a nonessential dirt road? Close it. Are "cherry-stem" roads invading a block of wild country from all sides? Shut them off at the periphery. Is the Forest Service building a logging road into old growth prime wildlife habitat? Wreck it. Are miners, seismographers, surveyors, trappers, or poachers threatening your area? Take their transportation away. Are bozos on their tricycles or dune buggies trashing out a wild canyon, roadless beach, or desert valley? Flatten their tires and make 'em walk out.

The most vulnerable portion of the industrial infrastructure is transportation. The ecodefender can safely, securely, cheaply and effectively disrupt it — and save wild country.

Most monkeywrenchers have focused on disabling heavy equipment, cutting down billboards, and — most recently — spiking trees. All of these are highly important, but road spiking and destroying roads have not received the exercise due them. With the United States Forest Service embarking upon a gargantuan road building program in currently roadless areas, monkeywrenchers need to make a major effort to close these roads. This chapter tells you how to do just that. An additional attraction of road spiking or road destruction is that it is much more difficult for the villains to protect hundreds of miles of road from sabotage than it is for them to guard a few pieces of heavy equipment or active logging sites. You are in much less danger of apprehension doing this kind of monkeywrenching out in the boonies than you are crawling around equipment yards. Nonetheless, do not neglect basic security precautions.

ROAD SPIKING

A modern version of the Vietnamese "punji stake" offers a simple means of closing an unsurfaced road. An angle-cut metal rod driven into the road's wheel rut will puncture tires while not harming people. The 1/2 inch diameter rod, protruding only about three inches, is too blunt to penetrate a shoe sole under a person's weight, while a heavy vehicle drives it through the tire. With this technique you can cure an ORV problem or make a logging or mining operation unprofitable. By harassing a survey or exploration crew with these you might persuade a corporation not to proceed with a mining or drilling operation. The possible applications are extensive since almost any exploitative enterprise requires roads.

One person can buy the materials to close a road for pocket change, and can emplace the stakes *alone* in a very brief time. By not involving anyone else, you can insure that nobody can rat on you. That peace of mind is worth more than the encouraging companionship. Since the stakes can be driven so quickly and easily, there is almost no chance of being seen, let alone identified, if you exercise even minimal caution. There is no reason that anyone cannot do any of this, even if he or she has not previously used tools or bought construction materials, by following these instructions.

Obtaining the Materials

Any piece of hard metal that can be sharpened and driven into the ground will work. For convenience and economy, we recommend 1/2 inch diameter steel rod used for concrete reinforcement, usually called "number four rebar" in the construction trades.

If you buy rebar pre-cut to length, you will order "so many one foot number-four dowels," and you will have to semi-sharpen one end.

If you decide to hacksaw the stakes from longer rods, the ends will be sharp enough. Cut the rods off at a sharp angle (at least 45 degrees) every couple of feet, then cut these pieces in half with a straight-across cut. Thus each stake is about one foot long, with one sharp end and one blunt end. Stakes longer than a foot are hard to drive deep enough in rocky ground; much shorter and they are not stable. Longer ones may be useful in very soft ground.

If you buy the longer rod and cut it, you should keep in mind that rebar is usually bought by contractors in quantity and delivered to a construction site. So, you should not call attention to yourself as someone who repeatedly buys small quantities of rebar and hacksaw blades in the same building supply store in an area where "road spiking" is taking the profits out of some local rip-off. But rebar is common, ordinary stuff and nobody will have the slightest interest in why you want it so long as you don't need a salesperson's help in figuring out what (and how much) to order. Order a length that you can easily transport (in multiples of two feet). When you select hacksaw blades, get the very best since cheap ones will only make a few cuts before dulling (they break easily, too). Buy the longest blades you can find in order to get a decent stroke. This will make cutting much easier.

Field/Expedient Method of Cutting Stakes

Secure one end of the rod (by clamping, jamming, etc.) and lay the free end across a crotched (or notched) piece of wood under the cut to be made, about one foot from the end. Grasp the free end in your left hand, pressing down and holding back against the forward/cutting stroke. Lay the blade alongside one of the retention ridges which run across the rebar at a 45 degree angle. Make several light strokes until the blade cuts into the bar enough to prevent slipping sideways. With a little practice you can cut more than a dozen road spikes an hour in this manner. If you cut up a rod or two in your spare time during the week, you will have as many as you can carry by the weekend.

Building a Jig

For ease, convenience, and to turn out more stakes in less time, you may want to build a jig to hold the rod steady and to guide the saw blade. Any kind of "miter box" that doesn't reduce the length of the stroke very much is okay. A simple method is to place two cement blocks on end and place the length of rebar to be cut in the grooves on the ends. Saw the rebar between the cement blocks.

Using an Acetylene Torch

A torch is the fastest and easiest method of turning out large numbers of stakes. Learning how to cut (as opposed to welding or joining) with a torch is very easy. It's only necessary to learn how to handle the gases and equipment safely, and to adjust the flame. Someone could show you in half an hour how to hook up and adjust the equipment well enough to burn off rods. (See the separate article on the **Cutting Torch.**)

Emplacing the Stakes

Make the "cap" illustrated here so that you can drive the stakes into the ground without blunting the sharp end. Buy two 3/8 to 1/4 inch galvanized pipe "reducers," one 3/8 by 5 inch galvanized pipe nipple, and one 1/4 inch nipple of any length (the shorter the better), and assemble as follows: Screw the five inch long pipe into the large ends of both reducers; screw the smaller pipe into the small end of one of the reducers; then cut it off flush.

The reducer with the flush-cut nipple in it is placed over the sharp end of the road spike and the reducer on the other end is hammered to drive the stake into the ground. If you simply put a piece of 1/4 inch pipe over the sharp end of the stake and hammered on it to drive in the rebar, one pipe end would deform very quickly from hammering and the stake would wedge up in the other end. The reducers hold their shape and make this a long lasting tool. Driving the first stake creates a seat (in the end that fits over the stake) into which succeeding road spikes should be fitted.

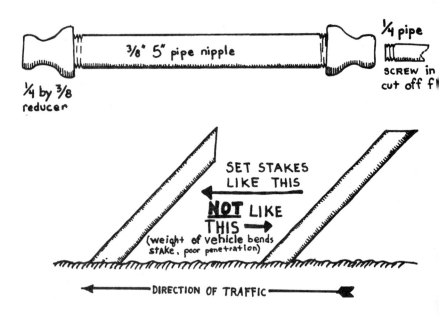

¼ pipe

SCREW in
cut off fl

3/8" 5" pipe nipple

¼ by 3/8
reducer

SET STAKES
LIKE THIS

NOT LIKE
THIS ➤
(weight of vehicle bends
stake, poor penetration)

◄————DIRECTION OF TRAFFIC————►

Where to Place Road Spikes

For effectiveness and safety, thought should be given as to where you should place road spikes. Avoid areas where a blow-out or flat from the stake might put the driver and passengers of the vehicle in danger. Roads or "jeep trails" with a sheer, long drop-off on one side are obvious danger zones. Choose, instead, a flat area or an area where the vehicle path bottoms out. Determine whether you should spike a long vehicle route at the beginning or in a remote location in the middle. Will a flat miles from nowhere endanger a typically overweight, soft ORV wimp (either young or old)?

Although road spikes are difficult to see from a vehicle (particularly a charging muscle-wagon), picking a spot where they will be even more difficult to see will increase their effectiveness. Choose a spot where vegetation to the side, shadows, a dip in the route, a curve or other natural camouflaging will obscure the three inches of dark rod protruding from the ground. Also, pick a site where there is a better chance of the road spike making contact with a tire. At some points along a vehicle route, there may be several feet of variance for the tires. Several road spikes may need to be used across the route there to flatten a tire. Instead, select a spot where ruts or natural constrictions keep the tire tread confined and where one spike is sure to make contact with knobby rubber. Crossings of streams and dry washes are also choice locations. Look at the terrain and previous vehicle tracks to determine where each of your spikes will wreak maximum (but not dangerous) havoc on vehicle tires that should not be there.

Consider the direction most vehicles will be traveling and incline the road spikes accordingly. It may be necessary on some routes to direct your spikes in both directions.

FIELD NOTES

* Check a dead-end jeep trail before you spike it. It is best to flatten someone's tires when they are going *in*, not coming *out*.

* Often a trustworthy partner can be useful for security. While one person drives the spikes in the road, the other can keep watch for vehicles or hikers. The use of radios can add to this security. See the section on **Tools** for a discussion on radios for security.

* Placing a rag over the head of the spike driver when hammering in stakes may help to deaden the noise of hammering.

* Rebar is cheap. A twenty-foot length at one suburban building supply store was only $3.50. Rebar also saws easily and quickly with a good hacksaw blade — don't be intimidated by the task until you try it.

* Disguise your spikes with small branches. This may be especially effective on logging roads. Soon, drivers will be afraid to drive over any fragment of dead tree.

* 3/8 inch diameter rebar cut in two or three foot lengths has been found effective for flattening the tires of dune buggies and the like on beaches and in sand dune areas.

* Free rebar can oftentimes be had by scouting around old construction sites where short pieces have been discarded.

* 3/8 inch rebar can also be used for road spikes. It is cheaper (79 cents for a ten foot length), saws easier, and is lighter to transport in your pack. Except for really macho tires, it should do an adequate job.

SPIKE DRIVER

This cheap, easily made tool is necessary for emplacing road spikes. The different parts are shown here in an exploded view. (See text for details.)

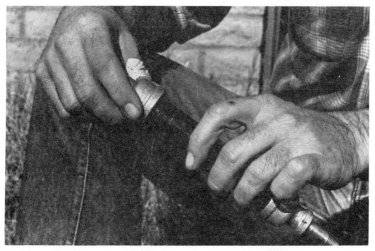

First, screw the reducers on the ends of the pipe nipple.

97

Then, using vise-grips, screw the 1/4 inch nipple into one of the reducers (as tightly as possible).

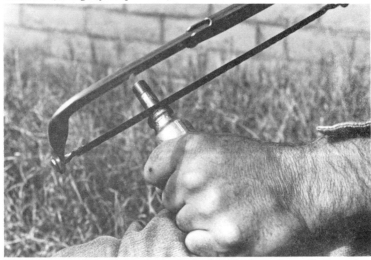

Finally, saw off the 1/4 inch nipple flush with the reducer. Your road spike driver is ready for use.

Use of the Road Spike Driver:

Place the driver over the sharpened end of the rebar stake and hammer it in.

Note the "seat" created in the end of the driver (the 1/4 inch nipple screwed into one of the reducers).

FLATTENING TIRES

Vehicle tires can be disabled by a variety of methods, causing damage ranging from cost and inconvenience to downright danger to the vehicle operator. The three methods are slashing, using caltrops, and emplacing road spikes (discussed previously).

Slashing:

Suppose your neighborhood is infested with off-road vehicle scum, or you chance upon an unattended muscle wagon where it shouldn't be. A quick slash job is in order. This is particularly annoying if all four tires are destroyed. Slashing the sidewall of the tire will often be non-reparable, while punctures of the tread can usually be patched. The choice is yours.

An excellent instrument for the job is a thick-handled, x-acto knife with a symmetrical "stiletto-type" blade (x-acto blade style 23x). These can be obtained cheaply at hardware or art supply stores. The blade design prevents the knife from getting stuck in the tire, and the sharp point allows easy insertion into the sidewall. This tool can be safely carried in your pocket if a piece of cork is used to cover the blade. Of course, one should also be kept in the glove compartment of your vehicle for use when the opportunity arises. While probably not as damaging as cutting the sidewall, an effective method of deflating a tire is to cut off the valve stem, or to pull the valve stem out entirely with a pair of pliers. Another way to puncture individually selected tires is to place small pieces of wood spiked with long nails under the tire of the parked car, or do the same thing with a caltrop. However, this method is more time-consuming, less certain, and best reserved for moving vehicles or situations where the sound of escaping air might give you away.

Caltrops:

Perhaps the best use of caltrops is for security in the event you are being chased, a use well-illustrated in *The Monkey Wrench Gang*. They may also be the best method of stopping traffic on *paved* roads, but road spikes are far superior and more permanent on dirt tracks. Caltrops are simply too tedious to manufacture and too unlikely to function on soft substrates to strew about the landscape in an attempt to stop ORVs. However, on secondary paved roads a large number dropped one-by-one from the back of a pickup truck would certainly cause a massive traffic

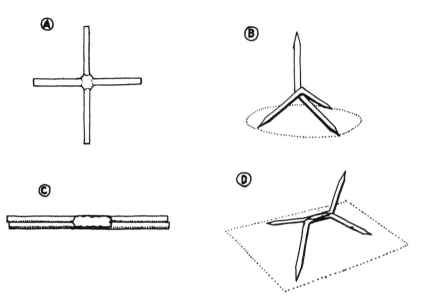

Two possible methods of making caltrops. Top: weld a cross, bend and sharpen. Bottom: weld side by side, bend and sharpen.

jam! How about on the route to the starting area of a dirt bike race on the evening of the race?

Caltrops can be constructed with a small investment in welding equipment. Adequate ones can be made with an arc-welding unit as small as 70 amps. Sears has a 20-70 variable amp unit that can be obtained as cheaply as $59. Higher-amperage units are substantially more expensive but will produce faster and more substantial welds. It is important to read the operating instructions carefully before arc-welding and to always use hand and eye protective gear (intense light can burn the retina).

Caltrops can be constructed as follows: obtain nails at least 4 inches long, the thicker the better (ORV tires are tough!), and cut off the heads with a bolt cutter or hacksaw. Sharpen both ends on a grinding wheel. Extreme sharpness is not necessary as the weight of the vehicle drives the nail into the tire even if somewhat blunt. Weld at least 3 of these nails together in opposing planes so that there is a tripod effect no matter how a thrown caltrop lands.

To perform the actual welding, place one nail in a vise, hold the other in a pair of vise grips, and use your other hand to hold the electrode. All this is made more tedious by the poor visibility through the protective eye gear. A better set-up for mass production would include clamps to hold the second nail firmly against the first during welding.

Before using, paint the caltrop black with spray paint so that it is less conspicuous on asphalt.

The ultimate in caltrop technology would be an automatic caltrop dispenser attached to the underside of your vehicle with controls in the driver compartment for release of the caltrops. Such a device might be made from a box constructed of sheet metal and bolted to the undercarriage of the car. Several caltrops could be released simultaneously by pulling the lever attached to an encased cable, such as used for automobile hood releases or bicycle brakes, thus releasing the hinged bottom of the box. Experiment with different designs.

FIELD NOTES

* Road spikes and caltrops may be of limited value against dirt bike tires because their narrowness presents a small target area. One possible method to flatten dirt bike tires is to drive numerous nails through a thin strip of plywood. Lay the plywood in a heavily-used dirt bike track and cover it with sand or soil so that only the nails protrude.

* Suggestions for additional methods of flattening dirt bike tires or otherwise stopping these highly damaging machines would be appreciated.

* Remember that many dirt bikers are children. Be careful. Many dirt bikes are traveling at a high rate of speed. Placement of tire puncturing devices should be done with the safety of the rider in mind.

* Many dirt bikers are of the most uncouth, violent and potentially dangerous variety of *Boobus americanus*. **Be careful.** You do not want to be captured by these slavering morons or even suspected of doing anything against them.

* A simple form of caltrop involves driving a half dozen long nails through a golf ball so that they stick out in all directions. Spray paint the whole thing a color similar to the surface on which they might be used. Remember that carrying a box of these around in your car or truck might look very suspicious to the policeman who, on a random traffic stop, decides to go poking around your vehicle in the hope of finding an open liquor bottle, drugs or stolen goods.

*Less incriminating than an x-acto knife and equally (if not more) effective is the "Opinel" knife widely sold at camping and surplus stores. The 4″ size is ideal. Sharpen *both* sides of the blade (make sure you get a model with a lockring). These knives are easy to get, extremely sharp, do not elicit suspicion and are cheap enough to become throwaways if that becomes necessary.

*An inexpensive tool known as a "valve core extractor" provides an alternative method for flattening tires. After the cap is removed from the valve stem, the extractor is inserted into the stem. Twist until you feel the tool engage the valve core. Then unscrew (counterclockwise) the valve core and throw it in the bushes. Doing this to all the tires on a vehicle would immobilize it, providing maximum harassment without permanently destroying the tires.

"Valve core extractors" may be purchased cheaply at most bicycle shops (the valves on most bicycle tires are the same size as the valves on automobile tires).

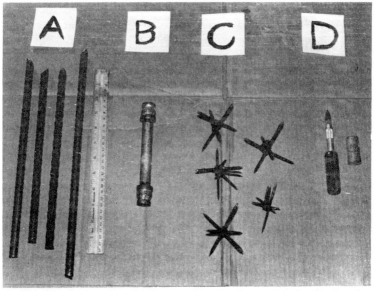

A) Road spikes made of rebar (with ruler for scale) B) Road spike emplacing tool C) Caltrops D) Tire slasher

BIGFOOT

Just when we thought we were having serious ORV problems, along came Bigfoot. No, I'm not talking about our large, hairy friend who lurks in the Siskiyous, rolling an occasional boulder onto a Freddie 'dozer. Unfortunately, this Bigfoot is a beast of another sort altogether.

I accidentally discovered Bigfoot a couple of years ago, while riding the bus downtown. There in a motel parking lot I glimpsed the biggest ORV I had ever seen. The cab and body looked like that of a fairly ordinary pickup, except for the obligatory rollbars and banks of off-road lights. But the cab and body looked grotesque and Lilliputian, perched as they were on top of the biggest tires I'd ever seen outside of heavy construction equipment. I guessed the size of the tires to be at least five feet high — which turned out to be a bit of an underestimate, once I was able to learn more about the vehicle.

Shocked and disgusted as I was to see this behemoth, I somehow was not surprised. Recent trends in ORV's have clearly been favoring the development of bigger and more destructive machines. I also had a gut feeling that this monstrosity was not just a freak; some madman's one-of-a-kind creation. I felt that I was merely looking at the latest fad among those cretins whose idea of fun is to smash through once-pristine wilderness behind the wheel of a multi-ton steel juggernaut.

I wanted to examine the vehicle more closely, but by the time I was able to return to the scene later that afternoon, it was gone — no doubt already out raping the desert outside of town. But as chance was to have it, my curiosity was to be answered only a couple of days later. While glancing at the magazine rack in a local supermarket I saw pictures of the same or a similar vehicle staring at me from the covers of no less than two of those sleazy publications which cater to the off-road crowd (like you, I'm not entirely sure that some of these yahoos can even *read,* but they do have magazines, nevertheless).

Despite a queasy stomach, I forced myself to read the articles. It was then I learned of the name "Bigfoot." What a libel against the original! I also learned a number of particulars about the vehicle. It weighs six tons, stands ten-and-a-half feet high, and is powered by an engine of over 500 cubic inches. Although the body is that of an ordinary 4x4 pickup truck, almost everything else is extra heavy duty — including axles and differential from a 5-ton truck, and ten heavy-duty shocks. But the tires — what tires! They are what truly make "Bigfoot" stand out above the crowd. The vehicle boasts four Goodyear "Terra" tires, sized 66 x 43 x 25 (i.e., five-and-one-half feet high). These tires do not come cheap — they cost $2,500 each, to be precise. These tires, together with all the other heavy-duty equipment, put the cost of one of these vehicles in the league of a classy motorhome, rather than that of a run-of-the-mill 4x4. However, don't count on the cost to prevent these monsters from spreading all over the landscape. While they are certainly beyond the means of the average peckerwoods millhand, I expect that the big city off-road crowd will make these their latest toy. After all, we are living in an age in which $40,000 motorhomes are as common as those dinkey little 12-foot travel trailers (most commonly seen now in junkyards) were back in the supposedly affluent '50's.

Judging from what I've seen in the press and on TV, I'd say that there might be several dozen of these oversize four-wheelers around today. A couple of years ago, when I saw those first magazine articles, there were exactly *two* in existence. Unless my whole concept of human nature is wrong, we've only seen the beginning.

While some of the owners of these vehicles are confining their destructive posturing to ORV shows (riding over and crushing old auto bodies is a favorite spectator sport), we can also expect to see "Bigfoot" cruising into some of our favorite wildernesses one of these days. Fortunately, these beasts' great height makes them topheavy in steep terrain, which will hopefully limit their intrusions into mountainous country, but in flat desert country or in river canyons with deep water crossings this height is an advantage. In fact, driving down previously impassable (to vehicles) river canyons is one of the things that "Bigfoot" is most suited for, and this was pointed out in the magazine articles which introduced it to the public. If "Bigfoot" should somehow get into water too deep even for its 10-1/2 foot height, it will *float,* thanks to those giant tires.

What can we do to defend the wilderness against this truly obscene machine? Ordinary spiking measures will probably not faze "Bigfoot"; in fact, the tires will likely crush ordinary caltrops and flatten small pieces of rebar. If you see one of these machines in the backcountry, remember that you are under no moral obligation to show restraint or to take half-measures. There is no possible legitimate justification for the possession and/or use of such a machine. Its use constitutes, plain and simply, a declaration of war against Earth and all her living creatures.

If one should be fortunate enough to come across one of these machines unguarded in the wilderness, there is no reason to stop short of total destruction. Burning is probably the most effective method, so long as it won't compromise your security. For techniques of burning heavy equipment, see the section entitled **Rags.**

Of course, most of us probably won't have such an opportunity handed to us, as if on a silver platter. We must instead come up with adequate defensive measures to discourage wilderness incursions by "Bigfoot."

The most vulnerable parts of these machines are their tires, and the fact that these tires cost $2,500 each means that you will be providing considerable financial incentives for the owner to stay out of the wilderness every time you damage a tire. Extra-large caltrops (made from half-inch or larger pieces of rebar welded together) just might be strong enough to hold up under the weight of the vehicle long enough to inflict serious tire damage. Such caltrops would require spikes several inches long, and obviously could not be placed in open areas without the risk of being spotted. The best place to place such caltrops would be in stream crossings, under water. Pick known vehicle crossings (or on rivers where the ORV's will be charging *down* rather than simply across a stream, look for narrow spots in the canyon where vehicles will not have much choice of route). If there is a rocky bottom, simply place the caltrops on the bottom — in places where the water is deep enough or opaque enough so they won't be spotted by the oncoming vehicles. If the bottom is sandy or muddy, find a flat rock and place the caltrop on top of it. There must be enough resistance beneath the caltrop to drive the spike firmly into the tire.

There is a definite hazard in using giant caltrops — yes, an unlucky hiker or passing animal could be injured by stepping on one. To reduce this likelihood, don't place these devices until you know of an impending vehicular intrusion. *Know* where you have placed caltrops (or other devices), and later return and retrieve them (that is, those that are left after some of them have done their duty puncturing those $2,500 tires).

The caltrops can also be placed in thick vegetation (high grass, brush, etc.) if you have reason to believe "Bigfoot" might be coming a particular way. Remember, this vehicle can crash through fairly heavy vegetation, and the cretins who drive it will no doubt take advantage of its power at every opportunity.

If you should find that caltrops are insufficient to stop these vehicles (the weld may be a weak point — it needs to be strong to hold up under the weight), there are certainly other methods with potential. A waterlogged railroad tie, studded with sharpened rebar, could be placed in a stream crossing. You could also take a two-by-six, drive numerous bridge timber spikes (see Field Notes to **Tree Spiking**) all the way through, and then nail the board, with the points of the spikes projecting upwards, onto a waterlogged railroad tie. Since it may take a while to come up with a waterlogged tie, other means of anchoring a studded board under water may be easier. For example, you could anchor it with rocks or fasten it to a heavy piece of metal. Whatever you do, remember to take precautions that your device does not injure the innocent, and remove it once the immediate threat has passed.

If readers have any other suggestions for dealing with oversize ORV's, the editors would welcome the information.

FIELD NOTES
* Although actual "Bigfoots" are still limited in number, they point the way of the current trend of jacked-up muscle wagons cruising the land with epicene youths at the wheel trying to impress others with their virility. We are in an ORV explosion today and every effort must be made to teach these yardbirds to stay the hell out of wild country.

SNOWMOBILES

It's time to haul out the old monkeywrench and turn the screws on the snowmobiling cult. As you are aware, the machines destroy the solitude of the woods with excessive noise, waste energy and resources, and wreak damage on plants and animals.

One way to deter snowmobiling in sensitive areas that have marked snowmobile trails (such as in the North Woods country), would be a committed but decentralized effort, beginning with the departure of snow, to remove and ruin signs and posts associated with snowmobile trails. Trail markers and trail identification and promotion signs should all be removed. Safety signs, such as stop signs at intersecting highways, should probably remain.

Equipment for sign removal is minimal — usually a box end or crescent wrench to turn out a couple of lag screws. Upon removal, the signs should be bent, defaced, or otherwise rendered unusable, then stashed under leaves or brush where they will eventually rot into the ground. If concealment is not a problem, a small pruning saw or bow saw would also be useful — to cut the sign post into several pieces.

Removing snowmobile signs will serve to discourage the cult by decreasing the accessibility of trails, eliminating the "advertising value" of sign posts, and siphoning away at least some of the funds that would go to trail expansion.

In one northern Minnesota county recently, eco-raiders removed over $2000 worth of signs out of a possible $5000 worth.

Maintenance costs for snowmobile trails can also be increased by pushing snags and dead trees over so that they fall across the trails. It's a good way to combine some low-commitment monkeywrenching with a hike in the woods.

If we all do our work this spring, summer and fall, the snowmobile trails should be in ragged shape by next winter.

FIELD NOTES

*It has been suggested that snowmobiles can be stopped by shoveling to bare ground a section of trail, preferably a section hidden by a bend in the trail. Drawbacks to this method are the amount of labor involved, and the fact that it would have little more than a "nuisance" effect on the snowmobiler.

*A more effective deterrent might be to go after the trailers that pull the snowmobiles, while they are parked unattended at the trailhead. Tires are obvious targets, although by no means the only vulnerable points. Trailers are also used to haul other destructive "toys" such as ATC's and dirt bikes. Be security conscious — it wouldn't do to have the owners return while you were trashing their trailers!

*Reportedly, monofilament fishing line spread out on the snow will suck into a snowmobile's track mechanism and cause it to jam. If anyone has definite knowledge of the effectiveness of this, please let us know.

*Remember that snowmobiles are often driven by overweight, out-of-shape, poorly-prepared wimps, who may be put into a life-threatening situation if their snowmobile is disabled miles from civilization. *Be very conscious of the situation you may be creating and be concerned for the safety of the snowmobiler.*

CLOSING ROADS

Most exploitation of the wild requires roads, and there is no way that the industrial machine can afford to constantly repair the road network on public lands if even a few hundred people across the country are making a spare time project of trashing it. Roads are difficult and expensive to maintain, especially in the areas we want to save. Selected areas, such as *de facto* wildernesses or roadless areas denied protection in the RARE II ripoff, can be protected by cutting the unsurfaced roads that are built and used in the process of exploitation.

Individuals can use the techniques described here, with simple, cheap tools, to prevent vehicle access to sensitive areas. You can deter the testing that is needed to prove commercial feasibility for proposed developments such as mining or oil & gas drilling. You can discourage the construction of a timber harvest road in a National Forest roadless area. You also can harass and render unprofitable an existing exploitative enterprise.

The simplest, and often most effective, way to inhibit vehicle travel is with "road spikes" (previously discussed). But for a variety of reasons, you may want to employ additional methods of stopping traffic. You might want to make the damage look like an act of nature (or at most, of vandalism). You may wish to prevent quick restoration of road usage. As each "road spike" is found, it can be removed, whereas some of these techniques will require a major effort to repair. On occasion, the money, equipment, and initiative to make the repairs will not come together, and they will be postponed. Numerous instances of damage to roads will multiply the effects and eventually large parts of the transportation infrastructure on public lands will be abandoned. In this era of high federal deficits, construction and repair of controversial roads, in remote, rough country, that are continually being sabotaged will be recognized as pouring money down a rat hole.

The well-known methods of cutting a tree across or rolling a boulder onto a road are of limited value. Trees can be cut out of the way and the intruder suffers no loss. Trees can be of use on footpaths where dirt bikes are a problem. Hikers simply step over, while the bike has to be dragged over the log(s). Of course the logs have to be placed in spots where dirt bikes can't ride around the ends and it must be done in many places to present a real deterrent. A tree across the road might be effective in conjunction with another operation to delay motorized pursuit.

Tools

Any boulder you can drag into the road, some 4-wheeler with a winch can probably move out. But for those occasions where you feel that a big rock can be placed in a hard-to-remove position, the most useful tools for maneuvering large rocks and logs are: a come-along, rated two tons or heavier; 2 or more chokers; 2 spud bars; a hydraulic (car or truck) jack; large and small rock chisels; and log-splitting wedges. You probably won't need all of these tools on any one job, but with a tool kit like this, you can do anything that is practical to do with hand labor. All of these items can be purchased cheaply at flea markets, and anyone who works in a construction trade can easily obtain the bars, come-along, chokers, and such.

A "choker" is a length of cable with a loop in each end: one loop is passed through the other loop and the cable is wrapped around the load to be lifted or moved. Pulling on the free loop pulls the slack out, choking the cable tight around the load, hence its name. You will need at least two chokers and four is better. Just buy fifty feet of good, flexible 5/16″ or 3/8″ stranded steel cable and have it cut into four equal pieces where you buy it. (It takes a special cutter to do a neat job on cable.) Now double the ends back to form a loop of about 6″ diameter. Then double cable-clip it. Cable clips can be bought in any hardware store and must be matched to the size of the cable they are to fit. They can be put on with a wrench or vise-grip pliers.

The "come-along," or hand winch, can be attached directly to the object to be moved or it can be used in conjunction with other tackle. You can use it to pull a rope or cable through blocks to multiply its rated power. The small reel on a hand winch will only hold a few feet of cable so you have to secure the load and get a new grip frequently. A logging chain is handy for this type of work. For one thing it acts as its own choker since it has a fitting on each end that grips on any steel link it is slipped over. Steel carabiners are indispensable for all rigging work, especially for work as "fairleads" (those with the Teflon rollers are best) to lead cables and ropes over and around turns. Any library should have books explaining rigging and the use of tackle in detail. Nautical books such as Chapman's have sufficient coverage of the subject.

"Spud bars" are just long, heavy-duty pry bars. You can make a nice one cheaply by using a piece of heavy-wall steel box tube. Cut a slot in the end of the box tube, slip a piece of leaf spring in the slot, and have a welding shop run a bead everywhere the leaf spring touches the tube. Use the come-along to pull on the end of a log as a giant lever if even a spud bar won't do the job.

The hydraulic jack is useful for raising something enough to get a bar or roller under, and it can be used for "pushing" as described below. The rock chisels can be used to start blocks of fractured rock, as can the thicker splitting wedges.

Undercutting a Bank

Undercutting a bank is only a little better than logs and rocks since the rubble can usually be cleared out of the way, or driven over with less trouble than it took to bring it down. However, it is possible to find conditions in which a modest effort applied to an unstable bank will fill up part of the road where there are no easy detours. Using the spud bar in the cracks of fractured rocks is sometimes feasible. After a bank is well undermined, a ditch across the *top* of the bank will help to bring it down. (Remain on the uphill side of the ditch and/or rope off to avoid becoming part of the landslide!) If, after undercutting the bank and ditching across the top, it still won't slide, you can lay a pole on each side of the bottom of the ditch. Lay the hydraulic jack on its side between the poles, and jack them apart. They will spread the load along the ditch and push the undermined bank off.

Removing the Roadbed

Much better than blocking the road is to *remove* part of the roadbed. This is especially effective on a steep hillside where more fill is hard to get and stabilize in place. One simple, small-scale way to do this is to ditch the natural water flow downward across the road. The best place to do this is where a gully or watercourse crosses the road on a slope. Such a spot may have a culvert or waterbreak to keep the run-off from washing out the road. You can dig out a waterbreak and create a ditch across the road. Running water will deepen it and eventually make the road impassable to vehicles. (If it is too wide, it can be forded, however, and if it is too narrow and shallow, it can be filled with logs or rocks by a driver.) A pick, pry bar and long-handled, pointed shovel are about the only tools you need for this kind of job.

Perhaps the best way to cut a road is to find the place(s) it is trying to slip off down the slope naturally. Clay slopes often do this as do fractured rocks bedded at a steep angle. On rocky slopes a spud bar and gravity should help you undercut the roadbed. This is especially effective on tight, outside curves and steep slopes. Don't bother to dig off the entire width of the road, since digging off just the outside will do the trick.

While clay slopes can be dug off, too, there is an easier method in some places. With practice you can spot a slope that is trying to slide off. The shoulders of the road will have cracked and slipped into a series of step-downs. If there is water on the uphill (inside) side of the road, stop up the drainage so that the ground becomes soggy. Dig holes to help the water penetrate the subsoil, and once the clay becomes saturated, it will slide.

Culverts

If the road has culverts, you can stuff the uphill ends with rocks and other debris. Then dig through the road fill to expose the top of the culvert. If this is done at the beginning of a seasonal rainy period or before spring run-off in snow country, most culverts will wash out, creating an excellent vehicle barrier. You can also *remove* the culverts, using the come-along or a vehicle to drag them out. First dig all the road fill off the top of the culvert and free an end enough to get a choker on it. Using pole A-frames and fairleads as necessary, get an upward pull on the end of the culvert, lifting it out of the road. Use the come-along or a vehicle to pull on the cable, through tackle as necessary, and then bend it when one end is free, leaving it half buried in the road.

Bridges

Wooden bridges are vulnerable and are a major effort and expense to replace. They can be burned but it takes more than a can of kerosene and a match. A huge pile of dry firewood must be heaped up under the load carrying timbers of the bridge to sustain a hot-enough fire for long enough to burn a soggy old bridge. Fill the available dry area under the bridge, or crib up a log platform covered with dirt, sand or rock on which to lay the fire. Several armloads of small stuff, topped with progressively larger limbs and finally logs should be crammed right up to the underside of the timbers. After the small stuff burns a little and the fire collapses, you should stoke it with big limbs and logs and stuff the openings with branches. Then you can walk away confident of the results.

You can also saw through bridge timbers from the underside with a chain, bow or crosscut saw. It is hard to avoid hitting nails — this can be dangerous with a chainsaw (see the **Tree Spiking** section). If noise is a problem, a bow saw blade cuts easily when sharp and can be quickly replaced when dulled. A few drops of kerosene will make it cut smoothly in resinous or creosoted wood.

Simple, safe and inexpensive methods such as these, done in your spare time, multiplied by dozens of similar actions by other ecodefenders in their particular neck of the woods, can effectively stop the destruction of many of our remaining wild areas by vehicle-borne logging, mining, poaching, and by mindless ORVing.

FIELD NOTES

* In the proper location, it is possible for a group of people, using only their hands, to fill a road with enough boulders and other debris to act as an effective barrier to most vehicles. While a vehicle with a winch, a bulldozer, or a crew of workers might be able to clear the road to permit passage, most casual ORVers will be stymied. If enough of even this kind of minor ecotage of roads occurred often enough and in enough locations, many marginal roads would be abandoned. This type of road trashing can be done casually by a group on a hike, taking care that they aren't caught by ORVers while doing it and being sure that they aren't trapping some poor old fogey in a jeep on a dead-end jeep trail.

* To effectively close roads, strike at numerous points along a single road, and at many roads within the road network surrounding a wild area. Maintain your campaign against the roads in the area — after they are repaired, strike again, and again, and again. Eventually it will become too costly for the Forest Service or whoever to continue repairing them and roads will begin to be abandoned.

* Keep in mind that as your campaign against roads becomes more effective and costly, your security precautions will need to become more stringent to prevent being caught in an increased law-enforcement campaign to protect the roads.

* If the West is entering a wet cycle, as many climatologists believe is happening, ecotage against roads will be aided to a great degree by nature. Now is the time to act. (Increased government budget-cutting is also a great ally.)

*Many Forest Service roads have gates which allow the Freddies to close the roads at will for a variety of purposes (wildlife protection is one reason, but these gates may also be used to keep protesters out of a timber sale area). You can cause confusion by getting cheap padlocks at a city hardware store and closing and locking such gates yourself. A little "Liquid Solder" in the keyhole prevents the lock from being picked. The design of the gate creates a casing around the lock which will prevent it from being cut with bolt cutters.

*Corrugated roofing metal or other types of sheet metal are ideal materials for blocking culverts under roads. Use your ingenuity to affix them to the culvert so they will stay in place in high water.

CHAPTER 5

VEHICLES AND HEAVY EQUIPMENT

There's more than one way
to skin a CAT®.

Jim Stiles
©1983

The classic act of monkeywrenching is messing around with a bulldozer. Probably the best known technique is pouring sugar or Karo syrup in the gas tank or oil system. But this doesn't really work! It just clogs the fuel or oil filter. There are better — and simpler — ways to "decommission" that piece of heavy equipment threatening your special place. The 'dozer is a tool of destruction. But like David and Goliath, a little ingenuity and chutzpah can go a long way toward stopping a monster.

There are, of course, more complicated ways to take out one of these behemoths. You can totally dismember one with a cutting torch. Or you can just cook one.

Be careful when doing this kind of "nightwork." People who own expensive equipment don't take kindly to having unauthorized maintenance done on their rigs and will encourage the police to do their best to find the culprits.

We have greatly expanded our treatment of this very important subject in this second edition of **ECODEFENSE.** With the new detailed instructions coupled with very clear illustrations, even "mechanical idiots" such as your good editors can accomplish night-time maintenance on heavy equipment.

DISABLING MOTOR VEHICLES OF ALL KINDS

All (motorcycles, cars, trucks, heavy equipment):

1. Jam door and ignition locks with slivers of wood, a hard tough cement like "super glue," or silicone rubber sealant.

2. *Sugar and syrup are ineffective in gasoline or diesel fuel tanks or oil reservoirs. At best, they will merely clog the filter. A handful or more of sand in the fuel tank or oil is much more effective and much easier. You also do not have to carry incriminating items like sugar or a bottle of Karo syrup.*

3. Pour a gallon or more of water or brine into the fuel tank.

4. Pour dirt, sand, salt or a grinding compound (like Carborundum) into the oil filler hole.

5. Pour water into the oil filler hole. Amount depends on engine size — at least 2 quarts for a V-8. The point is to make sure to use enough so that the oil pump will draw only water. The water should maintain "oil" pressure without lubricating at all.

6. Slash tire sidewalls. Sidewall stabs cannot be effectively patched, whereas tread stabs can be. On some tires, cutting the valve stems is an easy way to flatten them.

7. Smash fuel pump, water pump, valve cover, carburetor, distributor, or anything else except the battery (for your safety) or brake system (for their safety). Use a sledge and a steel bar for precision blows.

8. Pour water and/or dirt into the air intake (the big hole usually right under the air cleaner). The more, the better.

9. Pour gasoline or other fuel into the oil reservoir. It will break down the oil and the oil filter will not remove it.

10. Put battery acid or some other corrosive in the radiator.

11. Put Carborundum or other small abrasive particles in the gearbox.

12. Pour a box of quick rice in the radiator.

HEAVY EQUIPMENT

Large machines, in the form of earthmoving and logging equipment and haul trucks, are the most pervasive tools of land rape. Because of their purchase prices and maintenance costs, they are one of the most attractive targets for successful monkeywrenching. Down-time for repairs can exceed fifty dollars an hour, and a proper job of sabotage can idle a machine for days or weeks.

There are hundreds of different types and models of heavy equipment, from the classic bulldozer to the highly specialized harvesting and handling equipment found in the logging industry. Regardless of their specific use, they all have diesel engines and hydraulic systems that are the targets of the experienced monkeywrencher.

A good first step for the equipment saboteur is a basic familiarity with the more common types of machines. Effective teamwork can entail dispatching a friend to work on "that loader over there," or a check to see if that's a security guard parked behind "that scraper." A little basic nomenclature can minimize confusion and enhance your safety and security. Study illustration 5.1, keeping in mind that the descriptive names are somewhat imprecise, due to the tremendous variety of machine types.

Basic Tool Kit

Effective sabotage can be achieved with nothing more than a handful of sand on the spur of the moment. Ideally, of course, it entails planning plus a basic tool kit. In illustration 5.2 you will find the basic elements with which to begin. Since most of this mechanical work will be conducted under the cover of darkness, a good flashlight for each team member and rigid discipline in the use of the light are critical. The military surplus angle-head flashlight (A) is a good buy at most surplus stores. Note the red lens stored in the base that, when mounted over the light, increases your security. The red light is not only less noticeable from a distance, but it will not ruin your night vision. A cheap acrylic artist's red paint (B) will do in a pinch, as will some red cellophane, if you can find it. As always, make sure that every part of the flashlight, including the lenses, bulbs and batteries, is wiped clean of fingerprints. Also, do not use your flashlight indiscriminately. Cup your hand over the end, allowing only a thin sliver of light to illuminate the area on which you are working. Similarly, use your body to block the light from view. A lightweight cord can be used as a lanyard, to hang the

Bulldozer
(w/ripper on rear)

Bulldozer or
Crawler Tractor

Small Crawler
Tractor

Loader, Front Loader
or Front-end Loader

Articulated Loader
(pivots in center)

Grader or
Road Grader

Wheeled Tractor
(w/loader & backhoe attachments)

Scraper
(w/2-wheeled tractor)

Hydraulic Excavator

Power Shovel

5.1

Backhoe

119

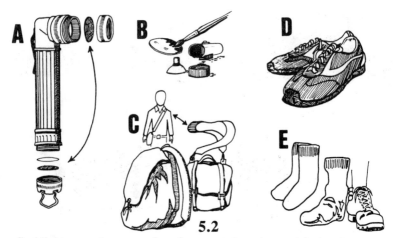

5.2

flashlight around your neck and prevent dropping and losing it.

A lightweight bag keeps your tools together (C) so that you don't inadvertently leave them as evidence at the scene. Nylon can be noisy, so canvas (like cheap army surplus) is usually best.

Lightweight running shoes (D) allow for more silent movement and quick escape. Deck shoes, with their relatively smooth, pebbly soles leave a minimum of distinctive footprints for matching with evidence at other monkeywrenching scenes. Never wear slip-on tennis shoes since they won't stay on when you run. If the terrain requires boots, they can be covered with large socks (E) to obscure their distinctive waffle print.

Your basic tool kit is shown in illustration 5.3. Cheap cloth gloves (a) can be purchased at almost any hardware or variety store. They can be disposed of after a single job, or after a few jobs, depending on the frequency of your monkeywrenching. Buy these only one or two pairs at a time, and get different gloves from different stores to further confuse the trail of evidence (in case a cloth pattern imprints on a greasy surface or a few fibers snag on a sharp edge or rough surface).

A common one-gallon plastic jug (b) is ideal for transporting abrasive material like sand to the equipment. The cut-away bottle makes a good shovel-like scoop if sand can be found near the equipment parking area. If, on the other hand, abrasive material must be transported in, any plastic bottle, cleaned with soap, dried, and wiped free of fingerprints will suffice. A screw-type cap is your best insurance against accidental spillage.

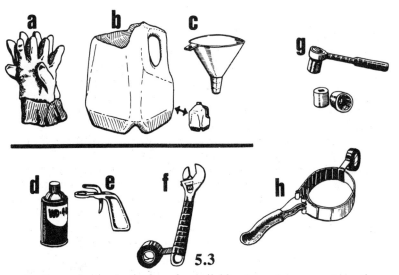

5.3

Lastly, a cheap plastic funnel, available at most grocery stores (or variety, hardware and auto parts stores) as seen in illustration (c) will allow you better access to the essential areas, some of which are not easily reached otherwise.

The advanced saboteur's kit includes a can of spray lubricant (d), used to wash away telltale signs of abrasive grit, and a spray handle for same (e) to improve your aim in the dark of night. In addition, a crescent wrench (f) wrapped in black electrical tape to eliminate its shiny metallic look and to silence it from banging inside your bag, is useful for gaining access to sensitive areas like oil filters that are rarely protected by padlocks. Make sure you are wearing gloves when you apply the tape, as it makes an ideal surface for fingerprints. Also useful for getting into diesel filter systems is a socket wrench and a selection of sockets (g) and an oil filter wrench (h) carefully wrapped with tape to prevent it from leaving telltale scratches on an oil filter housing.

Abrasives
We will assume that you have studied the other operational methods described in this book, and are now standing beside a large mass of slumbering steel. At this point, you can vent your frustrations and attack it in every conceivable way, cutting hydraulic hoses, pulling out electrical wires, hammering at delicate parts, and even slashing the operator's seat. At no small risk to yourself, you will have crippled

the beast for a few days at best, and the repairs will go rather quickly once the parts arrive.

But if you are a serious and dedicated saboteur who wants to have maximum impact, you will work in silence, and when you leave, no one will know you have been there. At least not for a day or two. When your trail has gone cold, and evidence of your presence has been destroyed or hopelessly contaminated, the engines of destruction will literally grind to a halt. Only major shop work will bring them back to life. You will have succeeded.

All experienced monkeywrenchers agree that the best and surest way to cripple heavy equipment is to introduce abrasives into the lubricating system. Illustration 5.4 will show you what typical filler caps look like. The glove in (A) will give you an idea of their approximate size. Be aware that there are a large number of filler caps that have nothing to do with the lubricating system. One that does is the dipstick shown in (B). However, not only does the narrowness of this access point limit the volume of abrasives one can introduce, but a quick check of the oil level first thing in the morning may reveal signs of grit on the dipstick. In (C) is a typical radiator cap, in (D) we see a filler cap on a small hydraulic reservoir, and (E) illustrates one of many styles of fuel tank cover, most noticeable for their large size.

Once you have found the oil filler cap, it is usually a simple matter to pour in dry sand with the aid of your plastic funnel. Illustration 5.5 shows the best procedure for those machines that combine the large

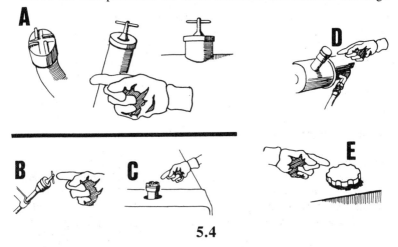

5.4

oil filler cap with the dipstick (a significant minority of heavy equipment). First unscrew and remove the cap/dipstick (a). Pour in your abrasive sand (b). Finally, use liberal amounts of your spray lubricant to wash any trace of sand down into the bowels of the engine (c). Re-insert the dipstick and pull it out again to make sure there is no revealing sand adhering to its surface. Many operators check their fluid levels first thing in the morning (Indeed, some companies are now requiring mandatory checks of all fluid levels each day before starting equipment) so there must be no sign of your work.

Gaining Access

One basic form of security used by equipment owners whose toys are left parked in vulnerable areas is the use of padlocks to secure every cap on the machine. Many manufacturers design caps that easily accept these padlocks. This will not stop the dedicated monkeywrencher. In illustration 5.6 we show how easy it is to use a crescent wrench to

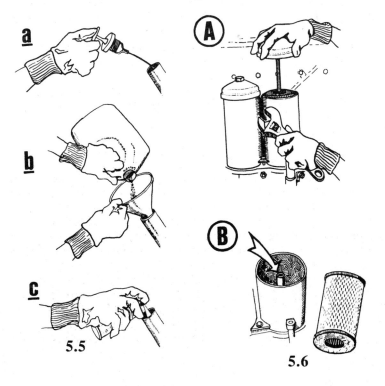

5.5

5.6

gain access to the oil filter housing of a Caterpillar bulldozer. The filter element can be removed and disposed of well away from the site. In its place goes a liberal amount of abrasive. Be careful not to get any abrasive in the tube marked (B). If this becomes clogged, you will not be able to re-insert the threaded rod that secures the lid onto the filter housing.

In 5.7 is another type of oil filter set-up. First use your socket wrench or crescent wrench to remove the small drain plugs (1). Use your open top plastic bottle to catch the oil and keep it from spilling everywhere. Next unscrew the filter case bolts (2) and the filter housing will drop into your hand. Dispose of the filter (3), pour in your abrasive (4), and re-assemble. Number (5) shows you an exploded view of the parts involved.

Another major filter type is the screw-on variety. These are gradually replacing the filter elements just illustrated. This type is removed with a good quality oil filter wrench found at any auto parts store. It's as easy as changing the oil in your car. If you don't know how to change the oil in your car, have a friend show you how. Once you learn this, you can adapt it to your heavy equipment night work.

Be careful to avoid too much oil spillage when removing the screw-type filter. Carry it well away from the machine before scratching out a shallow hole to receive the quart or more of oil inside the filter. Pour out the oil slowly and cover the hole to leave no trace. Fill the inside of the filter about 3/4 full of abrasive and screw it back on to the engine.

Oil-Access Points

Because of the large number of equipment manufacturers and the various models produced, it would be all but impossible to illustrate all of the oil-access points. The remaining illustrations provide a cross-section that will enable you to quickly learn what to look for. By all means, study whenever possible. When you walk by a piece of equipment, stop for a moment and practice spotting the oil filter cap. Keep your distance, though, so no one will suspect you of tampering. Once you have correctly identified a dozen or so filler caps, the rest tend to come very easily.

Remember that your equipment sabotage must not be noticed until the machines begin to break down. Carry a few dark colored rags in your bag to clean up any messes like accidental oil spills that may occur when removing filters. Don't leave things spotless, however, as an extremely clean area on an otherwise greasy, dirty machine is also a giveaway.

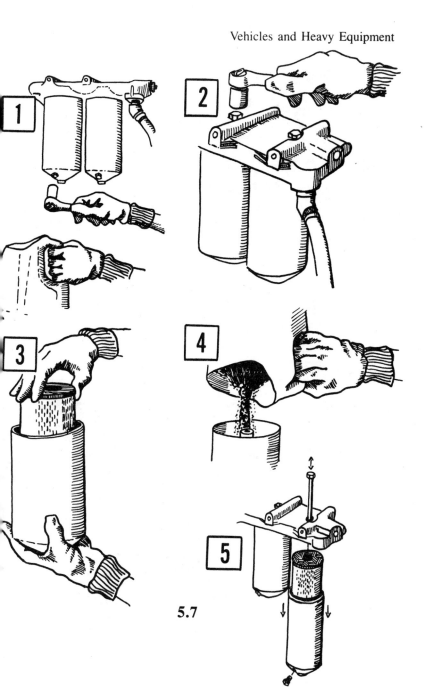

5.7

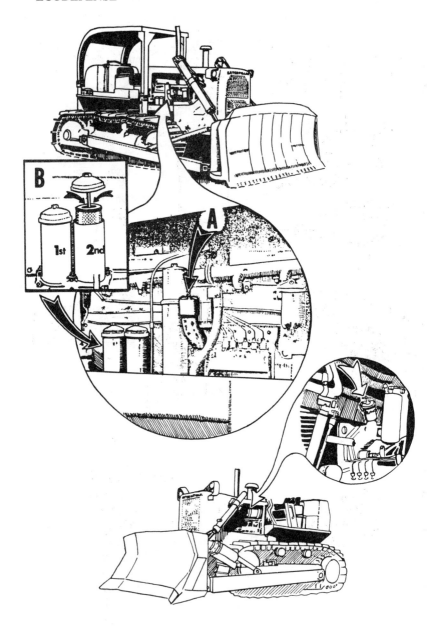

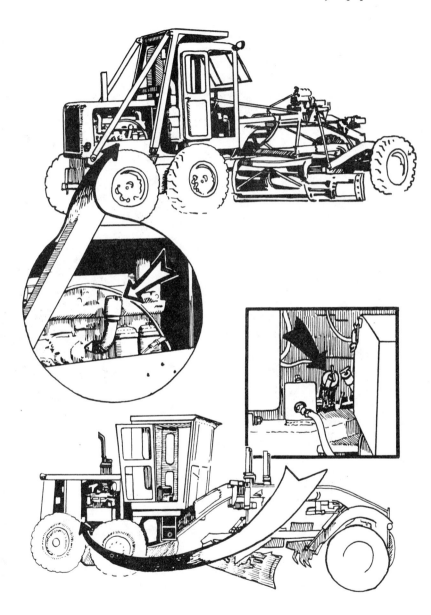

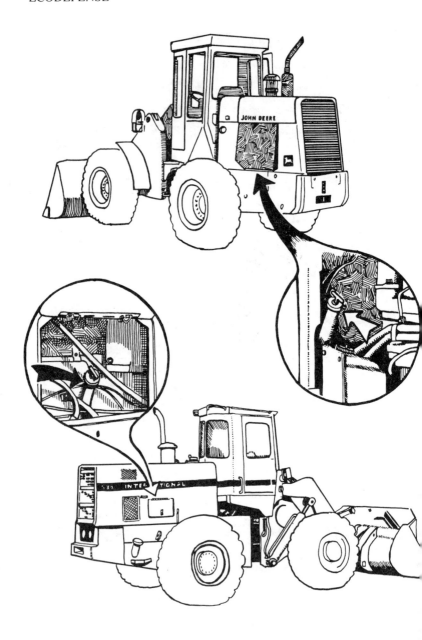

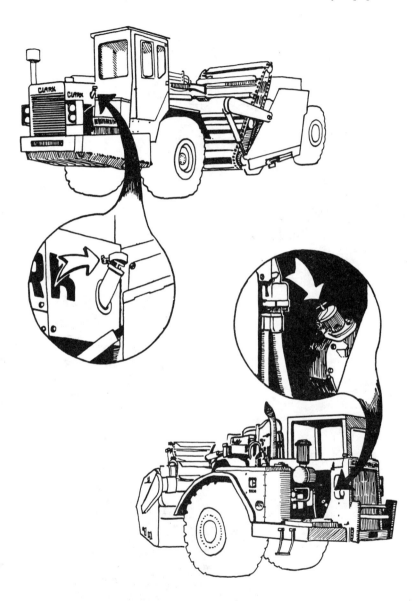

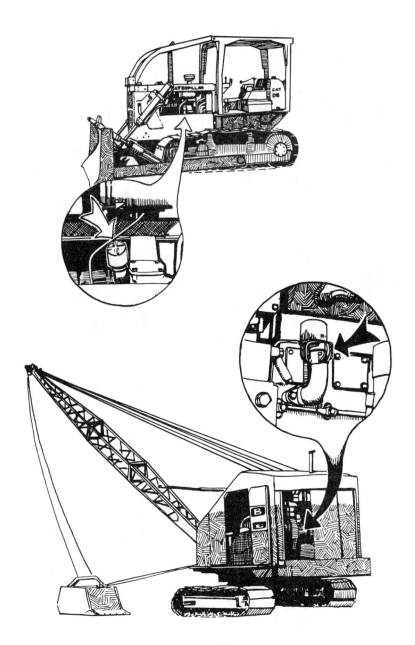

130

Lubrication Points

In addition to the oil filler caps, there are other lubrication points that can be creatively sabotaged. This becomes important when the machines are locked up and you are denied access to any of the points previously discussed.

Every moving joint must have some type of lubrication to prevent overheating and premature wear out. One tool you can find at any auto parts store is the grease gun (see illus. 5.8A), and with it you can introduce abrasives to these moving parts. First, remove about half of the grease from a standard grease tube. Replace this grease with sand or another abrasive and stir it to a smooth blend with a metal rod or dowel. You are now ready to "unlubricate" a machine at a dozen or more points. Look for the "zerk" fittings at every pivot point. Illustration 5.9 gives a close-up view of these grease fittings and shows a variety of locations where they can be found on typical machines.

A simple end wrench or box wrench can also provide access to these grease fittings. Begin by unscrewing the fitting as seen in (B). Use a stick or nail to remove some of the grease (C). After making room inside the hole, add a squeeze of highly abrasive "valve lapping compound" found in auto parts stores. These handy little tubes are easy to use and allow for precision application.

Other moving parts that must be kept properly lubricated are wheel hubs and transmission differentials. While simply draining the differen-

131

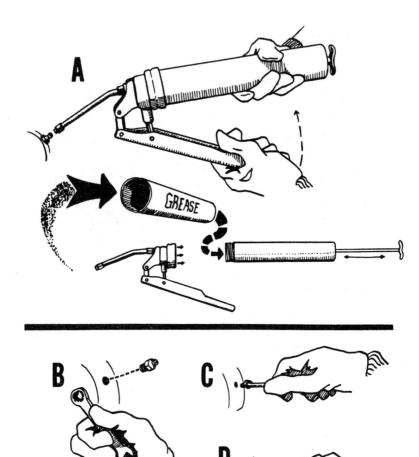

tial lubricant could cause substantial damage, operators in areas where sabotage has occurred have been known to even check *these* before firing up in the morning, so it is better to introduce abrasives into the lubricant. Access to these points is virtually guaranteed, since no one has devised a means of locking out access.

The most important tool for this work is the "breaker bar" and sockets

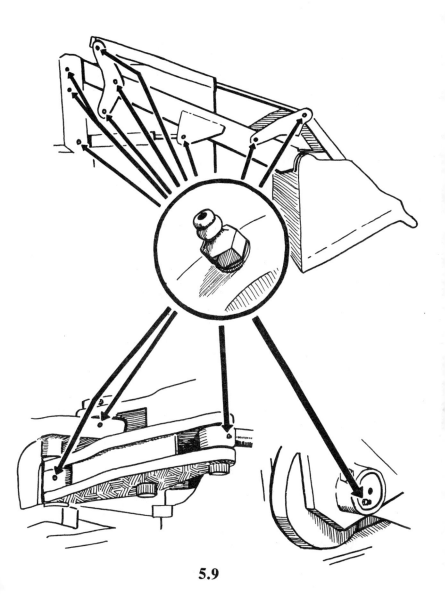

5.9

seen in 5.10A. The long handle provides the leverage needed to unscrew the caps. A short length of common pipe, called a "cheater" (B) can be slipped over the breaker bar handle to provide the leverage of an even longer handle. Various types of oil filler caps found on wheel hubs can be seen in C through F.

In (G) is a plug in a differential through which lubricating oil (and abrasives) is introduced. A neat job will ensure that even should the operator check, it will not be immediately apparent that abrasives are present.

Selection of Abrasives

Common sand is the best and cheapest abrasive for equipment sabotage. Ideally, it is dry and free of organic matter like leaves and twigs. A small piece of window screen or fine mesh hardware cloth can be used to remove rocks and gravel that would otherwise prevent smooth flow or even jam a filler tube on an engine. Simply pour the sand through the screen and into your plastic bottle.

The sand you use should not come from near your home. Forensic laboratory analysis might be able to determine the approximate area the sand came from. This is done by comparing it to samples collected in various drainages where the differing rock formations might lead to slight variations in the makeup of the sand. Although this is a complex laboratory procedure not likely to be employed, it is best to take this extra precaution. Ideally, your scouting will locate a source of clean sand in the vicinity of the equipment parking area.

For the sake of variety, and to make it appear as though separate groups of monkeywrenchers are at work, you can purchase abrasive compounds from suppliers in big cities. Look for a medium grit of silicon carbide. Lastly, lapidary supply houses are a good source of top-notch abrasives which are used to polish stones in tumblers.

Other Sabotage Methods

None of the following methods are as effective as adding abrasives to lubricating oils, but are mentioned in the event a monkeywrencher might want to break up her/his pattern by using differing techniques.

HYDRAULIC SYSTEM — Cut hoses with cable cutters or bolt cutters (a knife won't work because of steel reinforcements in the hoses). Smash hydraulic pistons and fittings with a sledge. *Don't tamper with the brake system.*

FUEL SYSTEM — Smash fuel injectors with a sledge and steel bar.

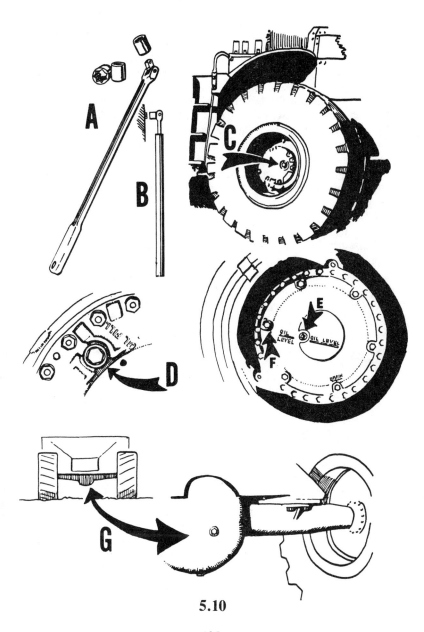

5.10

These are expensive and very hard to remove when effectively smashed "in situ."

TIRE PUNCTURES — Use a sharp knife blade to puncture the sidewalls of tires. A good-sized cut is not reparable, and those large tires are quite expensive. If you use a folding pocket knife, it should have a good lock to prevent it from closing on your hand while you are slicing through the tough sides of a tire. Remember that a knife blade cut can be matched back to a blade as evidence. Don't use your favorite blade, or a good quality knife you would hesitate to throw away if circumstances demanded proper disposal of evidence. *Be careful when puncturing high-pressure tires.* You can also cut valve stems, or even pull the valve stem out with a pair of pliers. Large tires on heavy equipment may have metal valve stems, which could be cut with bolt-cutters.

COOLING SYSTEM — Common table salt, and drain-opening compounds like "Drano" will cause corrosion inside an engine. Introduce through the radiator cap. A small amount will not do, as these big engines have large coolant capacities. The engine must be cold before you remove the radiator cap. Dry rice can be added to a radiator as well. The small grains distribute throughout the system and when they swell with water, the system becomes thoroughly constipated.

WATER — If sand is not handy, you can add water to either the oil or diesel fuel (see section **Water and Diesel Don't Mix**). One advantage of water is that it can be poured down the dipstick spout.

OTHER CONTAMINANTS — Each system of an earthmover's operating equipment requires different fluids to insure proper operation. The wrong viscosity of oil in the hydraulic system can cause serious damage. Diesel oil or gasoline added to lubricating oil will cause oxidation and loss of lubrication. Gasoline in excess of 90 octane will do serious engine damage if added to diesel fuel. Even simple overfilling of transmission fluid or engine oil can cause damage through lack of effective lubrication.

SUGAR — Sugar or Karo syrup in the fuel does little more than clog the filters and is a relatively worthless method of sabotage.

TRUCKS

Often neglected by monkeywrenchers are the fleets of haul trucks that are used in earthmoving and logging operations. Frequently these trucks are parked in a more secure area than the other heavy equipment,

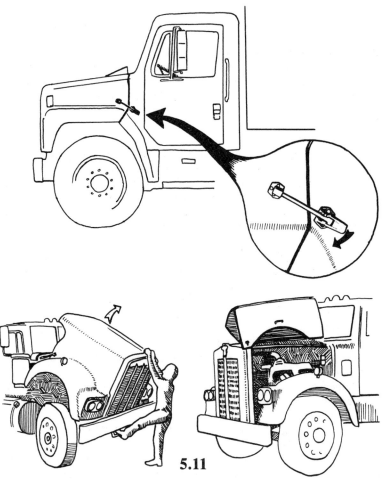

5.11

due to the ease of moving them around. Illustration 5.11 shows a typical hood lock and a couple of hood configurations. Many truck hoods are made of lightweight plastic or fiberglass materials and are easily opened. As illustrated, there are handles, and even hood ornaments, that are used to open these areas for access to the engine. Take a close look at the trucks you see around you before attempting clandestine access.

The engines in these trucks are the same or similar to the diesel power plants found in heavy equipment, so the same principles of introducing abrasives apply here. They also have large numbers of tires waiting to be flattened.

Never tamper with the air hoses or electrical wires that connect truck and trailer. These operate safety equipment, and a careless driver (the majority) who doesn't check his vehicle thoroughly before heading out in the morning can cause an accident. Do not sabotage brakes, lights or any other safety equipment.

Related Targets

CONVEYORS — Construction and mining operations frequently make use of conveyor belt systems to move and sort material. The belts are similar in composition to automobile tires, with thick rubber reinforced by fiber cords. The simplest form of sabotage is slashing with a sharp, thin-bladed knife. A common hardware store item, the "utility" knife, is ideal. Blades are inexpensive, replaceable and usually can be stored inside the handle.

Since cuts that run straight across the belt are easily repaired, all your slashes must be at an angle, and as long as you can make them. Do not attempt to cut completely through the belt. A number of deep cuts at different points will cause the belt to deteriorate rapidly under use. Breakdown and early replacement become necessary.

MAINTENANCE FACILITIES — If you can gain access to garages, fuel trucks or maintenance yards, contaminate any fuel and oil you find. Add water to diesel and dirt and sand to oil. Also, put diesel into any lubricating oils you find.

Remember that guards often hang around garages and maintenance yards.

SECURITY AND HEAVY EQUIPMENT

Because of the high cost of heavy equipment and its extreme vulnerability to sabotage, security efforts are often concentrated on its protection. Always be on the alert for guards around machinery. A security guard might park his pickup truck in amongst the equipment.

Often these machines are brought together at night where they can be more effectively guarded. They might be parked alongside a busy road so that passing traffic alone will discourage monkeywrenching. Or, they might be parked in a special compound, with the protection of a fence, lights and possibly even a guard dog. Remember that every security measure adds to the costs of raping the planet. Even driving the machines to and fro every morning and night adds to lost work time.

If you suspect the presence of a guard, you might want to force him to reveal his presence by using the decoying methods described elsewhere.

In addition, it is possible to wire heavy equipment with a "pager" type alarm system that will summon a guard by radio signal if someone tries to break into the cab. If you plan to force your way into the cab of a machine (perhaps to smash the instrument panel), check first for any antennas, and snap them off at the base when you find them. This will greatly diminish the transmitting range of the alarm system and limit its effectiveness. This type of alarm system has received some attention in logging magazines.

Also, if you are carrying a portable CB for communication with lookouts or driver, switch it on before breaking into the machine. An intermittent tone lasting 5 to 10 seconds can indicate an alarm transmitter trying to signal a pager in the possession of a guard.

If you chose to strike shortly after the end of the work day (often before a security guard arrives), be on the lookout for the maintenance crew. These fellows usually drive a truck loaded with fuel and lubricants. It is their job to top off the diesel fuel tanks to prevent water condensation overnight. Often they check and adjust the levels of lubricating oil. Because of this, they may work a couple of hours to service a large number of machines.

FIELD NOTES

* After repeated sabotage of heavy earth moving equipment, some companies have mounted heavy steel plates over engine and cab access points and secured them with padlocks. Lock jamming methods described elsewhere in this book can create lengthy and costly delays when operators arrive for work. A series of lock jammings, randomly occurring over a long period of time can bring about abandonment of this security measure or the imposition of more costly and time consuming methods, such as extra guards, fenced and lighted compounds for overnight parking, or complete removal of all equipment from the site each night. Any additional security precautions impose financial burdens on the opposition and therefore help to accomplish the monkeywrencher's objectives, whether they are reforms in the mode of operation, the abandonment of a project, or even the curtailment of future planned despoiling of the Earth.

*Silicon carbide or "tumbler abrasive material" (available at "rock shops" which cater to hobbyists) is more effective than sand as an engine abrasive. Enough grit to destroy the largest engine can be carried in a pants pocket, and if used just right it is not as messy as sand. *Very fine* grit is so powdery that it feels like white flour. It will mix thoroughly with oil, so it's easy to pour down an oil filler or dipstick hole. It also stays in suspension for a long time, so it will circulate nicely throughout the entire oil system to get into all of those little cracks. It can also be used in fuel tanks, because the tiniest particles are so small that they'll go through filters. For security reasons, take the usual precautions when buying this stuff, and don't leave any of it lying around your home.

*Semi-trucks are vulnerable to several forms of specialized monkey-wrenching. Refrigerator trucks (beer trucks, etc.) have a thermostat accessible from the outside. Simply by turning the thermostat all the way down, significant damage can be done to the contents (frozen and blown-out beer cans, for example). Many semi-trucks have their oil filler hole in the grill. This is convenient for those who wish to add abrasives to the oil.

*It is possible that both the oil filler pipe and the dipstick tube on heavy machinery will have caps which are locked. It may be possible to punch or drill a small hole (large enough for the tip of your funnel) in the filler pipe, dipstick tube or their locked covers. If this is done in an inconspicuous place and well camouflaged it might not be discovered until it's too late to save the machinery.

CUTTING TORCH

A cheap, light-duty cutting torch designed for artists and hobbyists is a suitable tool for cutting rebar for use as road spikes. However, a medium or heavy-duty torch (costing about $60 to $100 more) should be used for structures or heavy equipment. This set-up can handle larger volumes of gasses and therefore can cut larger pieces of steel faster (like bulldozer blade arms and railroad rails in less than a minute each). Since the use of a torch for monkeywrenching is a team operation anyway (an oxy-fuel flame is very bright — if you use it alone, you're asking to get caught), the additional cost for equipment may not be so burdensome.

How does one get the equipment and learn how to use it? Forget hardware stores — go to a welding supply store. They can provide the right equipment, the gasses, and the instruction manuals. Use of a cutting torch is fairly simple but certain safety precautions must be adhered to or torch use could be very dangerous. The instruction booklets I've seen are very thorough on both technique and safety. The only criticism I have is that they assume you are cutting clean metal. *If you cut metal contaminated with oil or grease, be careful. Oil and grease can burn explosively in pure oxygen.*

Get the largest oxygen bottle you can reasonably transport. The whole principle of flame cutting is to burn the metal in a stream of oxygen — the fuel is needed only to preheat the metal. Thus the amount of metal you can cut is directly related to the amount of oxygen you can dispense. Charts provided with the equipment give you the data you need on gas requirements.

On the subject of fuel, consider only acetylene or propane. Each has advantages and disadvantages. Both are equally effective for cutting. Acetylene looks less suspicious in the field because it can also be used for welding, but it's more expensive (unless you rent the bottle). It is also much bulkier to transport, a little trickier to handle, and can be obtained only at welding supply shops.

Propane is cheaper and easier to handle, can be obtained almost anywhere, and can be used in your camp stove. But it cannot be used for welding. The cutting torch attachment, handle, hoses, oxygen bottle, and oxygen regulator are the same regardless of fuel. Only the cutting tips, fuel bottle and regulator are different with different fuels (although an acetylene regulator is fine for propane, a propane-only regulator is cheaper).

If money is most important and you have no propane bottle already, go with oxy-acetylene and rent the gas bottles. If you have propane equipment already, or no need to weld, or if weight is most important, go with oxy-propane and either rent the oxygen bottle or buy an aluminum oxygen bottle. Don't buy a steel oxygen bottle — aluminum ones weigh only two-thirds as much as steel ones. A supplier of medical gasses would be the best place to start looking for one. You don't need to be a gorilla to backpack a heavy-duty oxy-propane set-up with an aluminum oxygen bottle of sufficient capacity to cut up a bulldozer.

Almost all of the above can be discussed with your local welding supply salesperson, but the following ought not to be.

What can you do with a cutting torch? If you must be neat or conserve gasses, use the right size tip for the thickness of the metal you are cutting. If you want to destroy something as quickly as possible, use the largest tip appropriate for the amount of gas you have.

Besides using it for cutting, you can use your torch to melt bearings, destroy hydraulic pistons, fuse joints, wreck gear teeth, etc. (watch out for grease and oil). In short, a torch may be the optimum tool for converting an expensive machine into a pile of scrap safely, quickly and quietly. You are not limited to iron and steel. Any metal that readily oxidizes can be cut with an oxygen torch. Aluminum burns very fast, copper burns slowly, and stainless can't be burned at all. Since you need to practice anyway, use scraps of the same material you'll be up against in the field and experiment with it at home. *Beware of volatile metals like zinc and cadmium (common plating materials) because they can produce dangerous fumes (cadmium is as toxic as mercury and is retained by the body longer.)*

While seldom useful or safe for the solo ecoteur, a cutting torch can be a very important tool for a monkeywrench gang. It is much more hazardous than other hand tools, but, in combination with other tools, it can virtually eliminate the need for explosives. Appropriate technology and safety are always important considerations when defending the Earth.

— *Robin Hood*

FIELD NOTES

* Remember that a cutting torch is very bright and makes you visible at a considerable distance. It will of course be more visible at night. Consider the use of a screen. Have lookouts that can warn of approach a considerable distance away.

* In case you have to abandon your equipment to escape yourself, be sure that there are no fingerprints or other identifying marks on it to link it to you.

BURNING MACHINERY

In some cases, burning a target is the most effective way of decommissioning it. This can be true of the most remote sites, such as logging operations on the edge of roadless areas, or in places where a quick get-a-way is assured, such as near a frequently traveled road or highway. Extreme caution should always be exercised in any action where fire is used, since it is a more serious offense than other types of "vandalism" (burning something is usually classified as arson). It can be dangerous to the perpetrator as well. Also, nothing draws attention quite like a fire.

To burn any object, the first requirement is fuel. Since most machines are made of non-combustible metal, fuel must be supplied if a hot enough fire is to be achieved. While there are many types of fuel that can be used, many, such as wood, are too slow to ignite, while others, such as gasoline, are extremely volatile, and should be avoided due to the increased risk involved. My favorite has always been diesel fuel.

Diesel fuel is also known as kerosene or heating oil. When used for aviation purposes, it is called jet fuel. While there are some very minor differences in purity, all of these names describe the same product. Unlike gasoline or Coleman fuel, diesel is much more stable and much less volatile. It is also denser, and therefore burns longer, but not as hot as gasoline. While the slightest spark may be enough to set off gasoline, sometimes a match held directly against an object doused in diesel will not ignite. This makes diesel fuel much safer to work around. When I was working in the oil fields of Oklahoma, we used to scrub the rig down with pure diesel while it was still running, and I never heard of an accident that resulted from this seemingly foolish practice.

Many large construction sites have an abundant diesel supply on hand, usually on a truck or trailer mounted tank, and all that is required is a large enough set of bolt cutters to remove the padlock on the valve. A 12 inch adjustable crescent wrench (or a monkeywrench!) may be needed to turn the valve to open, always in a clockwise direction. Be very careful when doing this because a large tank can produce very high pressure, and you risk getting yourself doused. Not only will this make you more flammable, but the scent of diesel can take days to wash out of your skin. This could be incriminating, unless you're a roughneck.

If you need to carry your own fuel, plastic milk jugs will do, but don't fill them full or they may leak. When finished, you can burn them along with the the 'dozer, and destroy the evidence. It may prove impossible to avoid getting any diesel on yourself, so coveralls or old clothes are advised.

It doesn't take much diesel to do a lot of damage if it is used properly. When the object in question is simply doused and ignited, most of the fuel runs off and into the ground, where it can do little damage, and the fire itself is short lived. To prevent this from happening, first cover the vulnerable areas with rags before dousing (sawdust or hay can also be used, as can many absorbent combustible materials, but rags are better and easier to carry). Put the rags on and under any exposed electrical wiring, rubber hoses and electrical parts such as meters and gauges. Also, put them inside the cab, under the dash, and, what the hell, leave some on the seat, too. In this manner as little as two gallons can accomplish the complete destruction of the electrical system, and, if the fire gets hot enough, also the gaskets and bearings, not to mention the hydraulic connections.

Once the rags are generously doused, the next step is ignition. This is the tricky part. Diesel fuel, being difficult to light — especially in cold weather — usually needs a large flame to get it started. As already mentioned, gasoline is much too dangerous for this purpose. The safest way is to soak a rag in rubbing alcohol, place it on the other already diesel-soaked rags and light it. Rubbing alcohol will not explode the way gasoline will, and the odor is neither as strong nor as long lasting. You may want to use a delayed ignition set-up that will allow you time to leave the scene. If so, be sure you test it not once, but several times before actually using it on the job. (See the article on **Burning Billboards** for one possible delayed ignition method.)

Never use rags collected around the house, because they may be traceable. A good source is a second-hand store such as Goodwill. 100% cotton is best. Rags can also be purchased at paint stores by the box, but these are usually made from polyester scraps, and are not as good as cotton.

AIRCRAFT

Helicopters

Helicopters are useful tools for the large scale Earth raper. They are used for dam building, logging, spraying toxic chemicals and other heinous practices. The monkeywrencher seeking to destroy or disable a helicopter should be especially cautious in this endeavor. Very few of the helicopters used in large scale construction operations come with a price tag of under a million dollars and anyone caught tampering with that kind of investment is likely to be treated mercilessly. Also, it would not be difficult to endanger someone's life. The idea is to protect the Earth, not to reduce helicopter pilots to blobs of protoplasm. The smooth, sneaky approach should give way to obvious destruction so as not to cause an in-flight accident.

Helicopters are generally made of light materials that are easily damaged by a sturdy instrument wielded by strong arms. Their rotor systems are extremely delicate. The slightest nick or dent on either a tail or main rotor will definitely mean mandatory replacement of the rotor. I once observed a helicopter main rotor latch onto a candy wrapper, and it sounded like a giant pterodactyl in the process of receiving a barbed wire enema. That chopper had to be shut down for a 12 hour inspection.

The air speed indicator is a little five inch projectile that sticks out of the "nose" of the helicopter. Be sure to give it a good whack. They're easy to ruin and expensive to replace. You should also do some damage to the cargo hook, which is on the belly of the machine. Remember, the more diversity in the damage you inflict, the longer the machine will be shut down.

Helicopters almost never fly at night and will generally be kept at a heliport set up somewhere near the construction site, or perhaps at the nearest airport. Be sure to check thoroughly to see if there is a guard before you commence with your duties.

The beauty of effective "helicopter management" is that one can generally shut down an entire operation while replacements are sought. At $250 to $2000 a flight hour, and big bucks for availability, a chopper is a heavy investment even for the likes of Bechtel.

In short, an individual with creativity and a crowbar can quickly and easily shut down a helicopter. But again, it needs to be stressed that on-the-ground action is by far preferable to taking pot shots at a helicopter in flight. Get the chopper where it sits, not while it's flying up in the wild blue yonder.

Fixed-wing aircraft

Light planes are used in a diverse array of destructive enterprises. Specific planes can be targeted by observing them at work and noting their general description and number. A check of local airports will reveal their home base. Sometimes a phone call to the airport can reveal the pilot and type of plane with experience in hunting predators, or ferrying oil exploration crews. Simply pretend you're a big shot or corporate functionary looking for an experienced pilot for a specific type of work.

Aerial predator control is becoming increasingly popular on both sides of the law. Once confined to lawless ranchers living out fantasies of being an ace, currently we are seeing state wildlife agencies gunning down wolves and coyotes from Alaska to Arizona. Winter is the favorite season for this, since the targets are easier to spot against a blanket of snow. Following are some of the gunners' methods:

RANDOM SEARCH: This involves flying low-level grid type patterns or scouting wide open expanses like frozen lakes. If you live in such an area, a decoy made up to look like a target animal and set on a stake in an open area might lure in gunners for identification.

RADIO TELEMETRY: Temporarily halted in Alaska, this technique will be used again to destroy whole packs. A wolf fitted with a radio collar after being caught in a leghold trap will later lead gunmen with radio directional equipment to the entire pack.

PREDATOR CALLING: A ground crew in a jeep or pickup will stop on a back road and turn on a siren. After a moment or two they will shut off the siren and listen for the answering howls of brother coyote. When they hear it, they will estimate the direction and distance. This information is radioed to the aircraft which closes in for the kill.

Both small helicopters and light planes are used for this type of slaughter. Planes are usually of the "wing-over" type, with the wing on top to prevent it from blocking the view of the spotter and shooter. In addition to the pilot, there will be one or two shooters, usually armed with shotguns (which requires them to get within 40 yards of the target).

If you spot this type of crime in progress, try to remain out of sight and use your binoculars to identify the plane or 'copter. Take careful note of the direction they fly when they leave, as this might lead you to the airstrip or airport where the aircraft is parked overnight. These fellows might return to a private commercial airport, or they might be temporarily or permanently based at a ranch airstrip.

There are a number of ways to sabotage a light plane, ranging from the silent and sneaky to the loud and severely damaging. If you use the louder methods, save them for last when you can immediately flee after 60 to 90 seconds of raising hell.

The illustration shows the vulnerable points on a typical light plane. Almost all significant repair on an aircraft is expensive because most of it, by law, must be done by certified specialists called A & P's (for airframe and power plant).

A. Control surfaces. These are the various flaps that control the plane in flight. They are carefully designed and must be properly balanced by an A & P before the plane can be certified. Like the rest of the aircraft skin, they are made of lightweight aluminum and are best damaged with a large axe. One good blow to each aileron, elevator and the rudder will ground the plane. These members are so precisely balanced that even the paint must be applied by a certified shop. Imagine what a good sound axe blow will do.

B. Antennas. Snap these off to prevent crucial radio communication.

C. Windows. Aircraft windows are made of plexiglas and are easily marred. An owner can, with considerable difficulty, replace side windows, but the windshield must be replaced by a certified mechanic.

147

The softness of the plastic makes sandpaper, or better still, sanding blocks, the ideal tool to quietly mar them to destroy visibility and require replacement. Even an oily rag and a handful of sand can be used to achieve the same effect, but with more time and effort involved.

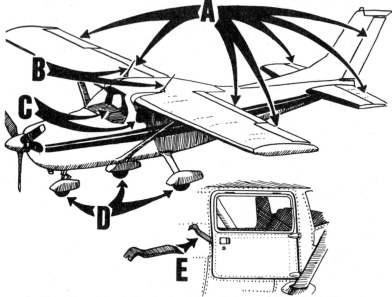

D. Tires. Punching holes in the sidewalls is a good method. Changing flat tires on a plane is much harder than on a car due to their unusual construction, split rims, etc.

E. Instruments. An everyday prybar from a hardware store can be used to force open the door of an airplane. Once inside, use the end of the prybar to demolish the instrument panel. Don't be satisfied with merely smashing the protective glass over the dials. As you strike each instrument, focus your energy on the idea that you are going to knock the back off. This will insure enough force to necessitate costly replacement.

Never tamper with an aircraft engine or its fuel. A mechanical failure in mid-air is extremely dangerous and life-threatening. The monkey-wrencher should aim to ground the plane with as much damage as possible, but without endangering anyone's life. *For this reason any monkeywrenching of an aircraft should be made obvious, with no attempt to disguise the work*. Keep also in mind that ecotage directed at an aircraft may entail felony violations of federal law or FAA regulations. Practice strict security on these operations.

VEHICLE MODIFICATIONS FOR THE SERIOUS MONKEYWRENCHER

PART ONE — ELECTRICAL

Sometimes you just don't want the dome light in your vehicle to come on in the "dark of the night" or those bright "tell tail" brake lights to flash as you stop in an out-of-the-way spot. The careful monkeywrencher may be interested in the following alternatives to factory wiring. I would suggest that a wiring diagram be located for your vehicle before you start any modifications, and that you ask for help if you have no electrical knowledge.

Dome Lights

Dome lights come in useful at times for map reading, finding the monkeywrench under the seat, etc. But the damn things also come on when the door is opened. The best way around this is to disconnect the door jam switches — either unclip them from their housings or cut and tape the wires (make sure no "open" or "live" wires can touch ground). Most cars and trucks have a light switch with an instrument light dimmer that when rotated all the way up will turn on the dome light — even with the door jam switches disconnected.

Auxiliary Headlight

The use of a small "tractor light" as a secondary headlight is a good way to navigate at night at slow to moderate speeds without using the headlight switch, which usually runs the tail and marker lamps as well. Tractor lights are low intensity lights commonly used on farm and construction machinery and can be bought at most auto parts stores.

A hood can be constructed out of almost anything and should be added to the light (see illustration). Large size tin cans or a small piece of sheet metal will work well as a hood. Paint this shield flat black. The hood will stop excessive up and side glare while the lamp is in use.

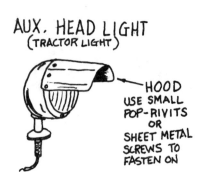

AUX. HEAD LIGHT
(TRACTOR LIGHT)

—HOOD
USE SMALL
POP-RIVITS
OR
SHEET METAL
SCREWS TO
FASTEN ON

Brake Light Lock-out

A switch to lock-out the brake lights can easily be installed. Most brake light switches are located on or near the brake pedal. The illustration shows a typical switch and how to wire it. Remember not to leave the brake lights off if you aren't "on the job." It's a sure pullover and ticket (I have a warning light on mine). Also remember that all other rear lights will still work — turn signals, emergency flashers, tail lights (see "Auxiliary Headlight" above), etc.

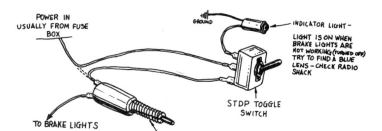

— BRAKE LIGHT LOCK-OUT —

POWER IN
USUALLY FROM FUSE
BOX

GROUND

—INDICATOR LIGHT—

LIGHT IS ON WHEN
BRAKE LIGHTS ARE
NOT WORKING (TURNED OFF)
TRY TO FIND A BLUE
LENS – CHECK RADIO
SHACK

STOP TOGGLE
SWITCH

TO BRAKE LIGHTS

BRAKE LIGHT
SWITCH

Back-up Lights

If your vehicle is in proper working condition, every time you put it in reverse, the back-up lights will come on. It is usually not worth the trouble to override this circuit. Each manufacturer incorporates this system in a different way. The back-up switch for most automatic transmissions is on the lower steering column and is usually incorporated with the neutral safety switch. Most standard transmissions use a sending unit in the transmission. The best way around the whole mess is to wire a new back-up light on the vehicle and disconnect the old system (just remove the bulbs). I use a couple of tractor lights which I find more useful anyway.

For added security, it might be advisable to disconnect the warning buzzers which tell you when you have left the key in the ignition or failed to fasten your seatbelt.

Coil Lock-out System

There have been times when I've wanted to either feign mechanical failure or disable my vehicle. This is when a coil lock-out switch comes in handy.

I like to put mine inside the driver's compartment in a panel with the rest of my "auxiliary switches." With the switch off, the engine will turn over but will not start. You should be careful not to flood the engine (keep your foot *off* the gas pedal) or to run the battery down. With the switch on, electricity hits the coil and the engine will start.

This switch is also handy when you're going to leave the vehicle — for hiking, camping, or "whatever." If the unit is to be left for a long period of time, it's wise to disconnect the battery and to somehow lock the hood (be creative). The illustration should be self-explanatory.

Remember to solder and insulate all connections.

COIL LOCK-OUT

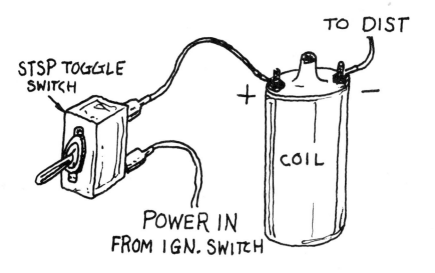

PART TWO — FUEL SYSTEMS

Most stock fuel systems can be classified as inadequate or poor for the serious eco-raider. The first problem is lack of capacity — 20 gallons doesn't go far in a 3/4 ton truck so extra tanks are in order. You should be able to carry 40 gallons in on-board fuel tanks. Most manufacturers have auxiliary fuel tanks as an option or they can be purchased from after-market dealers.

Jerry cans are a good idea and are more mobile and transferable, but mounting and space requirements make too many of them impractical and unsafe. However, 3 or 4 five-gallon cans and at least one on-board reserve tank would be ideal. If two auxiliary tanks are installed, mount them on separate sides of the truck in about the same location for balance. Use a brass tee so equal amounts of fuel will be drawn from both tanks at the same time. Always use locking gas caps for your own protection (hee-hee).

Most vehicles have only one mechanical fuel pump and one small and usually hard-to-get-to fuel filter. By adding an electric fuel pump and an in-line filter for each tank, you can stop trouble (i.e., plugged filter or bad mechanical pump) when you can't afford it (when you have to leave quick or "just can't stop now"). See illustration.

Everything needed to upgrade your fuel system can be bought at your friendly auto parts store. It is a good idea to mount a small fire extinguisher in the cab of your truck. $20 is cheap insurance.

—Happy Hunting,
Mr. Goodwrench

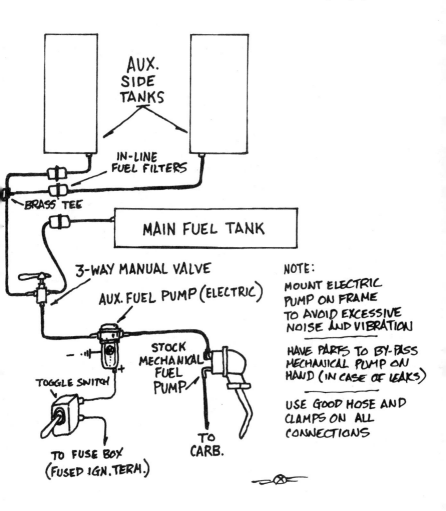

AUX.
SIDE
TANKS

IN-LINE
FUEL FILTERS

BRASS TEE

MAIN FUEL TANK

3-WAY MANUAL VALVE

AUX. FUEL PUMP (ELECTRIC)

STOCK
MECHANICAL
FUEL
PUMP

TOGGLE SWITCH

TO
CARB.

TO FUSE BOX
(FUSED IGN. TERM.)

NOTE:

MOUNT ELECTRIC
PUMP ON FRAME
TO AVOID EXCESSIVE
NOISE AND VIBRATION

HAVE PARTS TO BY-PASS
MECHANICAL PUMP ON
HAND (IN CASE OF LEAKS)

USE GOOD HOSE AND
CLAMPS ON ALL
CONNECTIONS

WATER AND DIESEL DON'T MIX

Well — here I am again — telling all you environmental blowflies how to hurt good yellow machinery. Now, you see, the problem is every time one of the tricks I know is printed, it warns all the pro-development people about what to look for.

Like if I say that diesel engines don't like water, then all the paranoid diesel engine guys who read this would figure out ways to protect their equipment. Well . . . I guess a lot of assholes wouldn't, so . . . .

The best way to use water is to get it into the fuel injection system (see illustration). Most (if not all) diesels have at least one water/fuel separator and possibly a warning system so you have to run enough water through the system to bypass it. Once the water gets to the fuel injection pump, it's history — time for R & R.

A simpler way to use water is to fill the air intake with it. Once water sucks into the cylinders (water can't be compressed), it will jam the pistons and the engine can't turn over — time for repairs (*down-time* for repairs, that is!). If the engine is running when the water is introduced to the cylinders, it will jam the pistons and bend the connecting rods — a lot of work for the poor bastard who has to fix it.

Another good way to use water is to push the machine off a cliff into a lake.

While I'm at it, let me tell ya why I like cement:

* Mix up a batch of cement in five gallon plastic buckets.

* Climb up on top of your favorite large piece of destruction equipment.

* Have your partner (yes, this is a family activity) hand you the buckets.

* Open the rain flap on the exhaust pipe and pour the cement in.

As long as we're on the subject of diesel equipment, remember that if the gear lube is drained from a transmission or differential, the engine noise will drown out the gear noise. By the time the operator thinks something is wrong — it's too late.

— *Mr. Goodwrench*

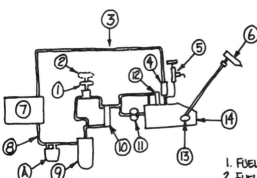

TYPICAL SCHEMATIC
OF THE FUEL SYSTEM
© CATERPILLER TRACTOR CO.

3208 SERIES
8 CYL. 636 C.I.D.
FIRING ORDER - 1-2-7-3-4-5-6-8
RIGHT HAND ROTATION

1. FUEL PRIMING PUMP - CLOSED
2. FUEL PRIMING PUMP - OPEN
3. RETURN LINE FOR C.B.V.
4. CONSTANT BLEED VALVE (C.B.V.)
5. MANUAL BLEED VALVE (M.B.V.)
6. FUEL INJECTION NOZZLE
7. FUEL TANK
8. FUEL INLET LINE
9. FUEL FILTER
10. BYPASS VALVE FOR PUMP PRIMING
11. FUEL TRANSFER PUMP
12. FUEL BYPASS VALVE
13. CAMSHAFT
14. FUEL INJECTION PUMP HOUSING
A. WATER SEPARATOR

Bulldozer. Note the smoke stack (exhaust pipe).

PAY
YOUR
RENT

CHAPTER 6

ANIMAL DEFENSE

I'll admit it right out front: I am a hunter and proud of it. But I'm not proud of much of what passes for hunting these days or what passes for a "sportsman." Slob hunters and poachers generally travel by pickup or some other form of mechanical conveyance and if you take their wheels out from under them, they're helpless. An even more sinister and despicable "hunter" is the trapper. Trapping is cruel, serves only greed and vanity, and disrupts the population balance of important carnivorous "fur-bearers." The leg-hold trap should be outlawed. But until that glad day, you can stop the trappers yourself in your neck of the woods. Be careful. These good ol' boys are armed and have the law on their side. Don't end up with *your* hide nailed to some yahoo's barn door.

By using the following, field-tested techniques, you can make trapping difficult — if not impossible — for even the most experienced and dedicated trapper. Remember the wolf.

TRAPLINES

One of the most widespread assaults upon the Earth and her creatures is the practice of trapping. Fur trappers kill whatever animals bring in the dollars, not the often-hyped "damaging" predators or overpopulated species. Regulation by state game departments masquerades as "scientific management," when in reality there are no reliable population figures available, no significant studies of the impact of trapping on target species, and virtually no enforcement of trapping regulations in the field due to the scattered and widespread nature of this destructive activity. In many states, there are no limits to the killing of coyote, fox, badger and numerous other species. The attitude seems to be "the only good one is a dead one." Only the strength and resilience of Mother Nature keeps many animals from following down the slow path to extinction of such once-common animals as the wolf.

To get some idea of the destruction and suffering wrought by trappers, examine these "body counts" for a typical Western state (Colorado) for the 1982-1983 season (a one year span):

Coyote — 14,419
Bobcat — 2,505
Beaver — 7,516
Raccoon — 4,800
Red Fox — 1,735
Badger — 1,832

These grim statistics are repeated in state after state, and must be added to the death toll of federal "predator control" programs that can destroy over 100,000 coyotes in a single year. Your state game department has published figures detailing the extent of the reported kills in your area.

How is this slaughter accomplished?

First, you must realize that the great majority of licensed trappers are amateurs, school kids, and part-timers whose technique leaves much to be desired. Rather than succumb to the temptation to exaggerate, consider what happens to a typical coyote when caught by a professional trapper of considerable abilities.

Mr. Coyote's first sign of danger is the snap of steel jaws as the leghold trap seizes a toe, foot or leg. The pain and fear causes an initial desire to flee. If the trap is chained to a stake, the attempted escape is short-lived. If the trap is attached to a drag (a hook or anchor-like

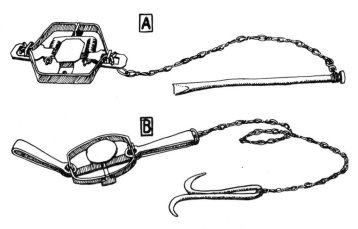

A) - *Coil spring-type trap attached to stake.*

B) - *Long spring-type trap attached to hook-type drag. Drags are also made from scrap metal, heavy rocks or combinations of all.*

device on the end of a short chain), the coyote instinctively runs for shelter, dragging the trap until the hook snags in brush to hold him fast.

At this point, the actions of a trapped coyote vary widely. Some lay down and quietly await death. Although most states require periodic checking of traps, there is no realistic way of enforcing such rules in the backcountry. It is not unusual for a trapped animal to spend two or more days locked in the grip of a leghold trap. When bad weather sets in, as it often does in the prime winter trapping season, the wait grows longer. Trapping authorities have often espoused the desirability of an animal who freezes to death while trapped, which eliminates the need for killing by gun or club and thereby insures an undamaged pelt for market.

Most trapped animals fight the trap to some extent. "Wring-off" is a trappers' term used to describe the animals whose twisting, biting, tugging, rolling and chewing causes them to sever or amputate the toes, foot or leg held in the trap. Although some animals crippled by their escape live to hobble around for many years, most die of infection or from starvation due to impaired hunting ability.

The coyote who remains in the grip of the trap until the trapper's arrival will usually be killed in one of two ways. If only a couple of toes are caught in the trap, the professional will use a .22 rifle to make the kill so that his approach does not frighten the animal into pulling free. Unfortunately for the trapper, this method can cause damage to the pelt, and hence to his pocketbook.

The most popular method of killing involves beating the coyote in the head with a long stick or club. Although some trappers beat the animal to death in this manner, the professional strives to merely stun the animal or knock it unconscious. He will then stomp on the rib cage or kneel on it in order to crush the chest cavity and cause death by internal bleeding (the blood often fills the lungs and causes death by suffocation).

Also common to trapping is the death and injury of so-called "non-target" and "trash" species. These are any type of animal, including house pets, that the trapper does not want to catch. Skunks are often the first animals to investigate a trapline laid for coyote and bobcat, and the trapper will virtually eradicate the skunk population to get to the furbearers he wants. Trapped skunks may be carved up and used as trap bait, so investigate the ground around any skunk remains.

With the professional and amateur trapper alike, the non-target animals constitute between one-third and two-thirds of the animals trapped, and include deer, squirrels, skunks, ravens and crows, hawks and eagles, pet dogs and cats, and others.

Perhaps most amazing is the way that trapping has persisted in the face of widespread public opposition. An extensive federally-funded survey conducted by Dr. Stephen R. Kellert of Yale University found that 78% of the public opposed the steel-jaw trap. In addition 57% disapproved of killing furbearers for clothing. Almost two-thirds of the trappers indicated that they did most of their trapping between the ages of 13 and 20, and a whopping 86.4% reported that trapping has never been a major source of income for them. Even a survey conducted by the American fur industry found that less than 3% of trappers derived most of their income from trapping.

Trapping is a hobby-like pursuit for most of its practicioners, yet one out of four trappers surveyed by a major trapper's magazine boasted that they would disobey any law that banned the leghold trap.

Where to Find Traps and Traplines

Locating traplines usually requires patience and practice. Many states have regulations that prohibit setting traps in those areas where the public is likely to witness the cruelty. The authors of *Fur Trapping,* published by Winchester Press, advise that "the trapper would be well advised to stay away from roads. This generates a massive amount of bad publicity against all trappers." In addition, "Public campgrounds are also an area that the trapper would do well to avoid . . . many of the campers have small children who might become caught in a trap and injured."

Begin your search with a trip to the local office of your state game department to obtain a free copy of the trapping regulations. This will give you an idea of where traps are to be found (for example: not within 25 yards of a public road or highway), when to find most of them (trapping season dates), and even information on the frequency with which the trapper must check his traps. If your state, for example, requires trap checks once every 48 hours, this may indicate the frequency with which the typical trapper takes to the field (an important security consideration).

Since most trappers prefer to drive instead of walk, a lot of traplines are found along rural roads, powerline easement roads, ranch roads, and roads that dead-end at abandoned mines and such. In tall timber, old logging roads and firebreak roads are favorites. In the desert regions, dry streambeds double as roads. Because of this, you should be suspicious of any slow vehicles cruising these types of roads. Favorite trapper vehicles include pickup trucks, assorted four-wheel drives, and station wagons. All of these provide a space to haul equipment and animal carcasses. Sometimes a peek into the back of a camper shell will reveal traps, chains and other indicators. Some trappers don't bother to clean off the telltale bloodstains on the backs of their vehicles.

Most trappers who work along roads observe their trap sites from their vehicle, sometimes with the aid of binoculars. Because of this, you must be on the alert for any sight or sound of approaching cars and trucks.

In more densely-populated areas, like the eastern states, a trapper is more likely to park his vehicle and make a walking circuit to check his traps. Some also use horses, dirt bikes and the three and four-wheeled all-terrain vehicles. Look for signs of a large pack or trap basket used to carry equipment and hides.

In the north country, many trappers use snowmobiles, often setting their traps near the snowmobile trails which are favorite travel paths of lynx.

Because the vast majority of trappers work their lines on a part-time basis, they often check their traps before going to work in the morning (this also limits the loss to trap thieves who steal the trapped animals). A hand-held spotlight can allow them to check their traps in the pre-dawn darkness. Also, weekends and holidays are when trappers are most active. You must be extremely cautious at these times, or avoid them completely.

Trappers range in age from 10-year-olds to senior citizen pensioners. Most live in rural areas and small towns. In many areas, state wildlife officers are among the most avid trappers, cashing in on their job-related intimate knowledge of wildlife habits and locations.

Some of the most lucrative trapping areas are around the boundaries of National Parks and Monuments, Wildlife Refuges, Wilderness Areas, Indian reservations and military lands. Within the so-called "wildlife

TYPICAL TRAP SETS

A) - Bait set using small animal or piece of meat suspended from tree limb.

B) - Set near where animal path crosses dirt road. Also used where culverts cross under roads.

C) - Traps set near where two streams or arroyos meet.

D) - Trap set on trail. Sharp rocks and sticks placed on trail force animal to step on clear spot where trap is hidden.

E) - Hole dug to simulate an animal's digging. Bait or lure placed inside hole. Large rock is sometimes placed on top to keep animal from digging after bait from above.

F) - A favorite. Trap(s) set at scent post (indicated by scratch marks left in dirt around bush, rock, stump, etc.).

G)- Trap set under remains of campfire (usually used to trap fox).

H) - Lure or scent sprayed under cow chip or flat rock propped up with stick. This keeps rain from washing away scent.

I) - Trap set at fence corner.

J) - Multiple sets used around dead animal (horse, cow, deer, etc.). Scent or lure also sprayed on nearby scent posts.

K) - "Cubby set." Branches leaning on tree force animal to approach bait from one direction only. Illustration shows bird wing nailed to tree as bait.

L) - Trap set on slide used by muskrat, otter or beaver along streams.

M) - Trap attached to log partially submerged in stream or pond.

N) - Trap set on beaver dam.

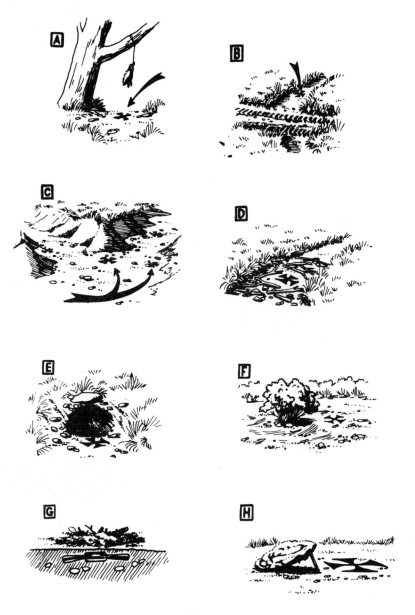

ECODEFENSE

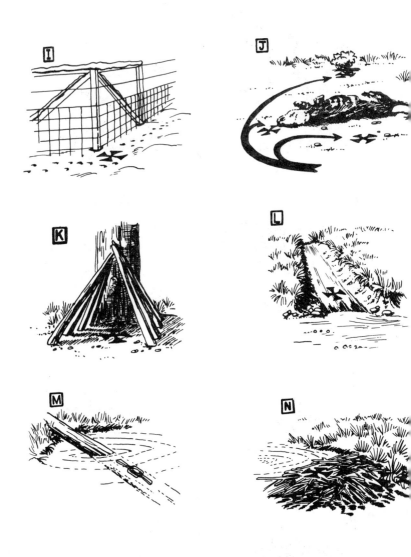

164

refuges," trapping is often hidden from public view behind signs reading "Public Not Permitted Beyond This Point."

Be suspicious of any small markers like strips of cloth, plastic flagging, or wire twist-ties that you find attached to barbed-wire fences or tree limbs alongside roads. These markers are used to sight along by trappers whose sets are back away from the road.

Experienced trappers favor trap sets near natural animal pathways like deer trails, cow paths, streambeds, fencelines and high observation points. In desert washes they favor piles of drifted brush and small brushy islands. Where other wildlife or livestock use the paths, the trap will be set off to the side to prevent deer and cattle from ruining the set. Small clearings, holes and bare patches of dirt on snow-covered ground are ideal for traps.

Sometimes a small piece of cloth or strip of light-colored fur will be hung above a trap to lure in the curious predator. Some trappers carry animal droppings and set them near the trap as an additional lure.

After a trap is buried, the surface will be restored to its normal appearance, making it difficult to spot. Use your foot *(Editor's note: this is OK so long as you are wearing heavy boots and not running shoes!)* to probe suspicious areas like slight depressions, small clear spots surrounded by twigs and rocks (designed to make the animal step on the attractive clear ground), or all around holes (any hole — animal or man-made). Many traps are set alongside a "backing" like a rock, bush, clump of grass or embankment to insure that the animal approaches the bait or scent lure from one side only.

Trapline saboteurs have also used leashed dogs and metal detectors to locate buried traps.

Where you find one trap, you will usually find more. It is not uncommon for traps to be set by twos and threes within a small area. As many as ten can sometimes be found within a 100-yard radius.

Trapline saboteurs can walk or drive through suspected areas. Cross-country skis can be used to quietly prowl along snowmobile paths. You might consider carrying a white bedsheet in your pack to use as quick camouflage if you hear a snowmobile approach from afar.

Motorized road patrolling is best done with two people, one of whom remains with the car or truck as a lookout. A cheap plastic whistle can make a good warning signal. Always have a good reason to give for being in the area. Props like binoculars, cameras, bird books and the like make it more convincing. One trapline saboteur carries a partial role of toilet paper as a prop to explain what he's doing back in the weeds off the roadside.

Mountain bikes, or just an old clunker from the Goodwill store, can provide a silent way of prowling roads and trails while keeping an ear cocked for the sound of an approaching engine. To avoid leaving telltale tracks, ride only in the other tire tracks so that the next passing vehicle will erase signs of your passing. If you wish to stop and check an area more closely, do not ride off the road. Stop in the track, pick up your bike and carry it into the brush, stepping carefully on rocks, twigs and clumps of grass to avoid leaving obvious footprints. Soft-soled moccasins leave a minimum of footprint, and you can quickly change them when you've found an area likely to contain traps.

Trap locations can be determined by careful surveillance of suspected trappers. If you witness activity that falls into the pattern described above, observe from a safe distance to see where the driver slows, stops, or uses a spotlight to observe trap locations. If the trapper checks his traps every morning, or on weekends, you can find yourself an observation post on some high ground and use binoculars and a note pad to chart his movements.

If you know where a trapper lives, you can piece together his route by following him a short distance when he goes out. Next time you pick him up again where you left off last time and follow another short distance. In this way you can gradually determine his trapline route without betraying your interest. Where roads are few, you can simply wait at the next road junction to see which way he turns.

Trappers' home addresses can be determined in many ways. Some states require the trapper to put his name and address on a plate on every trap. An inflammatory anti-trapping letter in the local newspaper may draw trappers out of the woodwork with their defensive responses. Telephone inquiries can reveal who is buying furs in your area. Sometimes these brokers will visit an area for a couple of days and purchase furs at a prescribed meeting point. These fur sales, and meetings or trapper clubs can be good places to obtain license plate numbers for use as described in the **Basic Security** section of this book.

Also, don't ignore the fur business infrastructure. There are about 30,000 "country collectors" operating in the U.S. who buy directly from the trappers. They in turn sell to a broker or auction company. *(Editor's note: In many small towns in the rural West, the visit of the "fur buyer" is announced in advance in the local newspaper or on community bulletin boards and is an event of major social importance.)* Once you have located these smaller buyers, call them to obtain the names of the next step, the brokers or auction companies. You could pretend to be an exclusive clothing shop owner or a clothing designer looking for a volume dealer. The "pretext" phone call is a tremendously valuable intelligence-gathering tool, so practice in advance to sound convincing. Don't hesitate to infiltrate a fur auction or the pre-arranged gatherings where trappers sell their goods. Pretend to be a novice trapper and keep your ears and eyes open. Use the intelligence gathering methods described elsewhere in this book to follow up leads like names and license plate numbers.

Trapline Sabotage

Any type of trapline interference is illegal. Because of this, you might as well do a thorough job and totally dispose of any traps you find, as this is no more illegal than simply tripping them and leaving them intact. Although no tools are necessary, a pair of "linesman's" pliers, with their dual plier/wire cutter head, can come in handy for cutting traps off chains or pulling out trap stakes. Do not carry them in plain view, of course.

Locating a trap with your boot or a stick will trigger it and render it ineffective until the trapper comes around next. This method is not effective for long, and if repeated regularly, may cause the trapper or state game agents to put the trapline under surveillance. It is also illegal (unless done on your own property).

Only removal or destruction of a trap will insure that it is not used again, and has the potential for imposing a crippling financial burden on the trapper. Such interference is of course illegal, but no more so than ripping up survey stakes or pouring sand into heavy equipment.

Since actual destruction of a trap can involve loud hammering or pounding, the safest method to use is quiet disposal. Traps can be gathered up and buried in well-hidden locations. It is important to remember that experienced trappers can follow your tracks and recognize disturbed ground. Your footprints at a trap set must be carefully brushed out and the site returned to a normal appearance. Practice walking without leaving obvious traces. Study your own tracks and those of others to learn what types of surfaces show sign clearly and learn to use rocks, logs, pine needles, clumps of grass, etc. to avoid leaving tracks.. Use soft soled moccasins if possible. Learn to walk slowly and carefully, applying your weight evenly to the whole sole to avoid leaving deep toe or heel impressions. Careful practice will keep you from leaving tracks that lead to your home or campsite. Tracking pursuers can also be thrown off by frequent and irregular changes of direction. When you *first* start back to home or to safety, walk in an entirely different direction and gradually zigzag back. Small deviations to one side or another of an obvious path of travel will fool no one. Think like a tracker. (Read Tom Brown, Jr.'s book *The Tracker.*) Also, make sure you know the area well enough or have map and compass to avoid getting lost in the woods.

If you know that you left distinctive tracks around the trapline (perhaps before you first discovered a trap) be sure to avoid wearing the same footgear in that area again. You might even consider leaving the area to camp elsewhere.

Unearthed traps can be disposed of by tossing them into ponds or streams where they won't be visible from the bank. Or they can be thrown into heavy brush as far off the trail as possible once you are well away from the trap line. Remember not to leave fingerprints on a trap. If you don't have gloves with you, use a bandanna, handkerchief, or even some toilet paper to handle the trap. See the illustration showing how to make a bandanna into a field expedient glove.

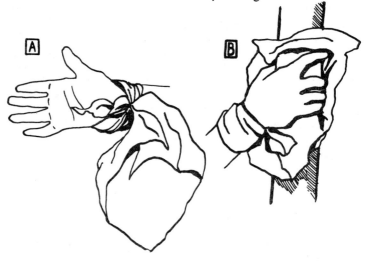

Improvised gloves using a bandanna: A) tie corner of bandanna to wrist; B) gripping an object to avoid leaving fingerprints.

After removing the trap from its set, restore the area to its *exact* appearance before your arrival. It could be days or weeks before the trapper discovers the loss, and by then your trail should be quite cold.

Keep in mind that where you find one trap, there are probably more. Always be on alert for the trapper checking his line. Take cover if you hear a vehicle or person approaching. Remember that some trappers check their lines from afar using binoculars. Be alert.

Because many trappers run their traplines along a primitive road, spiking such vehicle trails is an effective way of discouraging trapping as well.

Handling Trapped Animals

A simple walk in desert or forest might someday lead you to an encounter with a trapped animal. Naturally, trapline sabotage greatly increases the odds.

In some states, it is a felony to free an animal from a trap, although we know of no person being convicted of releasing a trapped animal for humane reasons. A visit to a state game department office (go to one in a distant city to better protect your identity) can yield a free copy of your state's trapping regulations and laws.

There are several ways to release a trapped animal, but we cannot recommend the method used by an elderly Texas woman who quietly approached a trapped coyote and released it without a fuss. A trapped animal can be frightened and in pain and might attempt to bite or scratch you. Every precaution should be used.

One release method involves throwing a coat or tarp over the animal's head to calm it down and put a barrier between its jaws and the trapped limb. If two people are working together, one should focus on restraining the animal while the other effects the release from the trap. Avoid any animal foaming or frothing at the mouth as this may be a sign of rabies (the odds of this are very slim). Once the animal is free of the trap, step back and allow it to run out from under the coat.

The best way to release the trapped animal is with the aid of a "noose pole" to restrain the animal and protect you from bites.

Commercially manufactured noose poles are available through veterinary supply houses that advertise in dog magazines. They come in various lengths, starting at three feet. One good pole is the "Snarem" (Ejay Veterinary Specialties, P.O. Box 1835, Glendora, CA 91740) whose five-foot models cost around forty dollars. The Cadillac of noose poles is the Ketch-All (Ketch-All Company, 2537 University Ave., San Diego,

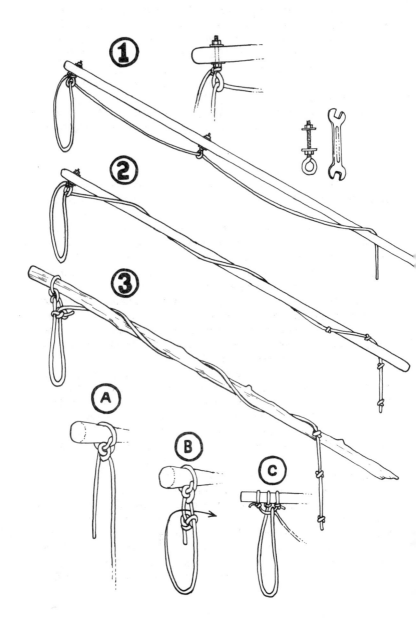

SIMPLE
NOOSE STICKS

#1) - Hardwood walking stick with two inconspicuous holes drilled in shaft to accomodate eye-bolt hardware. Carry hardware, rope and wrench in pack or pocket. Can be assembled in two minutes. Walking stick can also be used to probe for traps.

#2) - Variation of #1 using only one eye-bolt. In place of second eye-bolt guide, wrap rope loosely around shaft. Knots on cord allow for sure grip.

#3) - Field expedient noose stick. Be sure to select a strong and relatively straight stick or branch.
  A)Tie one knot leaving several inches free on end.
  B) Tie second knot to long cord which then loops back through.
  C) Variation using a short cord to make a loop guide for noose.

CA 92104) whose nifty five-footer can be had for just over sixty dollars. For those needing something inexpensive or compact, it is possible to make one's own noose pole:

The Earth First! Deluxe Noose Pole

Because of cramped spaces inside vehicles and the need to be able to conceal an anti-trapping noose pole in a small car or inside a backpack or sleeping bag, this collapsible noose pole was designed. Made of thick-walled PVC pipe, it is extremely lightweight and can be assembled in less than an hour with materials costing less than ten dollars.

All the materials can be bought at any hardware store, but to avoid suspicion, spread your business around to at least two different stores.

Materials: One length of 1/2 inch (internal diameter) Schedule 40 (thick, *not* thin-walled) PVC pipe (you will use only 3 - 5 feet). One end cap for pipe (illus. A). Two or three screw coupler sets (illus. D). Four feet of 1/8 inch braided steel cable. One cable "stop" for the above (illus. B). One cable "ferrule" for the above (illus. C). Four or more feet of 1/4 inch braided nylon rope. Lastly, PVC solvent and cement (for assembling pipe pieces).

As you can see from the diagram, the end cap is drilled with two holes to pass the noose cable through (A). Before gluing the cap to the end of the pipe, place the cable stop (B) on one end (crimp it to the cable with a couple of hammer blows), and crimp the other end into the ferrule, along with one end of the nylon rope (C). Pulling on the rope will tighten the noose.

Cut the PVC pipe into the lengths you require. Think about this first. If you plan to carry it inside a small pack or under a car seat, measure the space first. Then size your individual segments accordingly. If the sections are longer, you may want to go with three pieces, if shorter, try four segments. Don't be surprised if they don't screw together completely and some thread shows.

Into the end of the last section cut two notches about an inch deep to accommodate the nylon rope (E). Tie knots into the end of the rope at intervals of about one-and-a-half inches. When the rope is slipped into the notch in the pipe, the knot will not pass through and will lock the noose tight around the neck of the animal you are rescuing.

A sturdier, heavier and only slightly more costly version of this noose pole can be made by substituting galvanized pipe for the PVC (have it cut and threaded at the store where you buy it). Look for the less-conspicuous black-finish galvanized pipe.

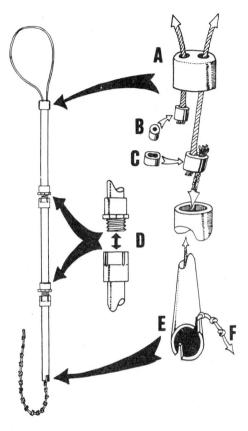

The lightweight PVC noose pole will bend and flex if an animal struggles. Do not use brute strength to subdue. Keep your distance and wait for the animal to calm down. If necessary, see instructions for tightening the noose until animal is unconscious.

Store your noose pole in a cloth bag to keep your fingerprints off and to keep dirt and grit from fouling the pipe threads. If confronted with it, say you carry it because you've had to release your pet dogs from traps before.

Using The Noose Pole:

Approach the animal slowly with your noose pole extended to the front. If the animal is agitated, softly talking to it or quietly humming can have a calming effect. Some animals will sit still, paralyzed with fear, while others will struggle and try to pull away.

Once the noose is tightened around the neck, the animal must be restrained to prevent it from injuring itself by struggling. Usually you can push the animal's head to the ground and step on the trap springs with your feet to effect the release. If the animal struggles, you may have to cut off its air by tightening the noose. The animal will pass out and go limp. Loosen the noose immediately, but only slightly, to permit the unconscious animal to breathe again. The animal will recover in a few minutes, after you have removed the trap. Remember, though, that they may revive at any time.

When actually loosening the trap by stepping on the springs, you may find that a previously docile animal begins to struggle. Sometimes the trap cuts off circulation, eventually deadening the pain. As the pressure of the trap jaws is released the revitalizing blood flow can cause extreme pain in a paw that is swollen, cut or possibly broken. Be prepared for an animal that suddenly struggles or attempts to bite (even pet dogs often react this way and bite their people). Before releasing an animal from the noose pole, make sure that it has a clear escape route away from you.

An additional aid for releasing trapped animals is a heavy coat or tarpaulin thrown over the animal to quiet and calm it. This can be especially helpful when releasing cats or birds of prey, as the cloth can prevent them from scratching with the free foot.

Special Release Problems.

EAGLES, HAWKS AND OTHER BIRDS — Some scumbag trappers still use dead animal baits that lure curious birds of prey, ravens, buzzards and others into the trap jaws (like the so-called "mountain man" Claude Dallas who murdered two game wardens in Idaho, and is running loose at the time of this writing — beware!). The claws can be dangerous during release, so grab the wing opposite the trapped leg and stretch the bird out as far as possible from the imprisoned leg before releasing the trap jaws. Eagles are very powerful and difficult to release. Cover the free leg with a coat or heavy cloth and hold it alongside the trapped leg to prevent scratching. Step back quickly when releasing an eagle. Heavy leather gloves can provide a little protection from scratching. The best type are heavy welder's gloves with gauntlets that protect the wrist.

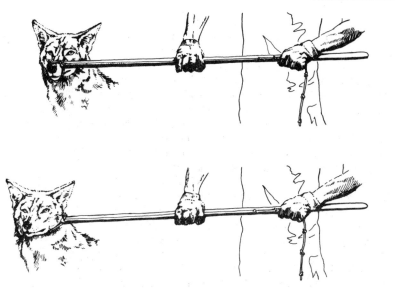

Two ways of using noose stick to immobilize trapped animals.

...eam of two using noose stick to release trapped wolf.

PORCUPINES — Gloves are no protection against porcupine quills, and you should never throw a coat or cloth over them as this can injure the animal by pulling out a large number of quills. A noose pole can be used to stretch them away from the trap by snaring the tail or a back leg. Since porky often protects himself by turning his back and raising his quills, one person can hold the tail down with a stick and then carefully grasp the long hairs and quills (when grasping, move your hand slightly to the rear, in the same direction as the quills). Lift the porcupine by the tail, using the other hand to support the abdomen. A second person can then release the trap jaws.

SKUNKS — Only the bravest and kindliest souls release skunks. Our experience with live-trapping skunks to remove them from civilized areas has shown that their temperaments vary. Some are calm as house cats, while others show total panic. It is possible to lure the skunk into several spraying attempts to "empty" it out (*several* times). Be prepared to move fast and remember that skunks can spray as far as four yards.

BADGERS — The badger is one of the toughest critters around and must be handled accordingly. Often just finding them can be a bit of a problem. A trapped badger usually tears up everything within reach, leaving a circle of torn-up earth around where the trap is staked. Sometimes a badger will succeed in burying itself in the loose dirt. If you find this torn-up circle and no badger, use a long stick to probe the loose earth. If no badger is found, it may already have been killed and taken away. Check the vicinity for new trap sets.

If you wish, you might buy a couple of different types of traps to practice learning how to open them for quick release of trapped animals. Of course, the best way is to practice with traps "borrowed" from a trapline. Most states require traps to bear a name or number identification of the owner, sometimes stamped into the steel of the trap. For this reason, do not keep "found" traps any longer than necessary. Always dispose of them properly.

For more information on trapping, consult your local library. Do your reading at the library, if possible, in order to avoid leaving a check-out record showing an interest in the subject. At bookstores look for a trapping book with the most thorough information on trapping the wildlife found in your area. The monthly magazine "Fur-Fish-Game" (which can be purchased anonymously at a newsstand or grocery store) regularly carries features on trapping tips, advertisements for suppliers, and dates and locations for trappers' conventions (use your imagination here).

FIELD NOTES

* When you discover a trapline of any type, careful surveillance of the trapper checking his traps may reveal still more sets. Watch to find out when and on what days he checks his traps. When following him, either on foot or in a car, stay well back and hidden. Don't try to do it all in one day. Follow him a short distance and stop. Next time, pick him up at that point and follow a bit further. Binoculars can be very useful for this. After a few days of this, you can cautiously and securely piece together his full route and routine. Check all possible locations for traps. Use a couple of short poles and your feet to probe sections of game trails. Check the entrances to culverts and under bridges. Look for low spots under fences. Bodies of dead animals, chunks of meat or feathers might be suspended from bushes over buried traps.

* Some trap saboteurs used a dog on a leash to locate traps set for coyotes. The traps were carefully buried next to small bushes or tree stumps that were sprayed with urine from captive coyotes, making false "scent posts" that attracted every curious coyote in the area.

* Two pairs of vise-grips make the job of extricating an animal from a trap quick and easy. Simply apply a vise-grip to each pair of springs on the trap.

* Perhaps coyotes under pressure from "varmint hunters" can be "trained" to avoid the gunmen. Hand-held varmint calls and instructional tapes are available through gun shops and sporting goods outlets. For those who don't want to learn the calling techniques, there are portable loudspeaker systems that one can use with cassette tapes in the field. There are many books on the market which describe the hunting techniques in detail. Armed with this information, the monkeywrencher can camouflage himself well, take to the field and call up coyotes, bobcats, etc. A rifle or handgun can be used to fire blanks or even send live rounds whizzing safely past the unwary predator. Rest assured that Mr. Coyote will take his education seriously and be more cautious in the future, much to the detriment of the varmint calling "sportsmen."

SNARES

Another insidious form of trapping, used against small game like rabbits and predators like coyotes and foxes, is the simple wire snare. This device consists of nothing more than a loop of lightweight cable or braided wire (as is used to hang picture frames) set in a place where animals will likely pass. (See illustrations.) The snare works like a miniature cowboy's lariat, tightening around anything unlucky enough to pass through it. It is draped over small branches around an animal trail or outside an animal's burrow. Stockmen and government trappers will put them in low spots that coyotes dig for trails under woven wire fences. Corners where two fences come together are especially popular. As the animal passes through the noose-like snare, it tightens about her/his neck and slowly strangles her/him. Smaller animals are frequently snared around the middle of their bodies and may be almost cut in half after a prolonged and fruitless struggle.

Usually a close visual inspection is required to spot snares. When found, it is best to cut the wire in an inconspicuous manner, perhaps close to the point where it is anchored or tied, or in a spot hidden by brush or loose dirt. This will insure that it cannot strangle any passing animal. If you take the entire snare, the trapper will simply and cheaply replace it. Make the snare look perfectly normal after disabling it, and the trapper will never be the wiser.

SNARES

The wire or cable snare is another trapper's tool designed to strangle an animal to death.

A) - typical wire snare.

B) - Snare set in crawl hole under fence.

C) - Snare set on trail. Tilted branch keeps larger animals like deer and livestock away from snare. This trick also used with leghold traps.

D) - Snare set on a log crossing a stream.

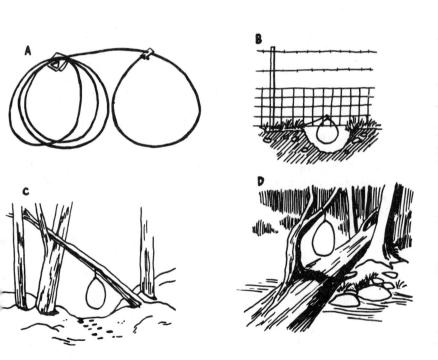

TRAPLINES #2

by The Head of Joaquin

"The fact is that my native land is prey to barbarism, that in it, men's only God is their belly, that they live only for the present, and that the richer a man is, the holier he is held to be." —St. Jerome

Those words were spoken over one-half a thousand years ago; yet barbarism still flourishes in our technologically advanced, "modern" 20th Century society. It can be seen throughout the world; it can be seen right here in southern Utah. I saw its hideous effect in the glazed eyes of a coyote yesterday afternoon, a coyote hopelessly caught in the wicked grasp of a steel-jawed trap. I hurried home to obtain the tools needed to extract the animal but when I returned an hour later the coyote had changed.

He was no longer alive. His face was as handsome in death as it had been in life just 60 minutes earlier. One very clean bullet hole penetrated his skull just below the ear. His eyes were wide open. And below his neck, every square inch of fur had been expertly removed, revealing the powerful muscles and tendons that had provided this creature such speed and grace.

Give that trapper twenty bucks. Death for fun and profit...what are we coming to? Here in southern Utah, these trappers have discovered that they can increase their profits by encircling the area's National Parks. The wildlife, protected by an Act of Congress, need only to step across that political boundary line, drawn up by politicians and bureaucrats in some faraway place called the District of Columbia, and they become targets and victims of these warped mental midgets.

What can be done about it? We must remove the traps. We must steal the traps and destroy them and make trapping economically unfeasible. *Profit* is what they understand, and *that* ultimately is what we must destroy.

Don't get caught. Use discretion — the trapper mentality is frightening. I honestly believe these creatures would consider murder a fair penalty for trap-taking. So, remember these points:

1. Work in pairs. When removing or destroying the trap, have your partner keep a close lookout. Bring binoculars.

2. Avoid trap-taking on weekends. Most of these people have regular Monday-Friday jobs. They let the animals wait days in the trap, starving

until the weekend, when the Great White Trapper can devote his time and pleasure to his "hobby."

3. Look for fresh tire tracks on roads near the search area. It might pay to follow these tracks just to avoid any surprises.

4. Don't save the trap as a souvenir for crissakes. Destroy it or bury it but don't keep it.

5. Don't brag about your exploits. "The deed is everything, the glory nothing."—Goethe

The trapping season does not last all year. In Utah it starts in December and runs through March. Generally you can contact the local wildlife officer for more specific dates. Sometimes, the wildlife officer will tell you which areas are being trapped since licenses must be obtained from him. Tell him you have a dog, that you intend to backpack in and near a National Park and that you would like to avoid these traps for your dog's sake. If he refuses, tell him it is your right to know as a citizen and *owner* of public lands.

You may also obtain information from Park Rangers. Generally they abhor trapping, and if a trapping problem exists near their boundary, they will probably tell you.

Once a trapping area has been defined, the traps themselves will either parallel a dirt road (usually within 100 feet of it—sometimes they are marked by engineer's tape or other flagging along the road) or be in a dry wash *near* a dirt road. Trappers are lazy bastards—they hate to walk. Look for white chicken feathers hanging on a string from pinyon or juniper trees. They scent the feathers, which lure animals to the trap. Often the trappers will cut juniper boughs and fashion a type of crude "run" or chute to channel the victim to the trap. The traps are usually buried—don't step in them yourself.

There is nothing more frustrating than to discover a trap and not have the equipment to remove it. A good pair of heavy duty pliers will probably allow you to do the job. A small pair of bolt cutters, however, will allow the trap-taker to totally dismember the steel monster.

The most difficult sight a trap destroyer may face is the wild eyes of a terrified animal already ensnared. Sometimes with the help of a canvas tarp, it is possible for one person to cover and restrain the animal while the other frees him. Sometimes it is too late and we are faced with the agonizing reality of having to end this animal's misery and pain. It will be one of the most gut-wrenching moments of your life.

There is no room in civilized society for such acts of cruelty and barbarism. This is one issue that cannot be defended—there is no "other side of the coin." Trapping must be stopped.

Postscript

Since publication of the original edition of **Ecodefense** I have learned some additional information about this wretched practice, which I will give here.

Types of Sets

A trap and all its trimmings is called a set, and if you find a set it's not too difficult to tell just what the trapper is after. Bobcat and fox traps are incredibly obvious; a coyote's is extremely difficult to spot. Bobcats, and to a lesser extent foxes, are very meticulous about where they place their feet. A cat moving along a canyon wall or a sandy wash will gingerly step over a rock or twig. They will stay close to the edge of the wall or stream bank. Trappers will try to funnel their victims toward the jaws and will frequently cut tree limbs and strategically place them along the intended route. That is your first clue and it is fairly obvious. The trap set itself can hardly be missed. The trapper will of course bury the trap, but will place rocks or twigs around the trap. The bobcat, not wanting to step on the rocks/twigs will walk between them, into the jaws of death. (See diagram.) But the trapper does not like to leave anything to chance; you can almost guarantee that a second trap will be placed just beyond the first.

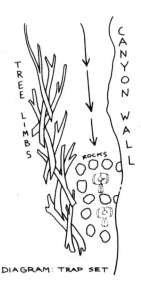

DIAGRAM: TRAP SET

Coyotes are so smart, they are so clever that a coyote would immediately cast a wary eye on a bobcat set and stay clear of it. Thus coyote sets are difficult to detect. They are buried with nothing to draw the coyote near. However, I have located several and they have always been under large cedar trees along sandy washes.

Where to Look

As I have already said, trappers are lazy bastards; they like to work out of their macho pickup trucks. Drive up the main highway and start checking intersecting dirt roads. Look for sandy washes that cross the dirt road, and intersecting canyons and narrow valleys. Bobcats will stay very close to the canyon wall. They will not travel randomly. A bobcat will pick its next point of cover as it moves downcountry. And it hates to walk in the snow. So check the canyon edge that receives more sunlight. It will pick that route.

Frequently the slob trapper will not even want to get out of his truck at all. He will instead rig up a lazy-boy, two sticks perched delicately against each other — if the trap has been disturbed, the lazy-boy will collapse. A good pair of binoculars will help you spot them.

Trap-lines

A trap-line rarely consists of more than two sets, occasionally three sets. (Remember, each set consists of two traps.) A trapper will run trap lines along several parallel routes. It is possible to work up one drainage and down the next, repeating the process and effectively clearing an area.

Be Careful

I cannot overstress this. These are not normal people. They are mutants. They are sub-humans who will not hesitate to use modern technology, a high powered rifle, to do very barbaric things to your body. If a trapper comes upon you messing with his sets, you have two choices:

1) You can give him a lecture on the barbarism of trapping, that this hideous practice has no place in the civilized world and that he should be ashamed of himself. He will probably kill you or beat you until you're no longer recognizable as a human being and you can become a martyr for a week or month or until your friends forget and go on with life.

2) Act stupid. Talk with an Arkansas accent. If you're actually holding the trap, ask him what it is. If you're prodding around, tell him you think there's buried treasure there. Speak derisively of hippies and tree huggers and say "by golly" a lot. It might save your life.

FENCE CUTTING

One of the ugliest sights you are likely to encounter while traveling about the West is the all-too-familiar dead coyote dangling from a rancher's fence. Never are you presented with a better reason to stop straddling the fence and start cutting it.

The tactics used will vary depending on whether you're in your neighborhood, or just passing through. Your primary consideration must be to avoid being caught, since small town juries and judges in ranching country are not likely to sympathize with a goldang coyote lover.

In Your Neighborhood

When you first spot the dead coyote, **DO NOT**, under any circumstances, stop or even slow down to look. Carefully look about to see if anyone might be observing you or otherwise working in the area. Drive out of the area and wait at least ten minutes before driving past the scene again. On this second, scouting run, use your odometer to measure distances from landmarks that will be visible at night to the scene of the crime. It's okay to make brief cryptic written notes of distances, but only if you will remember to burn the note after committing the key information to memory. Thus, your notes might read: "Hwy. junction 21.5 —gully 22.1 —m.p. 145 22.7 —X [marks the spot] 23.2 —bridge 23.9."

From these notes, you will memorize that the target is one and seven tenths miles from the highway junction, and five tenths — or one half mile — past milepost marker 145. If your approach is from the other side, you know it is seven tenths of a mile past the bridge to the target. This precise pinpointing of the target by distance will keep you from making the classic error of cruising the rural road or highway in a slow and conspicuous manner while you squint into the darkness hoping to catch a glimpse of the dead coyote. Always assume it will be hard to spot at night.

Wait for a suitably dark night, and have a trustworthy companion drive while you do the cutting. Make your approach run when there is no other traffic likely to observe your actions. You may have to drive by more than once to accomplish this. That is why it is important to have landmarks and mileages from both directions. If the area has a number of homes or ranches located next to the road, don't drive by more than a couple of times. It's safer to wait for another night. After all, that coyote isn't going anywhere.

When you make the hit, try to leave the vehicle on the road, rather than leaving traceable tire tracks on the shoulder. You will, of course, be wearing dark clothing, smooth-soled shoes and gloves. Your cutting tools will be thoroughly wiped clean of fingerprints in case you drop them or have to ditch them. A small pair of bolt cutters works best. Heavy wirecutters will also work, but are harder to use and slower.

Leave one of the top two strands of barbed wire intact. This will keep cattle from straying onto the road until the fence is repaired. In sheep country, leave a strand or two of the woven wire panel on the bottom intact. Barbed wire should be cut once between each set of fenceposts. Woven wire (usually a crisscrossed four by four inch welded smooth wire) should be cut on each side of a couple of fenceposts, and generally butchered. Do all of the cutting you can in sixty to ninety seconds and promptly leave. Don't try to cut the whole fence down. Just cutting it up near the dead coyote will convey the message. (Be careful when cutting tightly strung wire since it may pop back at you and take a slice out of your body.)

If the target is located near a house, consider having your partner drop you off nearby to let you approach it on foot. Carefully pre-arrange the time and location for your later pickup. Have a backup time and place in case anything goes wrong. You may also want to carry a pepper spray (see section on **Dogs** in **Security**) in case man's best friend gets too rowdy.

Drive away from the area at normal speed to avoid suspicion. You may want to bury or otherwise thoroughly dispose of the wire cutters since they are probably the only thing short of a confession that can positively link you to the crime. That safety and peace of mind are well worth a few dollars. Even if you are questioned as to why your car stopped out there that night, you can always say that you stopped to take a leak, or that something ran out in front of your car and you stopped so fast that you stalled the engine.

Just Passing Through

If you are traveling through the area, you may want to do your fence work immediately. Always carry a dark plastic bag with some dirty, empty aluminum cans in your car. Pull off the road and pretend to be picking up cans. When the coast is clear, check one last time. If it's still clear, whip out your trusty cutters and quickly, *but casually,* go to work. Don't ever run in broad daylight as this looks mighty suspicious even from a long way off. In daytime, you should only do as much cutting as can be accomplished in 15 to 30 seconds. Casually stroll back to your vehicle and leave at normal speed.

Do not stop anywhere in the area unless you are urgently low on gas. Leave the county. Cross at least two county lines before stopping for the night. If the state line is nearby, modify your plans and vacation in another state for a while. Changing to a different highway might throw off a deputy or highway patrolman checking travelers for the elusive coyote lover.

If all of this seems awfully elaborate for a little fence cutting, rest assured that your coyote-killing rancher will consider a crime against his property to be just about a capital offense. In Texas, where a lot of stockmen favor this type of fenceline decor, it is a felony, punishable by up to five years in prison, to cut a fence. This law is a hold-over from the old open-range fence cutting wars of the 1880's and 90's, but it is still on the books, and might be used on you if you get cocky or careless.

So, watch those fencelines, plan ahead, be careful, and STRIKE BACK!

COYOTE GETTER

This handy tool can be used while browsing through the fox, bobcat, lynx, badger, beaver, cougar, coyote, ermine, mink, muskrat, etc. coats at your "favorite" fur shop.

The "coyote getter" consists of an inexpensive air brush modestly customized. Badger makes one for around $35 (model #350) including hose and bottles. An 11 ounce can of propellant runs about $4.

Modify a cheap pair of gloves so you can conceal the brush and tip in them. Cut a small hole in the glove just large enough for the spray tip to be exposed. Paint the tip the same color as the glove. Use tape or rubber bands to fasten the brush to your hand and wrist (put the brush in your palm and use your thumb to press the trigger). Run the air hose up your arm and down to your coat pocket (the coat should have a hole cut in the inside of the pocket for the hose to come through). Fill the paint bottle (carried in your coat pocket) with your favorite fluorescent dye or paint, and hook up the hose to the propellant can.

While browsing, surreptitiously "decorate" the coats where they won't be immediately noticed from the aisle, and leave.

FIELD NOTES

* One can also browse through the fur coats on the rack at your local classy department store with a razor blade concealed in the hand. Simply slice the lining of the coats from the inside as you admire them.

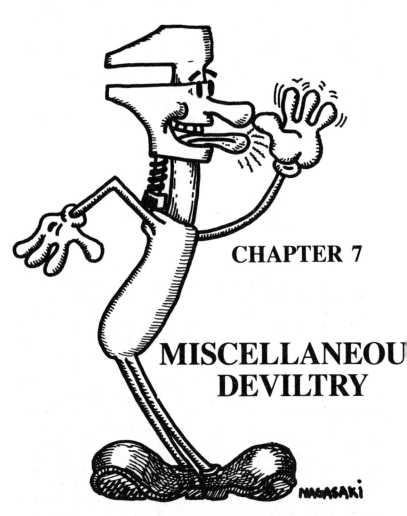

CHAPTER 7

MISCELLANEOU
DEVILTRY

NAGASAKI

In this chapter, we look at a potpourri of tricks in the monkeywrencher's bag. Smoke bombs and stinkers, lock jamming, political fun & games, returning trash — this is where the ecoteur can have fun! After all, we need to let our hair down once in a while. Enjoy. But don't forget security!

SMOKE BOMBS

SMOKE IN THEIR EYES!

Many times the object of an act of ecotage is to disrupt or delay an activity. A very useful tool in the monkeywrencher's bag of tricks is the smoke bomb or smoke grenade. A wide variety of these are available to the public with no legal restrictions on their purchase. These devices are safe to use and offer the imaginative monkeywrencher many options for upsetting or complicating the activities of the greedheads and others who destroy or damage Mother Earth for fun and profit.

While it is possible to make your own smoke bombs at home this is not recommended for two reasons: 1) if you do it wrong the things won't work and 2) if you really do it wrong you may blow yourself up. A wide variety of smoke bombs and grenades are produced and can be bought by mail with no record or legal hassles. The commercially produced devices are safe for the non-expert to use and offer a variety of choices to the monkeywrencher depending on the planned use of the smoke bomb.

The devices come in two basic types. The first type is designed to be ignited by lighting the fuse. The second type of device is designed to function like a hand grenade. The user pulls a pin and the device self-ignites several seconds later. These devices generate very large amounts of smoke (anywhere from 3,000 to 115,000 cubic feet), and will make smoke for up to ten minutes. These smoke bombs and grenades even come in a variety of colored smoke. White, grey, red, green, yellow and violet are the available colors. To give you some idea of the quality of smoke produced, burning crude oil has a TOP (Total Obscuring Power) rating of 200. Some of these devices are rated as having a TOP of 2100.

HOW TO USE THEM

The best way to make effective use of these devices is in the form of boobytraps and ambushes. Both of these uses allow the monkeywrencher to set up his ecotage and be safely away when the crap hits the fan. Examples: R.J. Hardhead calmly seats himself in the driver's seat of his dozer ready for another day of tree trashing. He is unaware of a fine piece of fishing line running from his dozer blade to the smoke grenade taped securely under the dozer. As R.J. starts up and lifts the blade, the grenade pin is pulled loose and the dozer and a very confused driver are swallowed in a large cloud of green smoke. After the smoke clears he and his buddies waste even more time figuring out what happened.

A. Motorhead, ace crosscountry motorbike racer, surges into the lead at the Annual Dirt Maniac Race. He doesn't notice the thin nylon line running from a firmly-planted stake to the pin on a smoke grenade taped to another stake a few yards away. As he and dozens of others yank the pins from these scattered grenades, clouds of multi-colored smoke fill the air forcing those behind them to stop short or risk kissing an unseen cactus or rock.

The smoke bombs with fuses can be used as in the first example but the fuse needs to be taped to a part of the machine which gets hot enough to ignite the fuse (exhaust pipe or manifold).

It is worth noting that these devices aren't cheap but when used well they're worth a lot. Besides after you've gotten R.J. and his buddies paranoid, think what a beer can painted the color of your smoke bombs and hooked-up to make them think it's real will do. By the time they get the bomb squad out there to collect the evidence they'll have wasted an hour or so. Then when they start up something else; POOF! goes the real one. Be creative. Rig the portjohn door: Use them for early warning devices on protests to slow the bad guys down and to let the protesters know where they are.

Keeping a couple of smoke grenades on hand to toss out the window while fleeing the scene of an act of ecotage might not be such a bad idea either.

The use of smoke bombs and grenades offers a very easy and effective method of ecotage that presents a very small risk of injury to either man or machine. Other than inspiring panic and high blood pressure attacks, the smoke poses a small risk of hurting people. I doubt that the smoke bombs would do much more than blister the paint of most machinery. Care should be taken with these devices though. There is no point in saving a forest from the bulldozer by accidently burning it down. A number of military handbooks are available which outline the uses of these devices in detail. Check your local military surplus shop or a paramilitary mail order store for copies.

— *Mooncrow*

Information Sources:
Bill More Publications, P.O. Box 1600, Cottonwood, AZ 86326
Paladin Press, P.O. Box 1307, Boulder, CO 80306

Smoke Device Sources
Superior Signal Co., Inc., P.O. Box 96, Spotswood, NJ 08884
Yankee Manufacturing Co., 59 Chase Street, Beverly, MA 01915
Aztec National Inc., Suite 341, 5365 Jimmy Carter Blvd.,
    Norcross, GA 30093
Phoenix Systems, Inc., P.O. Box 3339, Evergreen, CO 80439

BUSINESS REPLY MAIL

You can put otherwise wasted paper to good use by recycling business reply envelopes and postcards obtained either from magazines or from unsolicited mail.

Pick your favorite ORV or dirt-biker magazine and obtain its business reply postcard from a copy at a library or store. Kill two birds with one stone by filling in the name and address of another target (such as a local land developer, fur store owner, etc.), then check the "bill me later" box. Your second target will suffer the anxiety of incessant overdue notices while the magazine, corporation, etc. will waste time, resources, and goodwill, especially if your operation is on a massive scale.

Business reply envelopes from deserving bad guys may be stuffed with paper, scrap metal, or other dense objects to increase the weight and postage charges to the greatest degree. Or tape the envelope or postcard to a box of bricks, old magazines, etc. Who knows how far you can go before the post office lets the recipient off the hook for the postage charges.

DISRUPTING
ILLEGAL ACTIVITIES

It is quite possible that while you are out monkeywrenching, you will chance upon others committing illegal acts — environmentally harmful acts, that is. You should do everything you can (without jeopardizing your own security) to see that these offenders are brought to justice.

A common form of illegal activity you may observe in rural areas is the dumping of toxic wastes. Be especially alert for this if you live or are operating in an area which contains chemical plants and the like. Signs of illegal dumping include tank trucks or closed trucks (concealing large drums) leaving industrial plants after dark, or driving along deserted back roads (especially if creeks or rivers run nearby). In some parts of the country secluded sites in the desert are favored by dumpers.

If you see illegal dumping, carefully monitor the activity, using proper surveillance techniques. Information and evidence obtained should be passed *anonymously* to both state police and state environmental control officials. However, *be careful.* In many areas, the illegal disposal of industrial wastes has become a lucrative business for organized crime. These people will not hesitate to use violence to protect their interests. Do not discount the possibility that local police might be "on the take" and receiving bribes to look the other way. Always take whatever security measures are necessary to protect your own identity and involvement.

In the Southwest, monkeywrenchers might come across cactus poachers. Be on the watch for two or three individuals, usually in a jeep or pickup truck, driving slowly along back roads, jeep trails and even newly bulldozed subdivision roads. Look for signs of fresh digging in the area. If you witness the poachers digging cactus, or come across parked vehicles containing untagged cactus (cactus obtained legally under permit will be tagged), you might disable the vehicles (three or more flat tires should do it), then call the sheriff's office with an anonymous tip.

In certain National Forest areas, illegal timber poaching is a problem of considerable magnitude. Use similar tactics as with cactus poachers. Gather evidence surreptitiously, disable vehicles if it can be done safely, and make an anonymous tip to the authorities. While it might be argued that it is futile to report timber poaching, since the Freddies are hell-bent on cutting all the timber anyway, remember that in some areas, it may be that the *only* timber cutting being done is illegal. This is particularly true in some Southwestern areas in which illegal cutting for commercial firewood is a problem.

TRASH RETURN

Here's one that makes for a great hobby and might even be legal!

Scattered along the back roads of America are countless thousands of privately dumped trash piles blighting the land. Civic-minded and neighborly citizens should consider returning these "lost" items to their rightful owners. Since this "wildcat" dumping is illegal in many areas, the previous owner must have "accidentally" dumped his possessions there.

On with the basics: Dumping of organic matter is often more legal than the dumping of usual household trash. In most cases, it's not bad for the land, either. These piles of grass clippings, tree trimmings, etc. should simply be scattered about to hasten their return to the Earth. Brush piles left intact can provide good shelter for wildlife, so use your best judgment.

What one sees most often on the backroads, however, is the paper, glass, tin can, plastic variety of trash. Even a moderately enterprising sleuth (moderation in all things) can search through this type of refuse and find the identity of the original owner. Discarded envelopes, letters, magazine address labels and assorted junk mail usually point the finger. In the interests of fair play, you should find several such clues before firmly deciding on your target.

To return the material, collect empty boxes from behind your local supermarket and fill them (not quite to the brim) with the offending matter. Although returning illegally dumped garbage is probably not illegal, you should take all the usual precautions. The evidence you leave on this type of endeavor may lead investigators to other, more illegal, activities. Besides, you may inadvertently return some garbage to the chief of police or the county sheriff. Pick up your grocery store boxes after dark (in the early, not suspiciously late, evening) and always wear gloves when handling them and the garbage. This type of activity is good teamwork training for more serious capers later.

Scout your target thoroughly. Map the neighborhood, and make sure that your wheelman knows every way in and out of it. Every way. You'll understand why soon.

Plan your mission for the evening hours. In the wee hours of the morning there's usually so little traffic that you will stand out and draw the attention of patrolling gendarmes. Dress your team accordingly: dark clothes, gloves, and possibly hats (to hide your hair and to keep it out of your face). If you have a choice of vehicles, a pickup truck is best suited for hasty deliveries. The ideal team consists of one driver and two dumpers. More than this will get in each other's way and will not fit comfortably (and perhaps legally) in the cab of the truck.

Just before making your run at the target, have one team member use a canteen of water and a little dirt to make mud to smear on your license plate. Daub a little on the bumper so that you can claim, "It accidentally just got on my license plate, officer!" Save some water to wash it off later. If you get into the habit of doing this a lot, you may want to periodically spray the plate with a couple of light coats of a clear spray varnish. This will protect the paint from the abrasion of the dirt and mud which, with time, will start rubbing off the paint.

Cruise by the target at least once to make sure the coast is clear. You can drop off a lookout in nearby brush to quietly observe for about ten minutes and make sure no witnesses are about. Make your final approach run at normal speeds and brake normally. (Once our driver was so wired-up with a case of nervousness that she careened into a U-shaped gravel driveway in front of the target house, slammed on the brakes, and put us all — two of us riding unprotected in the back — into a four-wheel skid sideways that brought us to a grinding halt only inches from some steel posts set in concrete.) If possible, dump the trash while remaining inside the bed of the pickup. If necessary, one person can hop out and dump the boxes that the other hands to him or her. Usually we leave the boxes at the scene, since they're clean of fingerprints, anyway. We rarely get them from the same dumpster twice, further impeding any attempts to trace us. Besides, the poor slob who gets his trash back will need something to put it in!

At this point, it's good to leave the area. On one occasion, we were pursued by the irate receiver of his trash and it was only our knowledge of the neighborhood that enabled us to elude him without heading down any dead end traps (which are common in suburban neighborhoods).

As soon as it's safe, get everybody back up in the cab and wash that filthy old mud off your license plate, for chrissakes!

STINK BOMBS

Stink bombs have numerous applications for the ecodefender. These can range from the introduction of a foul odor into a corporate board meeting during a daring daylight raid, to the introduction of more insidious and lingering substances into offices via small holes in windows during nocturnal operations.

Among the chemicals with potential for stink bombs are the following, which can be obtained from school laboratories and over-the-counter chemical supply houses:

- Carbon disulfide
- Hydrogen sulfide (smells like rotten eggs)
- Skatole (feces smell)
- Ethyl amine (fishy smell)
- Proprionic acid (sweat-like smell)

Butyric acid will make a remarkably effective stink bomb. This is a weak acid (not dangerous) that has an incredibly powerful stench. It smells like vomit and thus is particularly appropriate for expressing opinions about land rapers. Only a very small amount is needed — 2 drops will produce a disgusting odor in a room. An ounce will perfume a building. The odor is resistant to cleaning and very persistent — it lasts for weeks.

Because of its power, delivery can be a bit of a problem. A medicine dropper can be used, but I use a hypodermic needle and a syringe. This allows small amounts to be delivered into areas that are difficult to enter (through the rubber seal around a truck window, under an office door, etc.). This also keeps the liquid off your hands — important, not only because it is incriminating but because it will cut down on your social life dramatically. The best solution for spills on clothes is to discard the clothes.

The only problem with butyric acid is acquisition. It is used in some tanning processes, manufacture of lacquers, and organic syntheses. It can be purchased through industrial chemical suppliers or scientific supply houses. It is not a controlled substance — no police records are kept. It commonly is stocked by college chemistry stockrooms and some high school chemistry classes. Collaboration with an instructor or graduate student at your local college chemistry department might be very helpful in getting some. You don't need much — the stuff is so powerful that a quart can represent a long-lasting supply for even the most ardent enthusiast.

Butyl mercaptan makes an effective stink bomb. This chemical is used to make natural gas odorous so that a leak can be discovered, and in higher concentrations has the odor of skunk. It comes from chemical supply houses, sealed in glass. If opened, the container needs to be resealed with a gas flame. A small container, broken in the ventilating system of a building, will certainly evacuate the place. But it will not stay long, and will soon be flushed out without harming anyone. *Hatpin,* a self-defense catalog for women (Hatpin, PO Box 6144, Santa Fe, NM 87502) sells "Repulse," a small glass vial of butyl mercaptan and a second vial of "neutralizer."

Pet and veterinary supply houses (check the yellow pages or the ads in national dog magazines) sell "animal trail scents" and "breaking scents." These are often foul-smelling liquids used to train hunting dogs. Sporting goods stores often sell skunk sprays in small aerosol cans, used by hunters to mask their scent in the field.

Also, don't neglect to visit the stores found in most large cities that specialize in novelties, jokes, magic tricks and the like (look in the yellow pages under "novelties" or "costumes"). Here look for "gags" like "Fart Spray," a wonderfully obnoxious 4-oz. aerosol. Read the labels closely, though. Some of these aerosol sprays are just room fresheners with funny labels. The truly foul-smelling ones usually say so on the label. Some of these gems are available through mail-order houses (as a last resort) like Funny Side Up, 425 Stump Rd., North Wales, PA 19454.

FIELD NOTES

*Most laboratory grade butyric acid can be diluted with tapwater by five or ten to one, stretching its use without diluting its effectiveness.

STINK GRENADES

This device is an adaptation of an aerosol spray can, making it usable as a "grenade," which can be thrown and will discharge its contents while the monkeywrencher escapes the premises. It can be used effectively with such commercially-available aerosols as hunters' masking skunk sprays and novelty "fart" sprays. Bear in mind that the design illustrated is approximate, since size and shape of cans will vary. The mechanism is basic and highly adaptable.

To change an aerosol spray can into a grenade, first remove the spray nozzle head (a) and with the aid of a C-clamp, glue it to a short (3/4 inch to 1 inch) length of 1/2 in. diameter wooden dowel (b) and a large, wide rubber band (c). The common cyanoacrylate "super glues" are ideal.

After a day's drying time, stretch the rubber band around the aerosol can and glue securely to *both* sides of the can (d). If necessary, the rubber band can be cut and the C-clamp used to hold it in place for gluing. The idea is to have a lot of tension on the rubber band when the spray nozzle head (a) is re-installed.

After another day of allowing the glue to set-up, install the spray nozzle along with the modified cap as pictured. The soft plastic cap has been modified with three simple cuts (e), one window to allow the spray out, and two smaller notches to accommodate the rubber band. The cap is not glued in place until the mechanism is tested and found to work. Before re-assembling, install a safety "pin," such as the nail (f), through a hole drilled in the wooden dowel. The pin holds the nozzle head up just enough to prevent it from spraying. This is a fine adjustment and must be made carefully. The spray nozzle must fit snugly in its hole in the can so that it won't accidentally go off.

The rubber band does not provide enough pressure (usually) to push the spray head down. It's purpose is to hold the spray head down after you push on the end of the dowel. This allows you to drop the "grenade" and leave, knowing the entire can will discharge. Test the mechanism out-of-doors for a second or two to insure its proper functioning before cementing the cap to the can. While assembling, NEVER allow the spray nozzle to point directly at you or your clothing.

Once you have a working spray you can do one of two things with it — glue the can to a flat wooden base, causing the can to stand upright while discharging, or glue on a piece of stiff cardboard as shown in (g). Note how the cardboard protrusion prevents the can from rolling to a position that discharges the spray into the ground or floor.

As a final step, carefully glue some cheap, coarse burlap to the smooth exterior surfaces of the can and cap. This burlap will not take fingerprints and allows you to handle the "grenade" without leaving any on it.

As a safety precaution, wipe all parts free of fingerprints BEFORE beginning assembly. Wear rubber gloves while assembling. When putting the mechanism together, wear safety glasses or goggles to protect your eyes from accidental spraying.

The stink grenade is delivered to the target site in the pocket of a cheap cloth coat or jacket bought at Goodwill or another second-hand store. The coat can be casually draped over your arm. This allows for a cheap, throwaway garment should it accidentally become contaminated with the odor. A cheap woman's handbag or shopping bag will do, but only if made of cloth (to keep from leaving fingerprints — avoid leather, naugahyde or plastic).

Drop the stink grenade to the floor just inside the door to an office or meeting room, in the fur section of a department store, or wherever appropriate. Walk away casually and leave the building immediately.

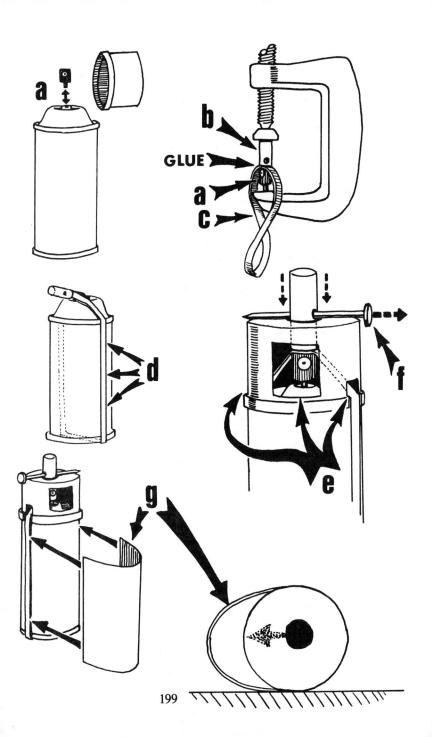

JAMMING LOCKS

One extremely effective means of hassling all sorts of villains is jamming the locks to their places of business or to their machines of destruction. (We'll leave it to your judgment who the proper culprits are in your area.)

Calculate the number of hours between your hit and the time when employees will first attempt to gain access to the building or equipment. Select almost any hard-drying glue or adhesive that will set-up within this time. The "liquid metals" are very good for this. Before the operation, cut or drill a hole in the screw cap of the glue tube so that the contents will come out in a stream thin enough to enter the lock's keyway. Cover this hole with a piece of tape until you are ready to use the glue.

Conduct the usual scouting of the target, establish a plan and prepare all your equipment in the standard manner to assure that no fingerprints, fibers or other evidence are inadvertently left at the scene. The drop and pickup method of delivery is usually the safest. (See the chapter on **Security.**)

Clothing worn should blend in with the locality and season of year. Gloves can be rather conspicuous in warm weather, so get some of the thin, tight-fitting surgical-type gloves in use in hospitals and some food service establishments. At night they pass at even short distances as being flesh-toned (for white folks). If you are working in daylight, your fingertips can be coated with clear fingernail polish to avoid leaving fingerprints. Be sure to stock some fingernail polish remover.

When actually jamming the lock, stand close enough to avoid ready observation by passersby. Force as much glue into the lock through the keyhole as you can, but don't smear it all over the padlock or door knob. Carry a paper towel to clean up any excess so there is no evidence to alert a passing security guard or policeman before the glue has set-up. (Of course, remove the used paper towel from the scene of the crime and dispose of it safely.)

Tapered hardwood shims can also be jammed into the keyway and broken off. A small screwdriver can be used to force the wood further into the lock. Properly executed this can accomplish the same basic mission as the adhesive/glue technique — necessitating the summoning of a locksmith to gain access. It does not cause permanent damage to the lock mechanism as does the glue, however.

Lastly, make sure that *all* entrances are similarly jammed. This may seem obvious, but out-of-the-way entrances are often neglected.

POLITICAL FUN AND GAMES

During the presidential campaign of 1972, one of Richard Nixon's henchmen named Donald Segretti perfected the art of political dirty tricks against a variety of Democrats, including Ed Muskie and Hubert Humphrey. There is no reason why the ecoguerilla should not adopt some of these techniques against anti-environmental candidates for any political office.

One way to give the candidate a bad name is to offer a free campaign party in his name. Cut words out of magazines or newspapers, fill in the small print with a rented or borrowed IBM typewriter, and layout on a sheet of paper: FREE—ALL YOU CAN EAT; FREE BEER & CHAMPAGNE; PRIZES; MUSIC; BRING THE KIDS; etc.; Hosted by (the candidate) on (dates/times in large lettering), at place (see below). Embellish with cut-out graphics of the Statue of Liberty, American flag, fireworks, or whatever is appropriate for your candidate. Make it look official. The location of your campaign shindig should be selected with care. If the candidate has a large, busy campaign headquarters, make it there during business hours to disrupt their operation. If a $100-a-plate dinner is planned for the candidate, why not add some unexpected non-paying guests?

Take your lay-out to a copy shop and have several hundred or more high quality copies printed. This is best done at another city in a busy shop where they may not even give a second look at you or your product. Many copy shops have high quality self-service machines where the risk of being noticed will be minimal.

The most time-consuming task of the operation will be posting all of the flyers on community bulletin boards, telephone poles, telephone booths, etc. Saturate the area. You might hire kids to do it, pay in advance, and disappear. If nothing else, you will generate some very bad publicity for the candidate.

Another scheme to disrupt the campaign of a worthless candidate focuses on tying up their telephones at critical moments, such as during election day get-out-the-vote efforts. If you infiltrate the campaign as a volunteer, you may learn of other important functions during which telephone lines should be kept busy, such as during major telephone fundraising events.

For this job, print another flyer, this time offering something for free that is desirable to most people but also within the realm of believability, for example $5 cash. Offer the item absolutely free, "no strings attached," in response to a telephone call as part of a "nationwide marketing test." Use plenty of graphics, $ signs to catch attention, and prominently feature the date(s) on which calls must be made. Then list all of the telephone numbers of the campaign. If there are many numbers, divide them up according to the first letter of the caller's last name, so that all lines will be jammed. This should keep those telephone-answerers busy!

With a little creativity, two targets can be harassed at no additional cost with this technique. Instead of offering $5 free cash, offer a free dinner for four at your local rainforest destroying fast-food chain (use their logo and advertising liberally on your flyer. Or choose a local business or corporation that is a major contributor to environmental rapist PACs, and state that they are offering a free item.

FUN WITH SLINGSHOTS

This versatile tool, available at large discount houses for a few dollars, can be used to knock out office windows from the relative safety of a passing car. In the illustration you will see the conventional type (a) and the more compact and easily concealed folding variety (b). Missiles must be small, dense and relatively round (c). Avoid irregularly shaped objects (d), as they don't fly true. Small rocks, steel bearings and large nuts (e) are quite suitable. In illustration (f) you can see how one or two slingshotters can hit a target from a passing car. The driver must signal when it is safe, ensuring that the hit cannot be observed by nearby drivers. Avoid using your brake lights or deliberately slowing down and then making a fast getaway. Try a couple of practice sessions on a remote country road first. To a passerby, the hit must be indistinguishable from the actions and movements of a typical passing car.

Accuracy with a slingshot is something that comes only through practice. Shooting into an empty cardboard box from gradually increasing ranges is good practice. Do this in a remote area, rather than leave your backyard littered with the same type of ammunition found at the scene of the hit.

When practicing from a moving car, keep in mind that the hand holding the slingshot must not extend outside the vehicle (f).

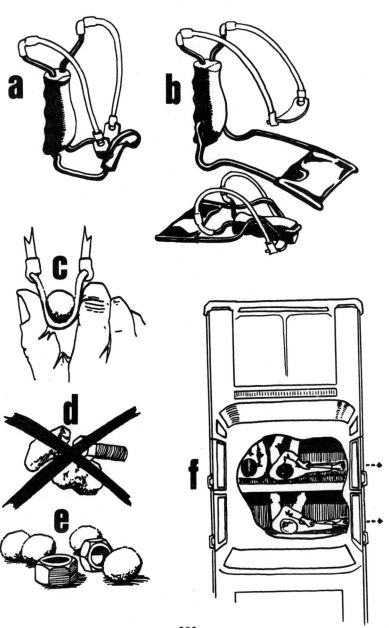

MOUNTAIN BIKES

While it is clear to me that there are many places where mountain bikes (and some of the dildoheads who ride them) do *not* belong, it is also clear to me that mountain bikes can be useful to those who use extralegal means of defending our Homeland from the Mad Machine. The bikes are light, quiet, portable, and will go almost anywhere, and have a fairly long range. Unfortunately, they have several drawbacks, such as cost and inability to handle certain types of terrain and they require hard physical labor. The following is a guide to help you use the mountain bike effectively in your ecodefensive operations.

Getting Started

For those with limited off-road cycling experience, or limited cycling experience of any kind, I suggest reading some of the books on the market which discuss how to buy, equip, and ride a mountain bike. Pay special attention to the sections on carrying gear. For non-camping outings, you will still need a *sturdy* rear rack, tool kit, tire pump, a set of rear panniers, and either thornproof tubes or a tube protector like "Mr Tuffy." Be sure you have "full knobby" tires. Many mountain bikes have tires with a raised middle ridge. These tires roll easier on pavement, but have limited traction on dirt. Choose tires which are appropriate for your area.

Advantages of Mountain Bikes

Unlike cars or motorcycles, mountain bikes are easily carried by people or cars. A group of people and bikes can be brought to within 10 miles or so of a work site in a van or truck, dropped off, and picked up someplace miles away. A bicycle can also be easily carried across washed-out sections of roads, or lifted over fences and gates. Many bikes can be carried in one vehicle, or hidden in a van or truck.

Bicycles can be easily hidden in the field as well, which is important when one is in a "closed area," or does not feel like making explanations to "authority figures." The bikes can be stashed in the bushes (be sure you remember where!) for a quick getaway after an action. They are also easy to hide if you hear someone coming. A person on a mountain bike can quickly scout out access and exit routes (most Freddie maps don't show all of the logging roads, jeep trails and connections). Most people in good shape can ride 20 to 50 miles in a day depending on terrain. Just about any jeep road or logging road can be ridden, along with many below-timberline hiking trails (see Editor's note) without too much pushing and carrying. Stay off Wilderness Area trails and any steep, erodible trails, please! (Unless in a *real* emergency.)

Disadvantages of Mountain Bikes

As one can see, mountain bikes can make ecodefense easier, quicker and safer. But they won't work in all situations. A good mountain bike is expensive, from $450 to $1,200 for the 15-speed low-geared light bikes. Not all of us are renegade yuppies with that kind of money. There are some bikes in the $250 - $450 range which aren't as chic, but they work adequately on the trail. Also check for used bikes.

Mountain biking, especially with a load of gear, can be *very* hard work. When I started riding, I was somewhat surprised by how hard it could be. Unlike pavement riding, you have to continually watch the road (or trail) ahead for loose rocks, ruts, holes, etc. A crash while on the job would be *no fun!* This means that it can be very hard to see or hear someone watching you from off the road.

Unless you're a shaved ape, you probably won't be able to carry many tools. Most mountain bikes weigh about 30 lbs., and you probably won't want to carry more than 30-40 lbs. of water and gear.

Consider the type of terrain in your area. If roads and trails follow sandy washes, or if they are frequently covered with deep, slick clay mud, you're better off walking or riding a horse. Loose rocks can be a lot of extra work.

Security

A *very* important consideration is not implicating yourself or your bike in any "wrongdoing." Paint everything on your bike flat black or camouflage. Wrap brake handles and other non-paintable areas in cloth or duct tape. Shiny paint and chrome can reflect headlights and sunlight. Be sure that all reflectors are removed (replace them for legitimate night riding).

Make as little noise as possible. Curse quietly if you do an "endo," or get stuck hub-deep in water or mud. Prevent the chain from slapping against the frame. Be sure all tools are wrapped and secured so they don't clink against one another. You'll be going over a lot of bumps. I don't know how to hide tire tracks, and mountain bikes can leave very distinct tracks. You do *not* want to be stopped with a muddy bike whose mud and tires match tracks left near a "boat anchor." The ultimate solution to this would be a stretch rubber covering with a different tread pattern which could be put on over tires, and hidden after each action. Unfortunately, such a thing is not available. Changing tires after an action would be awkward and difficult to do in the field, and dragging brush behind you wouldn't work on clay soil. Other ideas on this problem would be appreciated.

Finally, a word about night work. This should only be done on moonlit nights or on a road or trail on which you have been at night before. Be sure you know where all of the bumps or sandy areas are. A generator-type headlight gives enough light by which to see, but the generators make pedaling more difficult and are noisy on most mountain bike tires. Also, such a light is quite conspicuous.

With careful planning, mountain bikes can make fast, strike-and-run ecodefense operations possible in situations where the Enemies will be completely unprepared. However, *you* can also be caught completely unprepared (and lose your bike!). Good luck and happy riding.

— *the Mad Engineer*

Editor's Note

While we do not, as a rule, approve of the use of wheeled vehicles of any sort on mountain trails, and certainly not in Wilderness Areas, we *do* think that mountain bikes have great potential for the ecodefender, especially as a rapid and silent means of getting around on all those thousands of miles of Forest Service logging roads. There are certain security precautions one should take, however.

Tire prints *would* constitute serious evidence if an ecoraider were ever apprehended, even long after the fact, as long as that person still possessed those tires. Since getting rid of bike tires after each "hit" would be an expense beyond the means of all but the richest ecowarrior, we suggest that mountain bikes might be used only to ride to the general vicinity of the work site. The bikes then could be hidden and the ecoteurs would go the rest of the way on foot. It's cheaper to replace shoes than tires.

URBAN MONKEYWRENCHING

No campaign of monkeywrenching is complete without consideration of urban area targets. The corporations who ravage mountains, oceans, forests and deserts are headquartered in communities ranging from small towns to major metropolitan areas. The decisionmakers for these businesses feel secure and untouched by most monkeywrenching in the field, and their continuing callous actions reflect this isolation.

Attacks on urban targets will rattle the cage of the upper corporate echelon and force a more serious consideration of the issues involved. Such attacks also provide the monkeywrencher with a wider range of targets. As security is increased at rural target sites, ecoteurs switch occasionally to less secure targets previously left untouched. These include equipment yards, sawmills, warehouses, corporate offices and retail store outlets. Thus the offending business is forced to incur still higher costs as their penalty for earth rape.

Even individuals should not feel completely exempt from true justice. Sadly, the corporate structure routinely shields decisionmakers from the consequences of their greedy acts. Corporate presidents, board members and managers are rarely held accountable under the law, the usual recourse being a token fine paid by the corporation. Then it's back to business as usual, with violations of health, safety and environmental laws simply better concealed than before.

When conducting research to fix blame for callous corporate activities, it is important to avoid field level managers who are simply carrying out orders. There are occasional exceptions to this, however, such as a militantly anti-environmental logging supervisor. Sometimes a local or on-site manager will seek to enhance his or her standing with the bosses by cost-cutting measures. This frequently occurs in the case of improper disposal of toxic waste. A plant manager will arrange for illegal disposal of hazardous materials rather than pay for proper removal. This increases the profitability of the operations, enhancing the manager's chances for a raise or promotion. Even when following orders in a case like this, the local manager becomes a knowing accomplice who is shielded by the law.

Imagine the chilling effect on wantonly destructive business activities if the owners and managers knew that they might be held personally accountable. Because of this, it is important that some publicity accompany such hits. Every effort must be made to garner public attention through the press. Failing this, brief cautionary phone calls *(Editor's note: security!)* can warn key individuals that their office or home might be next. Raids on personal residences should be planned and executed carefully, so as to avoid any chance of injury to individuals such as might result from a face-to-face confrontation. For this reason, such raids should probably be limited to spray-painted slogans on walls and autos, and the like.

Remember that if every monkeywrencher is held fully accountable under the law, that same principle should be applied to the corporate power-brokers whose callous behavior makes monkeywrenching necessary.

There has recently been a great deal of concern expressed over the use of civil suits by corporations to silence legitimate opposition. Land developers, timber companies, animal experimenters, and billboard companies have all filed suit against private individuals and public officials to stifle dissent and subvert regulatory laws. The immense financial resources of these corporations can easily insure victory over their individual opponents. Even a victory in the courts for the activist/victim can lead to financial ruin, due to the high cost of legal services.

We may have already reached the point where only the monkeywrencher can act to deter this threat to liberty. The corporate decision-makers and their attorneys must be held accountable for their attempts to subvert the constitutional guarantee of free speech. They must be made aware that they face years of harassment if they attempt to abuse the court system to stifle opposition. If enough tension is generated, the legal system may actually move to curtail such abuse.

Attack on an Urban Residence

Any "hit" on an urban residence must be planned so as to avoid the possibility of a confrontation with the owner or a neighbor. Never use intrusive methods like window-breaking on any building where people live.

The best type of urban residential operation is embarrassing slogans painted on highly visible walls. They must be tailored to fit the crime, like "I poison your children" for the home of a toxic waste dumper.

Verify the accuracy of the address through at least two sources. The phone book and city directory may be of help, though these may not be up-to-date and many prominent people will not be listed in phone directories. Books like *Who's Who* and its various regional editions have bios of many corporate types, and while they do not give street addresses, they at least pinpoint the community in which they reside, so that a little additional detective work may turn up the actual address. When you have a likely phone number, you can verify if it belongs to the right person by making a call under some innocent-sounding pretext. Matching license plate numbers at the corporate parking lot and at home is a good way of being sure that your target actually resides at a given address. Another way would be to pose as a prospective property buyer and inquire at the county courthouse about who owns a particular residence. This information is a matter of public record.

Once you have a house pinpointed, study the layout of the neighborhood streets carefully. This will prevent your driver from inadvertently trying to escape into a dead-end street or cul-de-sac in an emergency. On scouting runs, check the layout both by day and by night. Decide ahead of time exactly what slogans will go on what walls. Unpracticed sloganeers do stupid things like running out of space for a full message.

Check the target at the exact hour and night of the week just one week before the hit. This will reveal any routine activity for that day and time that might interfere with your plan.

Take care to follow the basic security precautions outlined elsewhere. Make sure your license number can't be read. If possible, use a brief drop and pickup-style hit, but avoiding stopping directly in front of the target home.

If, on the approach to the target, a neighbor or passerby should see you, scrub the mission and wait for another time. Be patient.

Time the hit to coincide with a late hour or cold or damp weather, all of which will keep the neighbors indoors. But never strike in the wee hours of the morning when *no one* else is on the road.

Never tamper with the mail box, as this may be a Federal offense.

Private Automobiles.

The target's car is a legitimate target that can be hit at home, at work, or in the grocery store parking lot. Smelly liquids or aerosols can be used on the interior, and paint stripper can be used (carefully!) to make slogans in the paint of an auto's exterior. It is usually too dangerous to fool with the engine (like sanding the oil), but the tires are a most vulnerable target.

Attacks on Corporate Offices

Corporate offices may range from small "store-front" operations (such as might be used by a fly-by-night real estate developer) to the massive glass and steel office complexes favored by the big, multi-national corporations. Corporate offices are vulnerable to a wide variety of mon-keywrenching techniques, including some tactics which would not be appropriate for a private residence. For instance, a quick, night raid involving the breaking of windows (through which paint or stink bombs might be tossed for good measure) might be clearly justifiable for the offices of a corporate criminal, while a similar action at a private resi-dence might be interpreted as life-threatening vandalism. Other appro-priate tactics for corporate offices include lockjamming, the use of spray-painted slogans, the dumping of noxious effluent and the like. These techniques will be covered in more detail later in this chapter.

The "Daring Daylight Raid."

There are times when much favorable publicity can be obtained from an action against a corporate office in broad daylight and during working hours. Prime examples of this were the raids carried out against cor-porate offices in Chicago by "The Fox," involving the dumping of raw sewage on the carpets of polluters. However, urban, daylight operations are potentially more risky than night operations, and require absolute precision in their execution. Following are some proven methods to follow:

Study the target building and surroundings in detail. Among the most important details are:

*Locations of doors and windows.

*Building security (i.e., guards and closed-circuit TV cameras).

*Parking (for lookouts and getaway car).

*Lighting (mainly important for night hits).

*Approaches and escape routes (don't rely on just one of each).

*Out-of-the-way access (loading docks, parking garages, etc.).

*Locations of possible witnesses.

Use any available pretext to examine the building layout. Dress like a typical business user and stroll about purposefully. Stop in as a passerby to ask for directions to a nearby building. Conservative-looking team members can inquire about renting office or convention space, and perhaps get a tour of the facility from the building supervisor. Always have a prepared story in case you are questioned. For detailed informa-tion, one of your team could try to get a janitorial job in the building (quit well before the hit, needless to say).

Detailed building plans may be on file and easily accessible at the office of the city or county building inspector. Pose as a prospective buyer (or buyer's representative), architectural student, etc.

When possible, determine what conditions may be expected at the time of the action by scouting the target one week and one day prior to the hit (at the same time of day). This will reveal typical patterns of activity you might expect at the time of your hit.

Consider a dry run to check out all aspects of your plan. Timing is important.

Getaway vehicles must blend in with the area. If you require certain parking spaces, be patient and wait until they open. To be safe, get there well in advance.

When necessary, use diversionary tactics. A smoke bomb set off safely in a planter might distract security. A well-timed phone call might distract a solitary receptionist in a front office waiting room.

Some type of disguise is usually a good idea. The basic type is an eye-catching garment that tends to distract the eyewitness. A brightly-colored ski mask, scarf, shirt or the like has a tendency to dominate in the descriptions later given to police.

Wigs and fake mustaches can be bought cheaply at second-hand stores (like Goodwill) and at novelty shops. Use special wig cleaner (available at wig shops) to clean any second-hand wig. These can often be bought for five dollars or less.

Avoid elaborate disguises. Most don't look that good close up, and may make someone suspicious. Shaving real facial hair or wearing a fake mustache can be an effective but simple disguise. See books like Corson's *Stage Makeup* (in most college and university libraries) for details on how to properly apply facial hair.

Such disguises are most effective if they can be quickly removed before one escapes the area or enters the getaway vehicle. The simplest method is to discard a garment while exiting the area. For example, a light jacket or second shirt worn on top of the first shirt (both bought at Goodwill) can be discarded in the trash, an unlocked closet, elevator, restroom, etc. *Never* discard a wig in this manner as it will invariably contain some of your hairs. Another disposal/quick-change method involves passing the items to a confederate totally different from you in appearance (for example, passing a brightly-colored shirt and wig from a man to a woman), with the receiver smuggling the items out in a large purse, shopping bag, briefcase, etc. This same person can also smuggle the disguise items into the target area for donning just prior to the hit.

Escape is the most critical item in your daylight raid plan. If foot pursuit is possible, a sack of BB's or bottle of cooking oil sloshed on a tile floor can delay pursuers, particularly in the confines of a hallway. If using an elevator is necessary, arrange to have a confederate hold the door open to insure quick getaway. Also, don't neglect the fire stairs in high-rise buildings. Keep in mind that you can readily enter a fire escape stairwell, but locked doors prevent you from re-entering the building (without the aid of a friend to open them from the inside). If there is a lobby security guard who might block a front door retreat, a well-timed phone call might tie up the guard's phone and delay warning.

Yet another way to delay pursuit is to use a locking device on the door after you leave. A pre-positioned length of lumber can be run through door handles to delay pursuers. Study your prospective exit doors closely and use your imagination to design simple and quick methods to secure them after the hasty exit. The locking device must be concealed near the door just prior to the job, or be installed at the critical moment by a waiting accomplice.

Once you have fled the building, you must either walk inconspicuously to a waiting car or simply flee. If you must run, consider wearing a jogging suit and tennies to avoid suspicion. Similarly, a bicycle can be used for a quick getaway without arousing the suspicions of passersby. The bicycle is usually used for a few blocks and then hauled away in a car or truck, or passed on to a confederate of totally different appearance who calmly rides off.

Urban hits are far more effective if accompanied by a press communique. Such a communique must be delivered only *after* the successful operation. See section on **Media Relations** in the **Security** chapter for further information about secure press contacts.

COMPUTER SABOTAGE

Monkeywrenchers of the future will need to acquire new skills to keep up with the spreading computerization of industry. Virtually all commercial operations that rape the planet are to some degree dependent upon computers. A two or three week shutdown of computers can cost a large company between one and two million dollars, and even small companies and contractors are becoming addicted to high-tech services for planning, payroll, inventory, and countless other essential functions.

Within ten years, every congressional election will have become irreversibly dependent upon costly computerized direct mail campaigns.

There are three basic types of computer sabotage:

HARDWARE SABOTAGE: This is the simple, straightforward destruction of costly equipment. It requires physical access, forced or otherwise, to computer facilities.

RECORDS SABOTAGE: Because information storage and retrieval is the primary function of computers, the destruction, by physical means, of computer tapes and discs can severely impede many destructive activities.

SOFTWARE SABOTAGE: This consists of "borrowing" embarrassing information from corporate files, diverting company operations away from critical areas, and the planting of so-called "logic bombs" that use predesignated cues to trigger massive erasures of records and operating programs.

All of these methods are highly effective when carried out in a planned and intelligent manner. Major destruction of hardware calls for new equipment. Labor repair charges usually exceed $60 an hour, with down time ranging from several hours to a few weeks. Destruction of records requires prolonged and expensive reconstruction from non-computerized data, *if* it is still available. And the highly damaging "logic bomb" can destroy costly programs and shut down a system for extended periods while operators search for other "bombs."

Because the potential for extremely damaging sabotage is so great, computer operations are increasingly viewed as industry's most sensitive and vulnerable activity. Any attempt at computer sabotage must be well planned and thorough. The ideal hit would include combinations of the various types mentioned, so that newly repaired or replaced hardware would be immediately shut down by "logic bombs." The reason for this is simple. Your first hit on any particular target might be your last easy opportunity. Heightened security measures of all types almost invariably follow on the heels of successful monkeywrenching.

Hardware Sabotage

First, you must locate the target. See the "Software" section for details. Next, scouting of the target should reveal the detailed physical layout; multiple routes of approach and withdrawal; alarm systems and other security; access points like doors, windows, skylights, air conditioner ducts and the like; and the best hours for a hit.

Your first selection of tools should be those necessary for gaining access to the (usually) locked facility. Always carry pry bars and heavy screwdrivers in case you encounter unexpected locks that must be forced. Clothing should make you appear normal for the setting. Shoes should be soft and comfortable, with thick rubber soles that do not squeak on tile floors. Because some computer centers are equipped with closed-circuit television (often to monitor the employees), you should plan on making your entry disguised by hats that conceal your hair, and bandannas or ski masks to conceal your face. And, of course, don't forget your gloves.

Read the **Security** section, especially **Basic Security** and **Counter-Security**, before undertaking an operation of this nature.

Special tools for wrecking computer hardware might include the following:

*Large screwdrivers. Good for prying open access panels. These must have insulated (i.e., plastic) handles.

*Small pry bars. Also useful for gaining access to the guts of these machines. These must be insulated by coating all but the working tip in a product like "Plasti-Dip" (available at better hardware stores everywhere). Several layers of electrical tape will also do the job.

*Long-handled axes. These tools can be used to force access to computer rooms as well as wreak untold havoc once inside. The squeamish can substitute long-handled sledge hammers.

*Water balloons or water bottles. Nothing is better than plain old-fashioned tap water for causing short circuits in electrical equipment. Water balloons can be thrown a distance, keeping you safely away from the computer innards. Water bottles are also very useful (and easier to carry). They should be of durable plastic, leakproof and have wide mouths, like a jar, to allow you to toss the water from a short distance.

Depending upon the size of the computer operation, once you arrive on target you will be facing a variety of computers, terminals, disc drives and supporting equipment. A visit to a good library or bookstore can familiarize one with the appearance of various types of units pictured in countless books and magazines.

Start in right away on the largest computers. Pry off access panels until you are looking in at rows of circuit boards (again, study the pictures first at the library). Once you have gained access to the circuitry, locate the power switch and turn the unit on. Stand back and toss in your water, frying countless circuits. Most computer circuits do not carry dangerous electrical current, but one must never take chances. Your distance of a couple feet, the plastic bottle or balloons, and your rubber shoe soles will protect you if the water should contact a higher voltage.

Pour water into terminal keyboards after turning on the power. With disc drives, pour the water in at any handy access point.

The axe or sledgehammer can obviously inflict considerable damage, but only after you pry or pound off the outside panels. It doesn't do much good to simply dent the exterior.

The cathode ray tube of the computer terminal (like a TV picture tube) is a tempting target, but these should either be ignored, or saved until last. These tubes are costly but carry high voltages. Don't punch them out with anything but a long-handled tool, or other object that gives you a good distance plus the insulation of a wooden handle. Also, the vacuum inside the tube causes them to implode violently when broken, usually scattering fine shards of glass about the area. The danger to your eyes, if you are standing in front of the terminal or simply facing it at the time you hit it, is serious. Also, the fine glass fragments can lodge in your clothing (virtually invisible), and stay there until the clothes are laundered. This could mean "wearing" the evidence out with you.

If you plan to break the CRT's, take some golf-ball-sized rocks with you, and break them from a long distance just before you leave (be sure there are no fingerprints on the rocks).

Note: Although most parts of computer hardware carry only low voltages, always assume the greatest danger. Even a computer that is turned "off" can have substantial current stored in some components (like the cathode ray tube). Always use well-insulated tools, wear rubber-soled shoes, and avoid unnecessary contact with machine parts or other metal.

Records Sabotage

Computer data is stored on large reels of magnetic tape, or the newer discs composed of flexible plastic with a magnetic coating on both sides.

The most important thing to remember about computer records is that duplicate records are routinely made by most businesses, particularly when critical data is involved. These duplicates might be stored with the originals, or in a separate room, fire safe, at another building, or at the home of a company or organization officer. Whenever possible, locate these duplicates before planning a hit to destroy records.

Tape reels and discs are stored on various types of shelves, sometimes in ring-binder type holders, special shielded cases (to protect against accidental erasure by magnetic fields), or in fire safes that range from small strongboxes to multi-drawer cabinets. Although possessing locking mechanisms, these fire safes are essentially just heavily insulated boxes designed to survive fires. They can be forced open with the usual tools.

The best way to damage magnetic tape is to cut into the side of the tightly wound spool with a small sharp knife. You don't have to cut all the way through. Even a shallow cut through many windings of the tape will prevent it from feeding into the computer.

Discs are usually protected by easily-opened hard plastic cases. Simply gouge the face of the disc one time and move on to the next disc. The read/write head of the disc drive operates so closely to the disc surface that a speck of dust can cause it to "crash." A single deep scratch renders the disc, and the information on it, worthless.

Software Sabotage

This can entail simply snooping for secret information that can embarrass a corporation or government agency, changing recorded data to create a bookkeeping nightmare, or inserting "logic bombs" to destroy data at the time of your choosing.

To undertake these activities, you must first have a working knowledge of computer operation, and hopefully of programming basics. The necessary training is best obtained through community colleges or other state-sponsored schools where the cost is kept reasonable. If you spend enough time around school computers, you will usually encounter "hackers," those fabled individuals with an all-consuming passion for computers. Getting to know them can provide you with an education in the fine art of obtaining access (often illegal) to various computer systems. You must pretend to be interested only in computers. Never tell them your real intentions. Many of these people have a love of the machine that would define heavy-duty sabotage as a capital offense. Learn from them, but never trust them.

Once you have an education in computers, you can infiltrate the target by applying for a job, or attempt to set up a simulated remote terminal with telephone access to the target computer.

If you operate from the inside, be constantly aware of employee monitoring. More and more businesses are installing everything from closed circuit TV to sophisticated programs that keep logs of all users' work records, phone calls and the like. Remember also that most insiders are discovered when suspicion leads to interrogation and a confession. If questioned, assume that the interrogator is very sophisticated (especially if he or she doesn't appear to be) and consistently lie. Usually, only those who break down and confess ever get into hot water.

The most you should ever concede under questioning is that you "might have made an error." About 85% of computer data loss is caused by operator error. Ideally, you'll do your snooping or tampering in a way that can't be traced back to you.

Entering the system from the outside, or "hacking," is a complex and ever-changing field. For basic reference in this area, read:

Out of the Inner Circle by Bill Landreth, Microsoft Press, Bellevue, WA. This book is widely available in bookstores.

The Hacker's Handbook by Hugo Cornwall, E. Arthur Brown Co., 3404 Pawnee Dr., Alexandria, MN 56308. This book may be available at larger bookstores.

Software sabotage calls for locating the remote terminal access for the system (if it has one). Hackers obtain their information from the thousands of "bulletin boards" operated by individuals and computer clubs, from the professional "data retrieval services" set up to provide businesses with reports on competitors (pinpointing their various operations and narrowing the search for the computer facility), and sometimes by automatically dialing the phone numbers around the known company phone number until a computer answers.

Remote terminal sabotage should usually steer clear of the software which handles a company's finances since these often have the highest level of security. Other computer functions may be just as critical, but not as well protected since they are not as attractive to thieves.

The most damaging form of software sabotage is the "logic bomb." These hidden instructions are inserted into the operating program and will initiate erasures at a given signal. Further damage can be inflicted by hiding other "logic bombs" in the electronic data files. The storage capacity of computers, coupled with their high speed of operation, can make the detection and neutralization of logic bombs very time-consuming and costly.

Security Tips For Hackers:

The primary tool for investigation of computer hacking is the tracing of phone calls. This risk can be minimized in several ways:

*Minimize contact with the computer. Some security systems notify the operator when more than three consecutive attempts are made to insert a password (such as when you are trying different possibilities). Obviously, the more times you enter the system, the more chances there are for calls to be traced.

*Avoid leaving obvious long-distance phone records. Use gateway nodes to gain access to a system through a local phone number. Then you should leapfrog through several networks and switches before actually linking with the target computer. Initial trace-backs will end at the gateway node where the call goes local. At this point, they will have to stand by and wait for your next intrusion.

*Make your contact short.

*Use briefcase portable computers and pay phones to make tracing more difficult. Drive-up pay phones are even handier. Keep it short and leave the area immediately.

*Use someone else's phone system. Look on the outside of a house or office building where the phone lines come in from a pole. A small plastic box or soft rubber cover will be found on the terminal block. A telephone with alligator clips can be attached to the terminals holding the red and green wires. You then become one more phone on that system. In office and apartment buildings, the terminal block is often found in the basement or a closet, protected by a cabinet. Books on phone wiring for do-it-yourselfers will provide you with pictures of these key access points.

Be security conscious. Make sure no one else is "in" where you are using the phone line. Keep a lookout.

FIELD NOTE

Because computers store their information magnetically, passing a powerful magnet over either hard or floppy discs can erase or scramble stored data. One could break in as described above and use a magnet to destroy records and then leave without any evidence of your activity until such material is used later by the operator. It may also be possible to hide a powerful magnet on your person and gain access as a visitor to a company's or agency's computer room during normal business hours. By merely walking close to hard or floppy discs with a magnet, you may inflict serious damage to records.

CONDO TRASHING

The following method has been suggested for use against environmentally objectionable construction projects such as condominiums, shopping centers and the like. It involves action to "impair" the electrical wiring system and the plumbing during the construction phase.

After the concrete slab foundation is poured, the connections for the plumbing (especially sewer) are exposed. Usually these connections are covered by duct tape to prevent foreign objects from being accidentally dropped down the pipes. Should someone remove the duct tape and *deliberately* put foreign material into the pipes, and then carefully replace the duct tape, there can be interesting results. The material put in the pipes should, if at all possible, be designed to cause a permanent stoppage (i.e., concrete or epoxy). Imagine the consternation if the blockage is not discovered until the project opens for business, and sewage begins flowing out of toilets onto the occupants' rugs, etc.

Similarly, a monkeywrencher can go after the electrical wiring after it has been installed in the drywalls, but before the sheetrock (or other form of wallboard) has been hanged. One can go about, from wall to wall wherever wires are found, cutting them in inconspicuous places (for instance, behind studs or crossties, or under joists) and then replacing the wire ends, perhaps taping or gluing them into place so as to make them appear untouched. When the sheetrock crews finish, there will be no evidence that anything is wrong until the sad day when the tenants move in and try to get their microwave ovens to work.

Obviously, these tactics can be applied to a wide variety of construction jobs. Remember, though, to choose your targets well. Make sure that the "victims" of such monkeywrenching well deserve to be singled out as egregious environmental rapists. There is no place for aimless vandalism in the monkeywrencher's arsenal.

FUN WITH PHONES

Perhaps you will remember reading a recent news item about a little "prank" someone played on Jerry Falwell. It seems some enterprising soul programmed their home computer to dial Falwell's toll-free "800" number (which provides a recorded message and allows the caller to order a free bible and other literature). The computer would dial the number, hold the line open just long enough for the connection to be established, then hang up and dial again. It did this at the rate of one call every 30 seconds, to the tune of a reported *half-million* calls before Falwell and the telephone company were able to figure out what was going on and put a halt to things. Needless to say, this cost Falwell a lot of bucks. The authorities, according to the newspaper accounts, weren't even sure what crime they would be able to charge the prankster with.

Now, we're not advocating that *you* go out and give Jerry a call. The point of this story is that lots of nasty earth rapers have 800 telephone numbers — big real estate companies promoting mountain condos or "retirement havens" in the desert are a case in point. And while it may be beyond the means of most of us to pull off a "prank" as major as the one on Falwell, even a few judicious calls to such people will run up their costs. Incidentally, sometimes these people are so eager to find suckers for their schemes that they fly prospective customers out to look at the site, feed them and put them up in a hotel or motel — all expenses paid. If you have a little time on your hands and could use a change of scenery, you might well take them up on their offers. Then later, tell them just what rotten pukes you think they are.

CHAPTER 8

PROPAGANDA

Propaganda — psychological warfare, whatever you want to call it — has been around ever since the early agricultural cities of the Fertile Crescent began quarreling and pushing each other around. Half of your battle is won when your enemy is afraid of you.

Propaganda is a good way for the monkeywrencher to not only present her message to the public, but also to cause sleepless nights for the blackhearted Freddies, developers, subdividers, gutless politicians, sleazy advertisers, and others.

Besides the well-known act of cutting down billboards, there are other entertaining ideas contained in this chapter, which can leave the evil ones sweating and sleepless in their beds.

ADVANCED BILLBOARDING

Monkeywrenchers are rarely called upon to enforce the law, but with the lack of proper enforcement of environmental legislation, vigilante action is increasingly justified. A clear-cut case of this need is the subversion of the 1965 Highway Beautification Act by the outdoor advertising industry. This law, intended to eliminate the roadside clutter of billboards, has been systematically gutted by an industry which flagrantly displays a lack of concern for environmental and highway safety issues. Although American taxpayers have spent millions to pay for the removal of these eyesores, the sign companies have gone so far as to take the tax dollars paid them to remove signs and use those funds to erect new signs. Billboard industry lobbyists in Washington have insured that appropriations for sign removal are pared down to the level where new sign construction outstrips removal by a factor of three to one.

The demand for private intervention is compelling.

First, all billboards within 660 feet of the highway are technically in violation of federal law, although the sign companies have unabashedly used a number of loopholes to circumvent enforcement.

Secondly, with unprecedented federal budget deficits, the odds of Congress allocating tax money sufficient to the task is virtually impossible. The billboard-cutter will not only aid in law enforcement, but will contribute to the patriotic task of keeping a lid on federal spending. In addition, every time a billboard falls, a landscape is created.

Lastly, and perhaps most importantly, studies in Minnesota and New York have proven that sign-free highways are safer. The incidence of highway accidents was found to be related to the number of billboards and the distractions they provide to drivers. In short, roadside advertising is a threat to public safety.

The clandestine battle against this roadside blight began in 1958 as the billboard lobby successfully defeated an early attempt to regulate signs. In June of that year, unidentified billboarders, enjoying popular support, cut down seven signs outside of Santa Fe, New Mexico. A dozen years later, a group callled the Billboard Bandits systematically sawed down close to two hundred signs in Michigan. In mid-1971, six high school students, one a senior class president, were arrested for destroying numerous billboards. They were stopped on the main street of a small town where police found a saw and an axe in the trunk of their car. After a failed attempt to prove the signs (not the sign-cutting) illegal, the youths pled no contest to one count of malicious destruction of property and each were given a suspended jail sentence, three-and-a-half months probation and a $150 fine.

The lessons from this case are many. Six young men driving through a small town at night will likely draw interest from the police anywhere. In the previous three weeks, 35 signs had been downed in the area, and police were on the lookout for suspects. This case also shows clearly why tools not in use must be locked away. When police ask to search your vehicle, the answer must be a polite but firm "No." They may threaten to take you to jail or hold you until a search warrant can be obtained, but you must not give in to this intimidation. Once you consent to a search, anything found can be used to convict you. If the police conduct an illegal search, any evidence found can be excluded from use against you. (On the positive side in this case, by pleading "no contest," the teenagers avoided an admission that could have led to a civil liability.)

Other billboarders active in the early seventies included "Americans for a Scenic Environment," who once replaced a downed sign with a small tree. During 1976 - 77, the "Vigilante Sign Committee" in Jackson, Wyoming, dropped every highway billboard in Teton County. In Arizona, a group called the "Eco-raiders" cut down numerous billboards around Tucson. According to one member, "If enough billboards are cut down, it will become prohibitively expensive to advertise that way."

Only work with those who are ideologically committed to uncompromising defense of Earth. Billboarding is excellent preparation and training for more advanced forms of monkeywrenching. Those who are simply looking for excitement and action lack the necessary depth of commitment. All must be willing to study, learn and discuss the essential issues facing all Earth defenders.

Effective sign-cutting requires a three-member team: a driver and two cutters. With four, your cutting team can have a lookout who can also alternate with the cutters in shifts. A five-member team is the largest size for safe operations and permits two teams of cutters and thus faster work at the target site.

Target Selection

Your first billboard raid should be an easy target in a remote location, far from any houses and with good access. Limit yourself to one sign the first few times out. Group morale is built upon success, so insure that the first few jobs come off without a hitch. Only after learning efficient teamwork should you consider more complex targets like billboard clusters, lighted signs, or sign company headquarters in urban areas.

Once you are ready to begin your sign-cutting campaign in earnest, commence a period of information gathering. Map out your potential targets in adequate detail. In this way, you will need only a quick drive-by to confirm the current accuracy of your data and note any changes. This limits your exposure to possibly suspicious people while scouting for new targets. Land owners like farmers and ranchers, who rent space to sign companies, will be on the alert once the signs begin dropping in large numbers. Get as much information as far in advance as possible.

Avoid operating in one area excessively. Police, security guards and beer-guzzling posses will be alerted and may stake out possible targets in the hope of apprehending you. It's best to hit several signs in an area on one night and wait several weeks to a few months before hitting the area again. Time is on your side and there is no shortage of targets. Wear the opposition down slowly.

Some billboarders favor the crosscut-type saws used by loggers of old. Others use a D-frame (bow) saw commonly found in hardware stores. If you use this type, be sure to carry one or more spare blades. An axe can be used to notch the poles on the side of the intended fall, but be careful of the noise, especially if there are houses nearby.

Safety

Safety in billboarding is of utmost importance. Think of the sign as a giant fly-swatter and yourself as the bug. Get the picture? Never stand in the area where a sign can fall (front or back). Walk outside of this danger zone. Don't take short-cuts. Watch a sign closely the entire time you are cutting. Leave the outermost poles for last. Always have an escape route planned if the sign shows evidence of falling prematurely.

Sawdust can get in your eyes and prove irritating. A good pair of safety goggles, available at hardware stores, can eliminate this problem. They are essential for contact lens wearers. Remember that goggles are reflective. Always pull them off your face before looking at passing cars.

Sign-Cutting

Use the drop and pickup technique described in **Basic Security** in the **Security** chapter to get to the target sign.

When sawing, duck down while cars pass if they can see you in the periphery of their headlights. Stop periodically to listen for any indication of discovery.

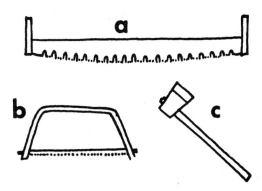

Tools of the trade: A) crosscut saw B) D-frame or bow saw C) axe

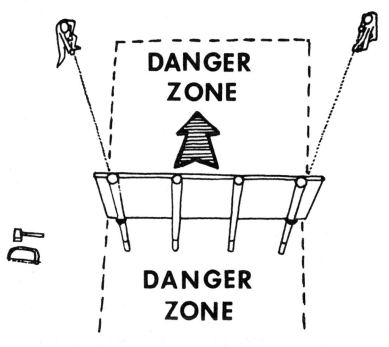

DANGER ZONE

DANGER ZONE

Felling with ropes; stay well outside the danger zone.

Felling is accomplished by pushing on the outermost poles, aided sometimes with ropes. See the illustrations for techniques on use of the rope. Use this rope(s) only for monkeywrenching since it may have to be abandoned if your work is disrupted — you don't want it accumulating fibers, dirt and oil stains that can link it with your home or workplace. Store it in a plastic trash bag between jobs.

Dropping a billboard face-up will allow you to inflict additional damage by spray-painting across the front of the advertisement.

Sign companies are adding protective metal strips to the sides of wooden poles to prevent cutting. Carry a crowbar to remove these. Sometimes it's possible to dig some dirt away from around the base of each support and cut the wood below the protective metal.

Billboarding is dirty work. Evidence that will remain on your clothing includes bits of brush, dirt on boots and knees, and sawdust. If you wear dark coveralls, remove them before the pickup and wrap your tools in them. Deposit this bundle in a locked trunk or camper shell in case you are stopped by a curious policeman. After a night's work, clean off your boots and launder your clothes. Vacuum your car trunk,

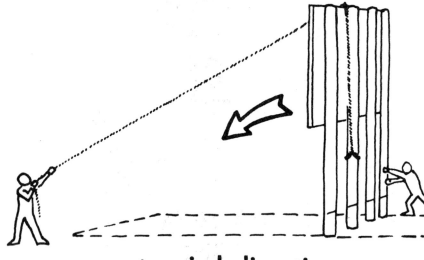

◄── wind direction ──►

Tie the rope high up on a pole and throw the remainder over the top (you may have to weight the end with a rock). Make sure the rope is long enough to keep you out of the danger zone

226

seats and floor carpets. Drop the vacuum cleaner bag in a dumpster or public trash can, never in your home trash.

Metal Posts

There is a definite trend towards all-metal posts, no doubt partly in response to the popularity of billboard monkeywrenching. While the smaller ones could probably be felled by a skilled team using a cutting torch, security problems would make this method extremely hazardous. The larger ones, which have a single tubular steel post sometimes several feet in diameter, are simply not practical for felling.

These billboards are susceptible to other forms of monkeywrenching, such as paint bombs and slogan alteration (described later). In addition, most large billboards are lighted at night, and there may be an electric meter and one or more electrical boxes affixed to one of the posts. The meter and boxes can be smashed with a large rock or sledge (stand back and be careful not to electrocute yourself).

It has been suggested that hollow, tubular-metal billboard posts could be rusted out with acid. Muriatic acid (an impure form of hydrochloric acid sometimes used as a swimming pool cleaner) and battery acid (sulfuric) have both been suggested. A clay dam could be constructed around the post to contain the acid, or a hole could be drilled into the post and the acid poured in. This technique has not been field tested, as far as we know. The use of a charge of thermite (a mixture of aluminum filings and iron oxide, which burns at an extremely high temperature), contained in a clay dam around the post, has also been suggested.

Other Targets

The headquarters of sign companies, located in every urban area, provide another source of targets. Additional techniques discussed in **ECODEFENSE** may prove suitable for making your point at these locations.

You might also plan action against the businesses that buy the billboard advertising space. Give them a warning, by phone, several months in advance. When the deadline passes and no remedial action is evident, bide your time since this will be their time of greatest vigilance. Do not contact them by phone again since they might tape record a second call or attempt to trace it. Wait them out and strike a few months later. A variety of actions, ranging from egg-throwing at a billboard-utilizing new car dealer's latest models to lock-jamming might discourage an advertiser from using the eyesores that make our highways unsafe.

Chainsaws

The use of chainsaws for billboarding is usually too dangerous due to the incredible racket that they make. Nonetheless, extremely remote locations, such as a sign miles from the nearest dwelling, and masking weather conditions, like wind blowing strongly or heavy rainfall, have brought out sign-cutters armed with these labor-saving devices. One must be particularly alert for passing cars when using a chainsaw.

Safety is the primary consideration with chainsaws, regardless of their use. Before using one to fell a sign, you should be able to operate it safely blindfolded, since the dark of the night adds to the danger. This is not a tool for novices. You should wear a safety helmet, goggles, heavy gloves and steel-toed boots.

Your first cut removes a wedge of wood from the side towards which you want the sign to fall. Repeat this on all poles, always starting in the center and working out to the ends. The third "felling" cut is made as shown in the illustration. Don't cut through the "hinge" of wood between the two cuts. Always cut the outer poles last because they will support the sign while you work. You should also consider wearing high-quality ear protectors to prevent the whine of the saw from deadening your ability to detect suspicious sounds. Simply remove them during security pauses to insure that your work is still undetected.

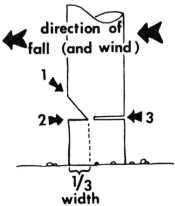

Chainsaw felling; note sequence of cuts.

FIELD NOTES

*Axes are the least desirable billboarding tools. Sometimes microscopic marks left on the wood can be matched to a specific axe in the possession of a suspect. Saw marks, on the other hand, are usually impossible to match up. Like files and grinding wheels, their surfaces are constantly changing, and so are the marks they leave.

BILLBOARD TRASHING

Billboards and other targets can be "painted" by the following simple method:

From a large paint supply store or hardware store, buy a gallon of a common brand of oil-based house paint and a gallon of paint thinner. Select a light color for dark targets and vice versa. From a grocery store buy several pairs of latex gloves and the thinnest sandwich-type plastic bags you can find (again, a major name brand). From the dumpster in back of the grocery store or a liquor store, get a cardboard box that contains a cardboard divider (used for separating glass jars of food or bottles of liquor).

Find a secure location to prepare your "paint bags." An outdoor location allows a little sloppiness in the preparation. If you are working indoors, spread a thick layer of newspaper about your work area. Dispose of the newspaper and incriminating paint spots by burning them or dropping them in a dumpster in back of a business.

In an empty milk carton or similar disposable container, mix a 50/50 batch of paint and thinner. Thinning the paint assures maximum spatter. Don your plastic gloves and open the box of sandwich bags. Lay out several for filling. Use a piece of heavy paper to improvise a funnel and pour the paint into the first bag. Do not fill it more than one quarter to one third full. Carefully tie the top shut, leaving as little air in the bag as possible. Do not use the twist-ties that come with some bags since the wire inside them can easily poke a hole in the thin bags.

Line the inside of the cardboard box with a plastic trash bag or two and re-insert the cardboard divider. Make sure the plastic bags have only been touched with gloved hands (the same goes for the box and divider — all of these surfaces are great for fingerprints). The plastic liner will keep a leaky bag from running all over you or your car.

Carefully insert the paint bag into one of the segments of the divider. The cardboard divider keeps the bags from sloshing around and makes them easy to retrieve when the time comes.

Repeat the above procedures until you have as many paint bags as you need, with a couple to spare.

These bags can be used to spatter billboards on saw-proof steel legs. Be sure to throw them at an angle from the side so that the spatter goes away from you, rather than splashing back on you. These bags can also be used to decorate vehicles, buildings, and even interiors (if you remember to toss a good, heavy rock through the window first).

At your earliest opportunity, check your skin, hair and clothes to make sure that there is no incriminating paint on your person. Keep a small can of paint thinner and some rags on hand just in case.

FIELD NOTES

* Screw-lid small bottles (like those for Mickey's Malt Liquor) can also be used for paint "bombs." Keep in mind that greater force is needed to break these than for the paint bags. Don't forget about possible fingerprints on the bottle and the lid.

* Glass Christmas tree ornaments make very good paint bombs which break easily. Remove the base, pour in paint and seal with duct tape. *Fingerprints!*

* Eggs are also very effective paint bombs. Take one large raw egg. With a needle, drill a hole in the top of the egg, gently breaking away a small amount of shell. Insert the needle and stir up the yolk and white. Poke another hole in the same end of the egg, about an inch from the first hole. Blow through the second hole so that the yolk and white come out the first hole. Have an omelette! Pour your paint/thinner mixture into a thin-nozzled, screw-top bottle (such as catsup comes in at restaurants). Seal the second hole in the egg with a pasty mixture of flour and water, or candle wax. Pour in the paint through the first hole and seal it. You now have a perfect-sized, semi-biodegradable missile. (*Editor's note: Thanks to BUGA UP in Sydney, Australia, for this technique.*)

*Another proven spattering technique involves "borrowing" a pressurized water-type fire extinguisher from a business or public building. Empty out the contents and relieve all of the pressure inside. Next, open the top and use a funnel to pour in a well-stirred 50/50 blend of paint and thinner or the preferred water and acrylic-type house paint. Pressurize the extinguisher secretly at a gas station; watch the pressure gauge to know when to stop. Use this spray gun to deface billboard ads. Do not attempt to cover the sign face, but make the most of your paint. Clean the extinguisher out after each use or it will clog up.

*When using either the sprayer or paint bags, be sure to wear grubby clothes (Goodwill is a good source of cheap clothes) or inexpensive coveralls, since you will occasionally get spattered with paint. Keep your hair pulled under a hat to keep out paint. A dark, wide-brimmed hat can provide further splash protection.

BILLBOARD REVISION

Even more effective than felling, burning or spattering billboards is *revising* them. A group in Sydney, Australia, BUGA UP (Billboard Utilizing Graffitists Against Unhealthy Promotions) has turned the revision of billboards into a major campaign. The following material is taken (slightly revised) from their 1981 Spring Catalogue (you can write them at BUGA UP, Box 78, Wentworth Bldg, University of Sydney Union, 2006, Sydney, NSW, AUSTRALIA).

Billboard graffiti is so simple you can organize it around just about anything. Even if you only paint one billboard a week, you'll be costing the corporate pushers between $500 and $5000 per year, depending on your thoroughness. It's a sad fact, but we've learned through long experience that money is the only language billboard advertising companies understand. Nothing will get those ads down faster than if their profits are reduced by escalating maintenance costs.

But even more important than this financial factor is the effect that the revised ad will have on those who read it.

First, select a billboard that 1) advertises a product from a notorious eco-raper (ORV's, for example), or 2) lends itself well to being transformed into an environmental message.

Purchase your can(s) of spray paint as discussed in the section on spray painting. For billboards, black and chrome are the most versatile colors, but red, blue, purple, and white are also effective on particular billboards.

Try to break down the power of the billboard ad by *answering* it, looking at the space available and the way in which the words and images lend themselves to addition, alteration or comment. Humor is extremely effective in exposing the advertiser's real intentions — turning the ad's message back on itself. (Be sure to avoid spelling mistakes!)

If the offending billboard proves too high to reach, you can either get a ladder (which isn't particularly convenient) or build a spray can extension rod:

Obtain a broom handle or another solid, strong but lightweight wooden pole (see illustration, #1). At one end, cut out a wedge, half the width of the pole. Fit a flat metal bar to the remaining wood (#2). About one foot from this bar (or the height of your spray can), attach a support clamp on which the can will rest (#3). Fit an angle bracket on each side of the pole, about 8 inches from the end (#4). The spray can should fit between these brackets. Tie a length of plastic coated wire to the flat metal bar (#2) and feed it through a hole in the support clamp (#3) and screw eyes attached the length of the pole (#5). This wire, when pulled, will press down the nozzle of the spray can and paint will spray out. An optional extra is the roll-top of a deodorant bottle, fitted to the support clamp (#6). This will help maintain an even distance between the spray can and billboard. You may have to experiment a bit to get the right measurements to fit a can of spray paint.

Although these spray paint can extension rods are clumsy to use at first, with practice they become very effective.

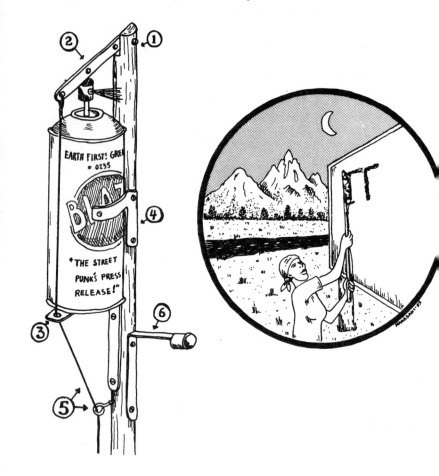

BILLBOARD BURNING

It is important to remove billboards. It is also important not to get caught (so we can remove more billboards). I have always felt that burning billboards (particularly in desert situations) is most effective. But it is somewhat "revealing" when a 50 foot high sign explodes in front of your very eyes, and those of who knows who else, lighting up everything around for half a mile. But there is a solution.

SCORE hair cream and swimming pool cleaner. I'm completely serious. My friend Oscar explained it to me. Now I will tell you. Here are the ingredients you will need:

1 envelope
1 tube *SCORE* hairdressing
1 canister "HTH dry chlorinator" (accept no substitutes).

Squirt about one and one-half inches of *SCORE* gel in one end of the envelope. In the other end, sprinkle about 2 tablespoons of HTH (It's granulated chlorine and will also clear up your sinuses if you get too close). Now, fold the envelope in the middle so the contents can't mix . . . yet.

Go forth into the night and find a billboard that particularly deserves cremation. Liberally douse the posts with gasoline. Now, it is time for the envelope. Unfold it and let the HTH mix with the *SCORE*. In fact, mush it up real good with your fingers (on the **outside** of the envelope, you idiot). Place the package at the base of the soaked post, get in your truck and drive away.

Four to five minutes later, about the time you're saying, "Yes, a pitcher of Bud, please," the envelope will start to smoke and hiss and produce a horrid, acrid aroma (air pollution) followed by intense heat and . . . Eureka! . . . spontaneous combustion. The flames race up the post spreading rapidly in the dry desert heat.

The next day you drive by and chuckle. But a word of warning: practice with this stuff first. It takes a while to get the right mixture. If it's not just right, it may simply smoke a lot. Remember, practice makes perfect.

—the Head of Joaquin

FIELD NOTES
*This delayed-action fire starter can be used for burning things other than billboards, too. Check the article on burning heavy machinery.

*Practice and experimentation are essential with this technique. In some tests, the "starter" ignited not much over 30 seconds after mixing. Even such a short time might give someone a chance to get far enough away from the target to avoid being seen, however.

*The active ingredient of "HTH dry chlorinator" is calcium hypochlorite. Other brands containing this ingredient may work; test them first.

SMOKEY THE BEAR CHAINSAW LETTER

Most Americans do not realize that commercial logging takes place in *their* National Forests. They believe that the Forest Service protects the Forest instead of destroying it. The Smokey the Bear Chainsaw Letter is designed to educate the average National Forest campground user about what is really happening on their National Forests.

These 8½ by 11″ posters (see illustration) can be quickly stapled or tacked to the bulletin boards in Forest Service campgrounds, picnic areas, trailheads, ranger stations, etc.

Rest assured that they infuriate Freddie timber beasts. In fact, when we first started using them, the Forest Service sent out a memo nationally to all their offices inquiring where they were coming from.

Of course you should be careful in putting these up, since the Forest Service would be more than happy to give someone a ticket for "defacing government property" for this heinous crime.

Some particularly nasty wilderness fanatics keep a box of "Smokeys" and a staple gun in their vehicle at all times and strike at every Freddie bulletin board they see.

If you would like a high-quality copy of the Smokey the Bear Chainsaw Letter that is suitable for making numerous copies at your friendly neighborhood self-service photocopy center, send a self-addressed, stamped envelope to Earth First!, POB 5871, Tucson, AZ 85703, and one will be sent to you *free*.

FIELD NOTES

Using staples or tacks to post your Smokey letters (or other message) to bulletin boards makes it all too easy for zealous Freddies to remove them. An alternative method is to coat the back of the paper using a can of permanent spray mount (available from art supply houses). Besides being an effective means of attaching flyers to signboards, walls and the like, materials so attached are most difficult to remove.

BE CAREFUL WITH CHAIN SAWS

ONLY YOU CAN PREVENT CLEAR CUTS!

Printed on 100% recycled paper-
to help protect the environment

CORRECTING
FOREST SERVICE SIGNS

This is for all of you frustrated artists who drive by the big "Land of Many Uses" signs and get pissed off because you know what the Forest Circus really means by that. Here is a way of making the signs more accurate.

You will need a sheet of 1/4″ plywood (other thicknesses will do, but they're heavier), some yellow paint (oil based), nails and glue. You will also need a router to engrave the lettering, and a saber saw to cut out the curves.

I assume that all of the signs have standard dimensions, but you should measure the sign you wish to modify, as some dimensions, especially those for the bolt holes, may be different.

Using the plan, lay out and cut the (replacement) bottom of the sign. It will be in two pieces, since most plywood is only 8 feet long. Paint it with a yellow paint as close to the Forest Service color as possible. Then, lay out the lettering from the plan, and use the router to engrave it into the wood. Make the letters in the same style as the Forest Service lettering so it will look as much like the original as possible. Use a drill or a hole saw to put two 1-1/2″ diameter holes in the board. These will accomodate the bolts which stick out of the existing sign. After the sign is finished, transport it as inconspicuously as possible to your target sign. Coat the back with glue. To hold it in place while the glue dries, use nails, preferably finishing nails. The corrected sign may not fit perfectly, but driving by at 60 mph, who will notice? Most people probably won't even notice your correction! (Except you and me, of course.)

Have fun with this. I hope to see corrected and accurate Forest Service signs as I travel. —*The Mad Engineer*

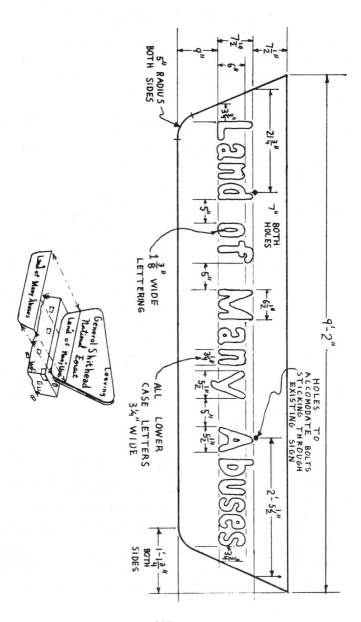

237

SILENT AGITATORS

Earth First! borrowed this tool from the Industrial Workers of the World (the Wobblies). "Silent Agitators" were merely little stickers that a Wob could stick up on a wall or on a piece of machinery in a plant. Other workers and the management would then know that the IWW was present and watching.

Earth First! Silent Agitators come in two varieties (see illustration) and have proved to be very popular. The "Coors" agitators are ideal for placement in the restrooms of bars that serve Rocky Mountain Mouse Piss, and they educate other beer drinkers about the demented politics of the Coors outfit.

The other agitators, featuring the Earth First! "fist" logo can be placed anywhere you want to leave a message that the rape of Earth will be resisted. They have proved particularly effective in Forest Service offices and a few have even been found in police paddy wagons and jails. During the Bald Mountain road blockade in Oregon, silent agitators were a constant source of psychological warfare against Freddie bureaucrats. The District Ranger finally began locking the restroom in the District office because he was tired of having to look at a silent agitator reading "No Compromise in Defense of Mother Earth" every time he took a leak. Forest Service personnel had to get the key to the bathroom from him and he would check afterwards to make sure nothing had been stuck on the wall.

The Fist Silent Agitators come thirty to a sheet and may be purchased for $1.25 a sheet postpaid from Earth First!, POB 5871, Tucson, AZ 85703. The Coors Silent Agitators are ten for $1.25 postpaid and can be purchased from the same address.

Some specialty Silent Agitators have also been printed. Be creative and have some printed for your particular issue.

Coors is Anti-Earth
Coors is Anti-Women
Coors is Anti-Labor
AND IT TASTES AWFUL!
BOYCOTT COORS
EARTH FIRST! POB 235, ELY, NV 89301

SPRAY PAINT

It has been said that the freedom of the press belongs to the man who owns one. In this day and age the press is owned by the corporations and access to it is limited by them to sanitized viewpoints. No city newspaper is going to present true alternative ideas of "no-growth" or biocentrism, or those opinions questioning control by the corporations. Fortunately, a can of spray paint and a little boldness gives anyone a press release that can reach thousands of people.

The limitation of spray paint is that you must reduce complex ideas to a few simple words: a slogan.

In selecting a slogan, you should be brief and to the point. Express a complete idea in two to four words. Make your best slogan your hallmark and use it often.

More complex messages may be your only way of being quoted in the media (which likely will be staunchly opposed to your illegal actions). Nonetheless, these longer spray painted messages are secondary to your major slogan.

The use of initials, such as the initials of a clandestine organization, can also convey a strong message of resistance. First, however, they must be presented repeatedly with the full name spelled out until people and the media begin to make the association. The single letter "V" (for Victory), for example, was used by the French Resistance during the Nazi occupation in WWII. It was quick and easy to paint (and therefore safer) and carried a complete message: "RESIST!"

Slogans and programs can be presented through flyers and small signs, but this requires secure access to printing or photocopying equipment, and will reach only a small audience. Bumperstickers are difficult to apply without leaving fingerprints (you must wear gloves *every time* you handle them) and are not easily manufactured.

The slogan hastily painted on a wall in full view of auto traffic on a busy thoroughfare, however, is the poor man's way of reaching a wider audience.

Your sloganeering operations should be as carefully planned and executed as any other type of clandestine endeavor (see the section on **Security**). Do not spray paint walls belonging to private individuals since this will unjustly aggravate them. There are plenty of "public" walls to choose from to use as your "newspaper." (In certain cases, of course, you may want to spray paint walls belonging to particular individuals or corporations.)

Select a common brand of spray paint that can be purchased through any number of retail stores or large discount houses. Shop at different places — spread your business around! Look for the inexpensive plastic pistol-grip handles that can be mounted on any can of spray paint. These insure that the paint always sprays in the direction which you want (not towards you!), even on the darkest night. A pouch worn on the belt is a good "hands-free" way of carrying it into the field.

If the target wall is in a busy location, the painter should be accompanied by at least one lookout. In quieter, or more rural locations, a painting team can consist of the painter and a driver who will deliver her to the target area and retrieve her later (in five minutes, say). Rarely is it safe to just stop the car and go to work. A half-finished slogan and a fast retreating car can lead you into considerable trouble. A lot of novice sign painters suffer from the jitters and are responsible for the hasty, illegible scrawls you see on many walls. The person chosen for the job must have the presence of mind to do a neat job.

After a while, it will be easy for the police to recognize the "hand" of a single sloganeer. It's a good idea to vary the look of your work to make it appear that your slogan is being used by many people and represents a broad constituency. Switch from all capitals to all lower case, then to a blend of the two. Change painters randomly since everyone will do it a little differently. Change color now and then.

A planned program of controlled variation can give the appearance of several groups at work. One area may have slogans only in black, another in red or brown. One painter will paint slogans in one part of town, another in a different part. The slogans themselves can be changed and attributed to fictitious organizations.

Radio communications via portable and mobile CB units can greatly aid in coordinating sloganeering efforts.

After a while, the opposition will discover that industrial strength paint removers will remove paint even from porous cement block walls. Sloganeering again on the same target can be a good psychological warfare tactic, but the danger increases accordingly and must be considered.

Sloganeering is as dangerous as any other form of ecotage but should not be approached too timidly. Anyone can paint a few small slogans on out-of-the-way walls or signs. The opposition will take you far more seriously, though, if your choice of targets clearly indicates boldness and competence.

FIELD NOTES

* Thompson's Water Seal spread over your spray-painted slogan may render it more resistant to industrial strength paint removers. Using it, of course, complicates and lengthens the job, thereby making it more dangerous.

STENCILS

A stencil can be very useful to the monkeywrencher for spray painting small slogans or logos in certain places — for example, an anti-cow message on the ubiquitous "open range" or "cattle guard" highway signs. Several groups made stencils which spelled "Watt" during his tenure as Secretary of the Interior and sprayed stop signs with them. "MX" stencils were also used in the Great Basin during the period that the racetrack deployment mode was being promoted there. In some Great Basin towns, every stop sign said "Stop MX."

Before making your stencil, visualize what you want to say (or the logo you want to use — say, a green fist), where you want to paint your message, how large it should be, etc. Linoleum is probably the best material from which to make a stencil. You can buy linoleum in various thicknesses, lengths and widths at building supply, hardware, or floor covering stores. Allow several inches of border around the cut-out message or logo on your piece of linoleum for sturdiness and to provide room to hold it so you won't spray paint your hands (or your partner's hands) while holding the stencil up to your target. (If you're using red paint, you can literally get caught red-handed this way!).

We've found that the soft, somewhat-pliable-but-somewhat-inflexible 1/16 inch thick counter top material with an unbroken surface works the best. It's comparatively easy to cut, but substantial enough to lay flat against your target — which is important if you wish to leave a well-defined spray paint image. When selecting your vinyl or linoleum material, try to visualize cutting holes into it with a utility knife and then being able to hold it up vertically against something without it drooping.

Cutting

On the rougher side of your material, sketch out your message or logo with a pencil and ruler, compass, protractor or whatever aids you need. Don't get too elaborate unless you want to spend more than a couple of hours cutting it out. Remember that any line that *encloses* a space, will cause that space to fall out, thereby leaving a hole in the stencil. Narrow "tabs" must be left for parts of certain letters and numbers (A, B, D, O, P, Q, R, 6, 8, and 9, for example). You can buy pre-made stencil letters to give you an idea or to use as a guide on making your stencil.

The actual cutting takes some concentration and time. With a good utility knife, carefully cut at a 90 degree angle along your lines firmly and gently. Start out slowly, even though it might seem like it will take forever to cut out the entire slogan. As you gain practice, the cutting will go much quicker and easier. A metal straight edge is useful for straight lines. Mis-cuts can be glued. With use, numerous layers of paint will help hold it all together, too.

Transport

After cutting out your stencil, you will need a way to protect it during transportation and to keep it from public view. It needs to be stored flat so that the longer, more narrow protrusions don't curl up. If this happens, it will cause the spray paint to blur. A good method is to sandwich the stencil between two pieces of 1/4" plywood. It is also wise to place the slick side of another similar sized sheet of linoleum next to the painted side of your stencil. If you don't do this, your stencil can stick to the plywood (even though the paint feels dry, it may not be) and you will have a horrible mess the next time you try to extract your stencil for use. Even with the extra sheet of linoleum or vinyl, you should always try to let your stencil completely dry before placing it against anything. This whole assemblage can be stashed in a vehicle and it will be safe from damage and public view. With proper use and storage, your stencil should last for hundreds of applications.

Painting

High quality, quick drying lacquer or enamel spray paint is the best to use with a stencil. Gloss white is the all-around most versatile and visible color, although other colors can be useful under the proper circumstances.

You should take the standard security measures, of course. Be particularly careful about fingerprints — you can easily leave them when working with spray paint. Wear gloves while using the stencil and for touching whatever you are painting.

With your stencil completed, there's nothing left to do but use your imagination. Go out and leave your message wherever appropriate.

THE TRAIL OF RISING
AND FALLING BIRDS

This is an account of one moment in an extended message-journey . . . a trail of art through the wilderness: wilderness, as original human nativity coerced by technographic cultural patterns; art, as it exists in one's complete spectrum of sensibilities from naive joy to educated rage; trail, as choice of direction; journey, as the process of forming a covenant of deliverance from Megaloization — the last stage in complete technography, immediately preceding which humanity will have its final opportunity to choose between eternal dehumanization and sweeping reformulations.

I arrived in Moab, Utah, on May 22, 1983, at 5:57 PM, with art and birds on my mind. Birds are the most universal symbol of the human spirit and man's bond with nature; they are environmental litmus and sense of harmless freedom. Art can serve as victimless weapon in defense of your beliefs. I was looking for maps and updated literature on the proposed canyonlands nuclear waste repository.

My rattletrap stationwagon was squirting green stuff from the heater hose and the transmission sounded like a rice grinder from Moose Jaw. I hadn't been to this neck of the woods for ten years and I couldn't help noticing that Moab had not become Salt Lake City as was promised in the boomdays of 1973. (But this goodbye-uranium slump will soon end, now that China and Japan have been suckered into bailing out the avarice and greed of our Czarist-family uranium investors.) I needed someone to talk to.

A prankster rockhound said I could find environmentalists across the street at the Poplar Place, infamous guzzle-hole to rafters and semi-solar types who like shouting. I sat for hours looking at maps while everyone around me looked at me like I was a fed. I learned, from two people who came over to investigate me, that around here no one says "nuclear waste repository." It's referred to as "the controversy," taboo-like as though the topic has been slurped up by an alien flying machine. "We burned out on that six months ago." "I'm just trying to get it together to live."

I spent two more days in Moab at a severe loss for ambience, having my mechanical conveyance worked on, and worked on. Meanwhile, the only "controversy" literature to be found was at park service head-quarters, of all places. The ranger at the counter encouraged me to fill out their "controversy" questionnaire with an *opposed* view. That heartened me, but I couldn't resist looking her in the eye and stating that if they put a rad dump in the canyonlands I'd never again come within one-hundred miles of the place.

Riled up, I marched down the street and purchased a fresh gallon of white paint and a spanking new single-action, armor-piercing brush. I flashed back to my *1979 Environmental Artists At War (EAAW!) Calendar* . . . triangulation laser sculpture in the Grand Canyon that shoots down sonic-booming jet fighters, purchased by the Museum of Modern Art . . . microwave-emitting March of Damns mural in the Elk Ridge Cafe in Blanding that permanently euphorized every heavy equipment operator and developer within 200 miles . . . .

At sun-up the next morning, on May 25, I departed Moab and headed south to the Needles country and the proposed repository site at South Six-Shooter Peak in Indian Creek Valley. Utah-211 first enters the top of the valley at a canyon narrows, at the petroglyph site called Newspaper Rock. When standing on the ground at this cool, sheltered close in the cottonwoods on the stream guarded by the undeciphered images from the hands of ancients, you can sense this place has a message. I continued into the valley past the caretaking eyes of Dugout Ranch, then the walls suddenly opened into a vastness of monumental space and formations parading from the dream-time into the physical reality of unspoiled land . . . Indian Creek Valley.

Halfway across the infinite valley, I met Six-Shooter Peak, heir-apparent to national radiation forever. I stopped at the entrance to Davis Valley road, adjacent to the peak in whose bosom the defiling material would be implanted. Technology has no wisdom. Technology is nothing more than ceasing to be nature. Dehumanization is the process of going away from nature toward dependent technologies. *Koyaanqatsi!* . . . life out of balance . . . a state of mind that calls for another way of life! This is landscape in utter distress, but no form of government or culture is inevitable.

In numbed mood and with solemn speed I got out my paint and brush. Something must be done for the humanization of this valley, to de-objectivize it from mere commodity. So I stepped onto the highway and painted a 22-foot long hex-on-the-inhumans-who-threaten-this-place. A falling man-bird: an infertile hybrid that no god would conceive; one who confuses science with nature and art. Jinx on Nuclear Waste

Repository! Jinx on Nuclear Waste Repository!

When someone dies we grieve because their mind is lost forever. If this valley is defiled we will grieve because its soul will have been lost forever . . . one more step toward Technocalypse, wholly devoid of redeeming or divine purpose.

I camped nearby, and at first light the next morning I returned to the site of the painting to photograph it, and to give the peak an understanding wink and well-earned salute, and then I turned to leave. As I exited the valley I stopped once more at Newspaper Rock, and I realized the message of the petroglyphs . . . "you stand in the portal to a religious place, if you have learned to see." This spot is the natural and intelligible entrance to the Canyonlands National Park. This is a message place.

Since his experience at Canyonlands in 1983, artist Lee Nading has traveled the highways and backroads of America leaving a "Trail of Rising and Falling Birds." A sampler of his work is presented here. If one of his Rising or Falling Birds is in your area, keep it repainted.

Lee Nading's jinx at Glen Canyon Damn.

Lee Nading's jinx on the Canyonlands Nuke Dump.

CHAPTER 9

SECURITY

It is important not to get caught. The information in this chapter comes from experienced monkeywrenchers who have studied police science. Don't take this section of **ECODEFENSE** lightly. It may be the most important chapter to *you* in this entire book.

There may be some seeming redundancy here. That is deliberate. There are rules of security so important that we want to hammer them home so that they become second nature to the serious ecodefender. As monkeywrenching becomes a more serious threat to the greedheads ravishing Earth for a few greasy bucks, they will force law enforcement agencies to crack down on Earth defenders. You can stay free and effective, by carefully keeping security uppermost in your mind.

Since the publication of the first edition of **ECODEFENSE**, at least two prominent monkeywrenchers have been caught and sent to jail. One, Howie Wolke, received six months in a tiny cell for pulling up survey stakes. He has publicly stated that he was caught because he was careless and let his security down. Don't follow his example to the slammer.

The Forest Service has also begun special anti-monkeywrenching training for their law enforcement specialists. Park Service and Forest Service cops have been identified at Earth First! meetings. They are taking monkeywrenching very seriously. But they can't touch you if you rigorously practice the security precautions in this chapter. It is your carelessness that will put you in jail.

Because of the crucial need for good security practices by monkey-wrenchers, we have expanded and updated the material in this chapter. Read it. Study it. Make it second nature — just like buckling up your seat belt when you get into your car.

BASIC SECURITY

Target Selection

Most activities worthy of monkeywrenching consist of a long chain of actions ranging from the corporate boardroom or government office to actual field operations or activities. Before selecting a target for monkeywrenching, one should gather as much information as possible on this "chain of command." Research may reveal better targets, or point to the most vulnerable link in the "chain." Newspapers and magazines, as well as physical surveillance of buildings, storage areas, work sites, etc., will help in the selection of targets.

Proper intelligence gathering efforts will insure fairness. One should not lash out blindly at targets without first making an effort to understand the overall situation. Make sure that an action is fully warranted and well deserved. There is a difference between monkeywrenching and plain vandalism.

Most damaging projects on public lands are more or less analyzed in public documents by the managing agency (Forest Service, Bureau of Land Management, etc.). These documents — environmental analysis reports (EA's), environmental impact statements (EIS's), land management plans, timber plans, etc. — are available free to the interested public and have fairly detailed information, including maps, on offending projects. Merely by contacting the National Forest or BLM District office in question, you can get on a mailing list to receive such reports.

Of course, the serious monkeywrencher may not want to be on such a mailing list due to security considerations. If possible, have a trusted friend, who does not plan to engage in monkeywrenching, get on the mailing list and then give the documents to you for your use. Perhaps you have a trusted contact in an environmental group who gets such documents and who can pass them on to you. Maybe you even have a contact within one of the offending government agencies — if this is the case, make sure it is someone you can trust, and for added security, *never, never* let them know what you plan to do with the information. If you do not wish to involve friends or acquaintances, however indirectly, you might receive the information from the agency under an assumed name at a post office box or addressed to your alias in care of one of the private mailing services found in big cities which provide confidential forwarding of mail. Or you might even go to government offices in person, well in advance of intended "hits." If asked to fill out a request form, use a fictitious name and address (just don't forget the name you give them!). Before going into an office to request information, leave your wallet with your ID's in your car, so that you can honestly say, if asked, that you left it in your car. If they persist in asking for ID, you can tell them you'll go and get it, leave the building, and never go back. *Note: avoid going in person to request information which later might prove incriminating if you are likely to be recognized by anyone in the office.*

Much of the work done by Federal agencies is contracted out to private individuals and small businesses, generally on the basis of competitive bidding — examples of this include some survey work and timber stand exams. It is possible to obtain information about many such projects by getting on lists to receive announcements of projects as a potential bidder. Again, it may be best to have someone else get this information to protect your security.

Any method of obtaining timely information on environmentally destructive projects in the area of your interest is valid, so long as you do not compromise your security in the process. A great deal of useful information on potential targets for monkeywrenching can be obtained from newspapers and periodicals. Publications of environmental groups (including the *Earth First! Journal*) are obvious sources of such information, but don't forget trade and industry publications, either. Local newspapers are an excellent source of information on what sort of development is currently going on or planned — this goes for big-city dailies as well as rural weeklies. (The latter often report regularly on government timber sales, permits for oil and gas exploration, and local mining activities.) A good place to read a variety of publications without compromising your security is the periodical section of your public library.

If you are interested in more detailed information, such as the names of individuals owning a business or owning a particular piece of property, a little bit of investigative work in the library or at the county courthouse can usually produce results. City directories or business directories (such as Cole's or Polk's) may tell you who lives at a specific address or who owns a business. In most states, the office of Secretary of State usually maintains records of corporations that are incorporated in that state. You may be able to obtain copies of these records for a nominal fee. Finally, your city or county recorder has public records on deeds which show who owns what land or buildings. The tax assessor has public records of property taxes which also indicate ownership of all properties. Also, the "Grantor" and "Grantee" books record all real property transactions alphabetically by names. Anyone can ask to see this material.

Finally, mining claims on the public lands are a matter of public record. They are usually filed at the county courthouse, where they may be seen. (These records are also kept at the state level by the BLM.)

Planning

Thorough planning for every step of the operation and all feasible contingencies is what will keep you out of jail. Every team member must fully understand the work to be done, individual assignments, timetables, radio frequencies and codes, routes to and from the scene, etc.

You should prepare for the fact that the best of plans can be quickly disrupted by unforeseen events. How to cope with and adapt to such problems is the ultimate test of one's monkeywrenching abilities.

The target should be reconnoitered in advance. If an urban target, know the layout of *all* the roads you might use during your withdrawal. Otherwise, you might find yourself at the end of a dead-end street should you have to make a quick escape. If you are planning a night operation, familiarize yourself with the target *both* during daylight and nighttime. This is because visible landmarks will be severely limited at night, and because there may be specific security precautions (lighting, security guards) used only at night. If your operation is in remote country, it is essential that you know the location of all trails, roads and natural drainages in the vicinity, in case you have to make alternate escape plans.

If it becomes necessary to use written notes and maps in preparing for an operation, be sure to destroy all such paperwork *before* commencing the action. The best way to destroy paperwork is by burning. Indoors, paper can be burned in a fireplace. If no fireplace is present, it can be burned in a large pan or bucket (place under a kitchen stove hood exhaust or a bathroom fan). It may be preferable to burn such material outdoors in a shallow hole. Since intact ashes can be analyzed in the laboratory to reveal something of their contents, even ashes should be crushed and disposed of. Outdoors, grind up the ashes and bury them. Indoors, flush them down the toilet.

The Team

In selecting people for an operation, one should keep the number involved as small as possible while still providing enough bodies to get the job done. Although there are activities in which a lone monkey-wrencher can engage, it is the small group of two to five members that is most effective. The group provides mobility through a driver, security through a lookout, and the sympathy of a friendly ear to relieve the inevitable tension of the underground. Usually it is just too dangerous for an individual to engage in some act of sabotage and look over his/her shoulder at the same time. So begin your organized monkey-wrenching with a friend who shares your values. Start small, with the simplest plans and easiest targets, until you learn to function as a team. (If you do not have an entirely trustworthy partner, it is, of course, better to operate alone.)

Recruiting new team members begins with evaluating your close friends as prospects. Bear in mind, however, that not everyone is suited for this sort of activity. A monkeywrencher should be someone who can function well under stress, but no test has yet been devised to predetermine just who is likely to crack under stress and who is not. The persons doing the selecting simply have to use their best judgment. It is a good idea to avoid the faint-of-heart, the excessively paranoid and the not-quite-thoroughly committed. Avoid the casual acquaintance you only see at a protest rally, especially the ones who "talk tough" (such people may well be police spies or *agents provocateurs*). The use of such infiltrators is widespread, both here and abroad. In Britain the authorities have attempted to infiltrate anti-hunting groups, and have even set up sham groups of their own to stage violent acts to discredit their opponents. In the U.S., cases in which the FBI or other police agents have infiltrated radical groups and even encouraged or participated in criminal acts are too numerous to mention — the history of the anti-war and civil rights movements are replete with such stories.

The success or failure of law enforcement lies primarily with the informer, known in police circles as the "confidential informant" or "C.I." These individuals are usually "turned" after their own arrest and aid the police in exchange for favorable treatment. Such persons produce perhaps 90% of all criminal arrests. The best way to avoid the informer is to work only with close friends, ideally of many years' acquaintance. A tight-knit group of friends, loyal to each other and careful to minimize leaving evidence at the scene, is virtually impossible to penetrate and apprehend.

Throughout history, secret societies have reinforced group cohesion with the use of an oath for secrecy and loyalty. The oath of secrecy was so successful during the Luddite uprisings in early 19th-century

England that oath-swearing was made a capital offense! Although it is not necessary to have a formal initiation with a swearing-in ceremony, it is important that group members openly and directly declare their willingness to protect one another. Psychologically, the act of swearing loyalty is of far greater value than the mere assumption of the same. The memory of such a moment can provide an added ounce of strength under police interrogation (when most groups come unraveled).

Once you have singled out a prospective recruit, use casual conversations to gauge the depth of her/his commitment to defending Earth. If all goes well, you will next proceed to carefully introduce the topic of monkeywrenching into your conversations, perhaps with the aid of a news broadcast or newspaper story dealing with environmentalist sabotage. This will help to measure whether feelings about conventional law and order might override deeper moral concerns. At this stage, you must be very patient. Never rush a recruitment. It may take months to find out that a certain friend is simply not suitable as a team member.

If all goes well, you will eventually suggest doing a "job" together. Perhaps something simple like spray-painting slogans on the outside walls of an offending land rapist. Do not, under any circumstances, tell the potential recruit that you have had experience in such matters. If they get cold feet at the last moment and back out, they will still have no knowledge that can harm you.

Once your first hit is successfully completed, you are bound together by shared danger and experience, and you may consider introducing the new recruit to the team. If the recruit seems excessively paranoid or expresses some doubts during or after the first hit, wait until they have a bit more experience before introducing them to other team members. The ideal recruit is one who responds with excitement and enthusiasm to the rigors of direct action.

Insertion

The team will most likely be carried to the vicinity of the target in motor vehicles (see also the section on **Mountain Bicycles**). The vehicle could be a motorcycle, car or truck. Whatever vehicle is used, it should be ordinary looking, and lack anything that might be conspicuous — such as a special paint job, provocative bumper stickers, personalized license plates and the like.

On most operations, one should not stop directly in front of, park near, or repeatedly cruise past the target.

When exiting the vehicle, do not slam the car doors. Instead, one should push on the door until it partially latches. The driver can stop briefly after leaving the target area to close doors properly. In rural and suburban environments, it is generally best to drop off the team well away from the target and let them walk to it cross-country. In built-up areas, the drop is usually made closer to the target to avoid being stopped by police patrols when walking down city streets. The basic principle is to avoid having a casual passerby witness the drop and later report a description of you, your car, or your license plate.

Parking near the target is usually dangerous for much the same reason. After the drop, the driver should leave the area immediately and stay away until the agreed-upon time for pick-up. Keeping the vehicle moving in evening traffic on major streets or highways could well be the safest way for the driver to pass the time. If you choose to park, do so only in busy areas near restaurants or movie theaters where you will blend in with the crowd. Avoid operating in the early morning hours when traffic is so light as to make you stand out. The best time for urban operations is usually from nightfall to midnight.

In a rural or sparsely populated area, it may be more dangerous to drive after dark, and you will want to conceal the vehicle by parking it in the woods or on jeep trails adjacent to the highway. Have such a parking place selected beforehand so you do not have to suspiciously cruise around searching for a good place to park out of sight.

Withdrawal

When a team is dropped off, it has a designated length of time to finish its work and withdraw to the pick-up point. The location selected for the pick-up should usually be different from that of the drop, in case the drop was observed. Timing is important, and the driver must not have to rush and break speed limits to arrive on schedule. If the team does not make the first pick-up run, the driver will return at pre-determined intervals of fifteen minutes, a half-hour, or whatever.

If there are police in the area, both the team and driver will make for an alternate pickup point located a few blocks or a few miles away, and up to several hours later if necessary. If there is imminent danger from police, the team members will conceal their tools for later recovery and leave the area without anything incriminating on their persons.

After a successful pick-up, the vehicle should leave the area at normal speed. Once safely away, the team should stop briefly to put all tools or other incriminating items out of sight.

In order to avoid leaving tire tracks as evidence, the pick-up vehicle should not leave the paved surface of the road. Of course, this may not be avoidable in rural areas or on forest roads. If you are utilizing a parked vehicle, it may be possible to sweep away tracks (both human and vehicular) with a broom or with branches.

The duration of a "drop and pick-up" type of operation may be anywhere from a few minutes for an urban "hit" (such as the delivery of a bucket of raw sewage to a corporate office) to several hours or possibly even days for a complex action in the field, such as a major tree spiking or road destruction operation.

For recognition of the pick-up point, the team can mark the spot by setting a pre-determined object on the shoulder of the road (such as a discarded oil can or beer bottle). Permanent landmarks, such as bridges or culverts, or road signs and mileage posts, are better. The pick-up vehicle can carry an extra light, like a powerful flashlight, on the dashboard so that the team will recognize it on its approach run. Use the brakes as little as necessary, since these lights can be seen from a great distance. One can avoid too much use of the brakes by stopping more quickly and using the parking brake more. The serious monkeywrencher might consider vehicle modifications (see section on **Vehicle Modifications**).

Radio communications are extremely valuable to coordinate the pick-up, or to advise the driver to use the alternate pick-up location due to unforeseen troubles. (See section on **Radios** for appropriate equipment.) The alternate pick-up can be anywhere from a few hundred yards to a couple of miles from the primary pick-up point. Whatever the distance, it must be out of sight of the primary pick-up point, out of sight of the target, and preferably, on an entirely different road.

Night Operations

Begin by reviewing your plan and equipment. Leave any unnecessary items behind. Do not carry any ID, wallets, loose change, or anything else that might identify you or make unnecessary noise. If you are carrying a car key, use a safety pin to secure it to the inside of your pants pocket.

Before heading into the dark, allow your eyes to adjust to the dark. Five minutes in the dark without looking at bright lights will usually be the necessary minimum, but it's best to wait half an hour before entering a dangerous area. Any bright light can temporarily ruin one's night vision. If it becomes necessary to look into a lighted area or use a flashlight, cover one eye so as to retain some night vision in the other. Using a flashlight with a red lens filter will not damage your night vision, but you should be aware that even a red light will be visible from some distance away. When looking at something at night, do not stare directly at it. Everyone has a blind spot in the center of their field of vision. By keeping the eyes constantly moving, it is easier to see an object at night than it is by looking directly at it. Practice by taking walks at night. And eat your carrots!

Travel at a steady pace and avoid running in the dark. Lifting one's knees higher than normal when walking will reduce the chance of stumbling over rocks, roots and low branches. To avoid being hit in the eyes by low branches, extend one arm in front of your face and well ahead. This is a safe way of "feeling" your way in the dark. If you encounter a situation in which you *must* run, use the following method: Run at a slight crouch, focusing your attention on the ground just two to three steps in front of you. The crouching position keeps you from taking long strides, which is dangerously uncontrollable at night. Concentrating just a short distance ahead alerts you to the smallest hazards, which are usually the ones that will trip you. As always, keep one arm extended to protect your face. Practice moving at night without a flashlight before you find this necessary on an action.

The sense of hearing becomes much more important at night and will often reveal as much or more than the eyes will. Always pause for several minutes before entering a dangerous target area to listen for the footfalls of a guard or passerby. Make sure that your hat does not cover your ears, and cup your hands behind your ears to help pick up faint sounds. Putting one's ear to the ground won't help.

Communication between team members is best done with hand signals. Tapping someone on the shoulder and pointing in one direction can indicate possible danger sources. If you must talk, try to cup your hands over your friend's ear and whisper. Night bird sounds, like owl hoots, should be used as danger signals only, to avoid excessive use. In addition, whistles worn on a cord around the neck can provide emergency signaling when the team is spread out over a large area. All team members should be assigned numbers or fake names for emergency shouting at night.

Rules of Security

Limit each team member's knowledge of operations to only what they have a "need to know." You can't slip up and talk about something you don't know about. This will protect your associates as well as yourself.

Don't openly discuss your illegal activities on the telephone. Not even on payphones!

Try to avoid storing potentially incriminating tools, clothing, paint, etc. in your house or apartment. (This includes documents and maps of the project in question.) If possible, hide them in the woods or in a rented storage locker (rent one under an assumed name). If you must keep anything potentially incriminating at home, hide it well. Keep in mind that a remote corner of your property away from your house can be legally searched without a search warrant.

Destroy potentially incriminating materials:

Tools — Periodically dispose of all tools which leave a distinctive mark (pry bars, bolt and wire cutters, etc.), and replace them with similar items from a different manufacturer. Right after a particularly "heavy" job is a good time to dispose of tools, although it is by no means the only time you should take this precaution. Remember, the cost of replacing tools is far less than what a good lawyer would charge you for an hour of legal services. Tools may be disposed of in dumpsters, buried in remote rural locations, or dumped into a deep body of water.

Papers, maps and documents — Burn completely and crumble the ashes. The crushed ashes can be buried or flushed down the toilet.

Paint — Dispose of in dumpsters. (Avoid fingerprints on paint cans.) Don't neglect to dispose of rags or clothing that may carry paint spots.

Shoes and clothing — All clothing, including boots and shoes, should be laundered and cleaned as soon as possible after a job. This can help remove incriminating dirt, fibers, plant debris and the like. Pay particular attention to grease spots from heavy equipment. If in doubt, dispose of shoes and clothing. These items can be discarded in dumpsters, buried or burned, as appropriate. Be especially wary of shoes. A distinctive footprint often can be positively connected to the shoe or boot that produced it.

Don't worry about the cost of replacing tools, clothing and the like. Freedom is priceless.

After using a vehicle on a job, vacuum the floor and wipe off the seats to get rid of incriminating soil, grease, etc. Don't forget to clean under floor mats, the crack in the seat, etc. After vacuuming, dispose of the bag. If you've been driving on unpaved roads, a thorough washing of the vehicle's exterior is also advised. Don't neglect the underside of the vehicle, especially the wheel wells and inside of bumpers. A self-service, commercial car washing establishment is a good place to wash and vacuum your car. Incidentally, spreading a little mud on your license plate before an operation to prevent it from being read at night is a good idea, so long as you are operating in an area in which mud would not seem out of place. Use common sense, though — a muddy plate on an otherwise clean vehicle would probably *attract* suspicion.

Never carry anything incriminating with you if it is not essential.

After completing your mission, resist the temptation to carry out survey stakes, surveyors' flagging, stolen or damaged pieces of equipment, and the like. If you should be stopped and searched (whether by an actual law enforcement officer or by an irate miner, logger, stockman or whatever) such items would likely be legally admissible as evidence against you.

Always have a story prepared to tell the police if you're stopped in the target area. Keep it short and simple and avoid unnecessary details.

Operate with a small group of trusted friends, and never have more people on an operation than are absolutely necessary.

Consider assigning each member of the team a fictitious first name or number for operational use. Memorization of these *nommes de guerre* will take concentration and practice; otherwise, during the stress of an operation it will be too easy to revert to using real names. Never use your fictitious names in public when not on a mission.

It is wise to limit talking when on an operation. Practicing a few simple hand signals in advance is a good idea, at least if there will be enough light to see them during the operation.

Try to avoid the nights of the full or nearly-full moon. A quarter to half moon should ordinarily give enough light for night movement.

Don't keep a diary or other written records of illegal activities. Don't get drunk and shoot off your mouth down at the corner bar. Bragging has put more people in jail than any other factor.

If you are engaging in serious monkeywrenching, avoid overt political activism, rallies, demonstrations and the like. When the police begin looking for suspects, they will begin by consulting existing records of activists, especially those with records of arrests and convictions. These records are very detailed, never destroyed, and are available to any police agency requesting them. Investigative detectives will visit known "hangouts," attend workshops and demonstrations, and make "radical" statements to elicit invitations to clandestine circles. The head of the local Sierra Club chapter or another "respectable" environmental group may be questioned, and he/she may cooperate fully, even to the point of suggesting suspects. Keep a low profile.

Let knowledge be your greatest ally. Go to the public or university library and study police investigative techniques.

Avoid patterns. This is easier said than done. You will tend to establish patterns as to type of target, days of the week on which you are active, times at night at which you strike, etc. Police investigators will look for these patterns and can be surprisingly good at predicting one's moves. This can lead the unwary monkeywrencher into well-laid ambushes.

Make a conscious effort to keep your actions as random as security permits. Periodically lay low for awhile. If you have reason to suspect that the police are intensively investigating your activities or conducting stakeouts, cease all activity for a few months. Limited personnel and budget will force the authorities to assign their investigators to more pressing matters.

Time spent laying low is a good time to dispose of tools, intelligence files, and other possibly incriminating materials. Be clean as a whistle in the event that investigators get a lead on you or otherwise become suspicious enough to haul you in for questioning or obtain a warrant to search your home.

A final rule: Don't hurt anyone. Respect all life.

Avoiding Arrest

If you have been active in one area for any length of time, the police will consider baiting a trap to catch you. In setting a trap, the authorities will look for any patterns you may have inadvertently set. Perhaps you only work on certain nights. Perhaps you hit certain targets more than others. Perhaps your routes of approach and withdrawal to your targets are known. Monkeywrenchers have narrowly escaped from police traps on some occasions simply because they were silent and alert, while the opposition was bored with weeks of fruitless waiting. The best way to avoid traps is to hit your target *one time only,* but with maximum effectiveness.

Sometimes a trap will be baited by deliberately leaving heavy equipment temptingly parked along rural roads. In such a situation, chase cars will be carefully hidden in the area, often on back roads and dirt lanes, sometimes one on each side of the "bait" but a good distance away, ready to intercept suspect vehicles. If you see such a tempting target, be careful! Instead of striking immediately, scout the area carefully ahead of time, carrying nothing incriminating.

In cases where construction equipment has been successfully sabotaged repeatedly, the owners will often move it at night to a more public location, such as a roadside, to facilitate protection by police or private guards. Be sure to check for the vehicles of private security guards, which may be concealed among the pieces of heavy equipment.

Be aware that monkeywrenchers may run afoul of the law in a completely unexpected manner. Don't break the speed laws when going to and from an operation — you could fall victim to a speed trap or police radar. A simple rule to follow to prevent most routine traffic violations is to have the front seat passenger (i.e., the person in the "shotgun" seat) act as an observer and check on road hazards, and caution the driver if the latter's speed becomes excessive. If the driver is over-sensitive about this, he/she shouldn't be driving.

Another conventional law enforcement activity to which unwary monkeywrenchers could fall victim is the local game warden on the lookout for jacklighters or poachers. A frequent tactic used by game officers is to park on a hill which allows a long view of a road frequently used by poachers at night. Be aware of the type of vehicles used by the game officers in your vicinity (a drive by the local office of the Dept. of Fish and Game might help). If you are out on a job at night and think you have spotted a game officer in the vicinity, you had best scratch your operation and wait for another night. These men and women are providing a valuable service in fighting poaching and should be helped, not hindered or distracted. Remember, game officers are full-fledged law enforcement officers with all the power of the state behind them, and may enforce other laws besides game laws. Since they may stop you at night, you should never carry rifles, spotlights, or anything else that might make you look like a poacher when on a monkeywrenching operation.

Another thing to keep in mind is that every time a law enforcement officer stops to check any suspicious person or thing, a record is made of the event. Even if you are merely briefly stopped and then released, that record may later be used to place you near the scene of an illegal activity. If you should be stopped by a cop before you hit a target, *cancel the mission*. If stopped after you have already carried out an operation, go to special pains to destroy all evidence as soon as you arrive at a safe location.

FIELD NOTES

*Exposure to bright sunlight on the day before a mission can impair your night vision. Wear sunglasses in bright sunlight to prevent this.

CAMOUFLAGE

The importance of proper clothing should not be underestimated by monkeywrenchers. Bear in mind that what is ideal for one type of operation might not be best for another. Whether an operation is urban or rural, whether it is a day or night operation, what time of the year it takes place — all of these are factors that might dictate which type of clothing is best.

As a general rule, one should avoid the exotic and unusual. One should not stand out. Dress like the locals, be they construction workers, loggers or corporate executives. It may be necessary to blend in with the local scene to escape from the target area.

Camouflage may be of many types. In a wilderness operation (tree or road spiking, for example) it may be desirable to wear traditional, military-type camouflage clothing. There is no shortage of this type of clothing available. It ranges from expensive, tailored gear available from fancy sporting goods firms to used, genuine military uniforms sold by "war surplus" stores. Military camouflage comes in many patterns designed for different geographical regions, such as woodland pattern or desert pattern. The reader is advised to consult the specialized literature, such as military training manuals on the subject or how-to books for bowhunters (which also give instructions for using camo face paint).

For many operations military-type camouflage is not only unnecessary, but might actually make the monkeywrencher stand out as suspicious. In operations around construction sites or machinery, coveralls and a hard hat might be best. Even if someone were to observe a monkey-wrencher so attired, they might think that they belonged. Used coveralls can be purchased for a reasonable price at many linen supply companies. The serious monkeywrencher might purchase several pairs, in different colors.

Dark clothing is the rule for night work. Long sleeves protect the arms and cover light skin (visible on moonlit nights). Avoid too tight clothing that restricts movement, and too loose clothing that snags on branches, barbed wire and the like. Avoid nylon because of the loud swishing noise it makes. A good source of cheap clothing is second-hand and thrift stores, like Goodwill.

Clothes can leave minute fiber deposits as evidence, although this is rare in outside work. Still, because of this you should avoid unusual, exotic clothing, and should consider discarding clothing after a particularly "heavy" operation.

Light Reflections

Light reflections off the face are rarely a problem in nightwork. Still, if for certain jobs you feel that this could be a problem, tone down these bright spots by rubbing a little burnt cork across the forehead, on the cheekbones, on the top of the nose and on the point of the chin. Never spread the blacking all over the face — hitting the aforementioned high spots lightly is sufficient. This form of night camouflage is rarely used, mainly because it makes the user stand out, and anyone observing an individual so made up would almost certainly conclude that they were engaged in some illegal activity. In certain wilderness operations, however, it may even be beneficial to use camouflage face paint (available at sporting goods and bowhunter supply stores). Again, how-to books for bowhunters may be your best guide. Anyone using either of these techniques is advised to carry a couple of packets of moist towels (like "Wash 'N Dry"). These should be carried carefully safety-pinned into a pocket (make sure that the pin does not pierce the inside of the packet, or the towel will dry out). At the end of an operation these can be used for quick cleanup.

Footwear

Proper footwear is important. Remember, shoes and boots leave prints which may constitute valuable evidence. *Such prints do not produce leads on suspects, but they do constitute physical evidence that might be matched up later when other means produce a suspect.* Cheap tennis shoes that can be thrown away after a major job or series of minor hits are ideal. If it's not too awkward, one can buy shoes a couple of sizes too large and wear extra pairs of socks to fill them out. This will confuse the investigators who may photograph and/or take casts of footprints at the scene of the "crime." If it's possible to obtain shoes with smooth soles, do so. If you do not throw your monkeywrenching shoes away, at least do not wear them for any other purpose. Do not ever wear them around your home, since the dirt around your house and driveway will be the first place that the authorities will look for matching footprints.

For some operations, lightweight shoes will be impractical. For work in rough terrain or at night, where the danger of falls and sprains is real, sturdy boots are generally called for (though some people even backpack off-trail in light-weight running shoes — one possibility is to tape your ankles and wear running shoes for night or rough ground work). Since it may be costly to throw away boots after a "job," one might consider covering the boots with oversize socks (dark for night work). Carry several pairs if operating on hard or stony ground. Socks should be disposed of after an operation, since minute fibers will have been left as evidence. You could also make boot coverings out of heavy canvas.

Clothing

For night work, clothing should be dark. Long sleeves will cover light skin. If stealth is particularly desired, nylon and plastic clothing should be avoided, since it makes a "swishing" noise when one moves. Wool is quieter than cotton. However, woolen garments are particularly susceptible to leaving fibers behind. Brush, cactus, barbed wire fences, and even rough brick can snag clothing and cause the ecoteur to leave fibers. Clothing should not be too loose or baggy, as that increases the likelihood of snagging it on adjacent objects. Again, coveralls (dark) may be best, although "work" shirts and pants are probably adequate.

Used clothing stores such as those operated by Goodwill or the Salvation Army can be sources for cheap, throw-away clothing (don't set a pattern of frequently buying such items at one store and becoming known by the clerks). It is probably best to throw away clothing after a particularly heavy job, in case evidence in the form of fibers was left at the scene.

Gloves

Gloves are a must to avoid leaving fingerprints. Each type of glove has its own characteristics:

LEATHER — Good, highly durable and suited to general purposes. However, leather can leave distinct prints like fingerprints, especially if it becomes contaminated with oil or grease.

CLOTH — Not as durable as leather, but adequate for most work, and cheaper to buy. The low cost makes it practical to dispose of cloth gloves after an operation; a desirable thing to do. Cloth patterns can be left under the same conditions mentioned above for leather.

PLASTIC OR RUBBER — Usually good for light work only. They will make one's hands sweat. When disposing of this type of glove, one should keep in mind that the insides carry a perfect set of one's fingerprints. Burning them in a fire insures thorough destruction by melting.

Regardless of which type one uses, dispose of any manufacturer's labels before heading out. Make sure your gloves cover the entire palm, as any part of the palm can leave distinctive prints for investigators.

Headgear

Headgear is important both for keeping warm and as a disguise. Knitted wool watch caps are both commonplace and comfortable. Wide brimmed hats hang up on brush and tree limbs and should be avoided. Ski masks and bandannas can be used for disguise, but their use may constitute an additional violation of the law. *Do not lose your headgear at the scene of an action. It will contain samples of your hair.*

If you have long hair, tie it back. Ponytails and braids can be stuck down inside a coat.

Vehicle Camouflage

For lower visibility, paint your truck, van or whatever one color with a good automotive "semi-gloss" or flat paint. Good colors are white, yellow, orange, green or brown.

It's not a bad idea to install a CB antenna or two, even if you don't have a CB radio.

Paint the wheels the same color as the vehicle, or else flat black. Avoid tires with raised white letters, and any other custom accessories. Avoid "suggestive" bumperstickers on the vehicle. An American flag decal or NRA sticker might be a good idea, if you want to fit in with the local "good ol' boys." (Scotch tape them to the inside of a window so you can later remove them.)

Cover any packs or other camping gear with a plain canvas tarp. Tool boxes, torches and other "working gear" left out in the open are a good idea if your purpose is to look like you belong on the job.

A set of official-looking magnetic door signs might also be useful.

Make sure your registration, driver's license, and vehicle identification number are all legal. A recently-purchased car might not be in the computers yet, and thus give cause to detain you. If ownership of a car can't be established, that alone is sufficient cause for a police agency to obtain a search warrant for that car.

Tires, windshield, blinkers and brake lights should be in good condition, to avoid giving the authorities probable cause for stopping you.

Switching license plates is not advised. Make sure that your front and back plates match. Incidentally, Idaho plates are the hardest for officers to read, while Utah plates are the easiest to read. Colorado, Arizona, Nevada and California plates all fall somewhere in between.

TOOLS OF THE TRADE

The number of tools used in an operation should be kept to an absolute minimum. Useful tools may include adjustable pipe and crescent wrenches, hacksaws with spare blades, heavy duty wire cutters or bolt cutters, pliers, pry-bars, screwdrivers and crosscut saws. Especially noisy tools should be avoided. Hammers fall into this category, although they are essential for certain types of work, such as spiking. Chainsaws are out of the question for any clandestine type of activity. Insulated handles (tape may be used for this) minimize the sounds of tools clanking together.

If only one or two tools are to be carried, you can secure them to your wrist or belt with a short cord, to prevent loss by dropping them in the dark. Otherwise, tools can be carried in jacket pockets or in canvas bags slung from the shoulder or attached to the belt. If bags are used, they should be easy to open and close. Before heading out, shake the bag to insure that the tools don't rattle or bang together. A dark towel or rag can be used to deaden any noise. A towel will also prove useful if there is wire to cut: drape a couple of layers of towel over the wire and then cut. The towel will deaden the sound of the wire separating. Be sure the ends of a taut fence wire don't snap back and cause noise. A shallow cut followed by flexing the wire back and forth should allow the wire to separate quietly. Practice.

All tools used should be of common manufacture and should be purchased with cash at large retail outlets or discount houses where the cashier is not likely to remember one's appearance. If asked for name and address, even for a warranty, give false information or none at all.

If one must buy special tools, materials, books or the like by mail, don't leave a "paper trail" for investigators to follow. Don't use charge cards or personal checks. Send postal or bank money orders instead, and DO NOT fill out your name and address in the part labeled "sender." Remember, bank accounts are accessible to the police, and provide a detailed account of purchases, travel, and even political opinion. All checks cashed are required by law to be recorded on microfilm.

Microscopic marks left by tools can sometimes be used to link a specific tool to the scene of a "crime." Also, paint flakes or other material from a "crime scene" may be found on a tool and be used as evidence to link that tool to a specific site. Because of this, it is prudent to dispose of tools regularly and to replace them with tools of a different brand, size or type.

Before beginning a "mission," prepare the tools to be taken by donning gloves and using a rag to wipe them free of fingerprints. Store the "clean" tools in a bag to prevent accidental handling (cloth laundry bags are good). All surfaces must be wiped off. In the case of a flashlight, for example, you must be certain that no prints will turn up on batteries, bulb, reflector or any other part you might conceivably handle.

Miscellaneous

Flashlights may be helpful, even essential, for night operations. See the section **Eyes of Night**. Watches are essential to coordinate the timing of actions, drops, pick-ups, etc. Any reliable watch with a lighted or luminous face will do. Particularly useful are waterproof digital watches that feature an alarm, a stop watch with an alarm, and a timer with an alarm. Get one with a button to light the face. Black, of course. A flexible terrycloth wrist sweatband, available at sporting goods stores, will cover up the telltale light and protect the watch from abuse.

Every team member should carry at least a couple of quarters (in separate pockets to prevent noise) for emergency phone calls. If you become separated from your team or miss a pick-up, you must be able to walk to a pay phone and call for an emergency pick-up. (Set up such an emergency phone number with someone on duty at it as part of your planning.)

Radios and Communications Equipment

While not actually a tool of sabotage, a radio is perhaps the best tool a monkeywrencher can have to avoid getting caught. They allow you to place a lookout miles away on a mountain top or along an access road. This changes warning time from moments to minutes and allows a clean getaway. A warning is in order, though — the use of any radio equipment for illegal purposes or to aid anything illegal is a violation of FCC regulations and is therefore a federal offense. This should be taken into account, especially in cases in which the act of monkeywrenching itself is relatively minor in the eyes of the law.

CB's — A basic piece of radio equipment is a full-power (5 watt) citizens band (CB) hand-held transceiver ("walkie-talkie") with multi-channel capability (preferably all 40 channels), an internal 12-volt battery supply, and a high-low power switch.

Five watt transmitters have an effective range of from one to a dozen miles or more depending on local terrain, weather, and electrical interference. Greater power is rarely necessary, and even this amount of power could be easily overheard by the wrong people in many areas. Thus the high-low power switch. Its use will save batteries and minimize the chance of being overheard.

CB's are recommended because they are relatively cheap, easy to get, and common enough to be only minimally suspicious. Also, because they work in the low frequency AM mode, their signal bends easily and is thus more suitable for rugged terrain than higher frequency FM.

A 12-volt power requirement for the radio allows the unit to be plugged directly into a vehicle electrical system for mobile use. For portable use, the power supply is usually either 8 standard AA size alkaline or 10 AA nickel-cadmium batteries in series. Alkaline batteries have about twice the electrical capacity of nicads and cost about half as much, but they cannot be recharged (I've read that some kinds of alkaline batteries can be recharged, but I've never seen them). Nicads can be recharged hundreds of times, offsetting their initial cost of about 3 dollars apiece.

Nickel-cadmium batteries are especially convenient when they can be charged from a vehicle's electrical system. A special charger for this purpose can be built for less than 10 dollars from parts obtainable from any Radio Shack or other electronics store. Using a transistorized voltage doubler circuit solves the problem of the vehicle battery being the same voltage as the radio battery pack. Complete plans can be found in the 1982 edition of *The Radio Amateur's Handbook,* and assembly requires little knowledge of electronics.

Regardless of whether they are charged on a standard home battery charger or on a vehicular battery charger, nicad batteries should be fully discharged before recharging each time. If they are only partly discharged before recharging, they tend to develop a "memory" at that point and may not provide service beyond that point in the future.

A basic radiocom set-up can be purchased for about one hundred dollars. This includes a mobile CB for vehicle mounting (as low as $40 new through *Scanner World)* and a hand-held transceiver with choice of three crystal-controlled channels (selling as low as $60). Even without shopping around for the best price, you can get good quality equipment for a total cost of under $200. As always, think of this cost in comparison to fifty to one hundred dollars an hour in attorney's fees.

PAGER — There are types of radio equipment other than the regular CB "walkie-talkies" which may be appropriate for monkeywrenchers. One relatively low-cost system entails the use of the pager-type alarm systems designed for use as a "silent" car alarm. These consist of a compact CB band transmitter and pager-type receiver that beeps when a signal is received. These can be used as a one-way communications system between a lookout and a team of saboteurs. Avoid the Radio Shack alarm of this type, as it is underpowered and virtually worthless for this application. The best model is the "Page Alert" available at large auto parts stores. The transmitter can be mounted in the vehicle permanently, as for an alarm use, or can be made more portable. For portable use, carry the transmitter with a portable CB antenna (commonly available magnetic or gutter-mount types) and a portable 12-volt power supply. This portable power supply can be made by wiring two 6-volt lantern-type batteries (the large ones) together in the following sequence: connect the positive (+) terminal of one battery to the negative (−) terminal of the other; connect the remaining positive and negative battery terminals to the appropriate positive and negative leads as indicated on the wiring instructions for the transmitter. Tape the batteries together, side-by-side, place them in a small cardboard box and fit the box into a small pack or pouch for easy carrying.

If you intend to use the transmitter from a vehicle but do not want to mount it permanently, use the same types of antennas mentioned above, but instead of the battery pack, wire the unit to a cigarette-lighter type plug (available at any electronics store) to enable you to set up quickly and easily.

To transmit, simply flip the switch "on" and the unit will send out a signal for five to ten seconds and automatically shut off. The signal transmission can be repeated by flipping the switch "off" and then "on" again. The "Page Alert" system broadcasts at four watts and has a range (ideally) of one to two miles. Test it in the field to determine realistic ranges. Also, keep in mind that the pulsing signal sent out by this unit can be picked up by other CB radios and even by TV sets if they are close enough to the transmitter.

On the receiving end is the pager-type receiver about the size of a pack of cigarettes. The unit has a clip on the back for affixing to a belt, but this is most unreliable when put to rough use. It is best carried in a shirt or jacket pocket with a button-down flap. When the signal is received, the pager will emit a loud "beeping" tone until shut off. This sound can (and should) be muted by putting several layers of electrical tape over the small opening on top that emits the tone.

Although this system allows only one-way communication, a system of repeated transmissions can be used as a crude form of sending two or three different messages (pre-arranged). One of the chief advantages of this system is that you can set it all up for under $150. One warning should be noted, however. The pager-type receiver cannot be relied on to receive transmissions inside a building containing large amounts of metal in walls or frame.

WALKMAN-TYPE — Yet another kind of radio equipment that is becoming increasingly popular is a short-range unit the size of a cigarette pack (designed to be carried on the belt) equipped with lightweight headset and microphone. Look for a unit that allows you to choose between a "push-to-talk" switch and a "vox" switch (this activates the microphone automatically at the sound of your voice). These units are available from Radio Shack as well as the survival supply houses.

These "walkman" type units have a maximum range of about a quarter of a mile under ideal circumstances (rarely achieved under field conditions), so their use is not suitable for all operations.

Practice and Use

It is essential to practice with radio equipment before undertaking an operation. It is especially important to learn how buildings and topography affect the range of your equipment. A pre-mission "dry run" to test radio communication may be a good idea on some jobs.

A very real danger which occurs with the use of radios is the possibility that a casual listener or radio buff may pick up your transmissions and become suspicious. Due to the vagaries of radio transmission, such a listener might be miles away. To make such interception meaningless, develop a simple code that will make your conversation sound commonplace, even boring. *NEVER, never use real names on the air.* Be wary — sheriffs and rangers often have CB scanners in their cars.

Perhaps the greatest danger in using radios on an operation is the chance that security guards or passersby might hear the user's voice (rather than the transmission itself). Using the earphone headset of the "walkman" type radios will keep the messages you hear from being overheard, but the sender's voice is another matter. To keep one's voice from carrying, cup your hand around the mike and hold it as close to your mouth as possible. Speak in a low voice, slowly and calmly, pronouncing all words very clearly. If you have trouble hearing or being heard, remain calm. Never raise your voice as this will be more likely to reveal your location than to help the transmission.

The larger portable CB units ("walkie-talkies") with their external speakers present a greater danger of being overheard. Nevertheless, they are invaluable for operations requiring long-range communications. A few precautions with this type of equipment will lessen the chances of being overheard. A small terrycloth towel (dark color!), worn like a scarf under shirt or jacket, or carried in a pouch with the radio unit, can be used to muffle the sound of your voice. When transmitting and receiving, observe the following procedure: Post other team members as lookouts, and to warn you if your radio or voice is too loud. Sit down cross-legged or kneel down with your back to the area of greatest danger. Cover your radio and head with the towel and/or a heavy jacket. Bend low to the ground, keeping the antenna straight up, and switch the set "on." Avoid long transmissions. Always use pre-arranged codes.

When using radios for key parts of an operation, such as calling the pickup vehicle after a mission is completed, always have a backup plan in the event of radio failure. (Your driver might swing by the pre-arranged pickup point at certain times, or automatically fall back to an alternate site.) Pre-arranged times for radio checks (example: every half hour at ten minutes and forty minutes after the hour) will help to insure proper radio links and build confidence.

Military Surplus Radios

Army surplus PRT-4's (the RT stands for "radio transmitter"), PRR-9's (RR = "radio receiver"), and PRC 25's provide a low-cost, high quality communications system which might be of interest to monkeywrenchers.

The PRT-4's and PRR-9's are Army squad radios that operate in the 47-57 megahertz bands. The transmitters use two 9-volt batteries (alkalines are a must!) and the receivers use either four 1.5-volt n-cells or a 9-volt battery with a 6-volt adapter. The transmitters put out about 450 milliamps of power which is pretty good when you consider that the radio shack headphone mini-radios put out about 100 milliamps. Range for the PRT-4/PRR-9 is easily 1 1/2 miles line-of-sight. Two PRT-4's with two PRR-9's cost the military 1,600 bucks but can be purchased surplus in excellent working condition for 150 dollars plus shipping (which is an extra five dollars).

Since these radios were constructed for the military they have been considerably over-engineered and can take plenty of abuse. Transmitters have worked even after klutzy paratroopers dropped them from a thousand feet! Since these radios do not have an FCC approval stamp on them, it is illegal to use them — *but not to own them*. However, enforcement is difficult since the FCC would have to catch you in the act of transmission. Another advantage of these radios is the fact that the transmitter and receiver are separate units. This allows two people to have a duplex system, i.e. I transmit on one frequency while I receive my friend's transmission on a second frequency. This decreases the possibility of someone scanning and picking up both sides of a conversation. Another advantage is that for another 70 bucks you can pick up a piece of equipment called an ID-1189 which is a test machine which allows you to change frequencies once you buy new crystals which are about 6 dollars each.

Another advantage of the PRT-4/PRR-9 combination is that it can net with the larger 920-channel PRC-25. A few weeks ago while out testing radios, I was in a river bed and easily transmitted and received transmissions with a PRC-25 that was over 5-1/2 miles away with three intervening ridges. Unfortunately, the PRC-25 is $650. For those with a Doc Sarvis in their back pocket, however, there's the PRC-77 for $800, a solid-state version of the PRC-25 with crypto-capability, meaning that with the PRC-77 you can encrypt your transmissions so no one can figure out what you're saying even if they do hear the transmission.

These radios are rugged, inexpensive for the quality, lightweight and dependable.

Police Band Radios.

It is impossible to overstate the value of a radio capable of picking up police calls. These units can tip you off to a surveillance or warn you of a patrolman or deputy dispatched to the scene of your recent hit.

Before buying, it's a good idea to read up on the subject. Look for books at your local library, bookstore or radio shop. One excellent reference is *The Complete Action Guide to Scanners and Monitors* by Louis A. Smith II. It is published by Tab Books, a major "how-to" book publisher. Additional valuable reference data is found in the *Betty Bearcat Frequency Directory,* which has an eastern and western edition. It provides an extensive listing of frequencies, including many used by police agencies. Look for it at radio shops or in stores that sell scanners. Still another volume of this type is *Monitor America,* which contains fewer frequency listings but has a number of partial police radio codes that can help you understand police communications. An excellent source of police frequency information is the series of "call books" published annually by Hollins Radio Data which break the nation down into regions covered by ten separate volumes. As always, check all the radio shops in your nearest big city, where they retail for $6.95. As a last resort, they can be mail-ordered from the following sources:

Police Call, Dept. 1, Lebanon, NJ 08833

Chick Ryel & Company, PO Box 762, Woodland Hills, CA 91364

Perhaps the best scanner frequency listings are to be found in the "Fox Scanner Radio Listings" available through CRB Research (PO Box 56, Commack, NY 11725). As of this writing, 28 area directories are available, with more in preparation.

Radio specialty shops are often the most expensive source of these radios. Look for them at department stores or the catalog showroom type of store (like Best or La Belle's). Also, the ads in specialty magazines like *Amateur Radio* and *Popular Communications* can lead you to mail-order suppliers. Good units can now be bought for under $150. One low-cost supplier is Scanner World USA (10 New Scotland Avenue, Albany, NY 12208), with an extensive catalog of scanners, CB's and frequency directories.

There are two types of radios for monitoring police calls. The older type is crystal-controlled, and requires buying a separate crystal for every frequency you wish to listen to. Because of the security problems associated with purchasing these crystals, this type of unit is not recommended.

Your best choice is a "programmable" scanner which has a keyboard on it which allows you to select the frequencies you are interested in. Once programmed, these units will scan a large number of frequencies, stopping on one when a transmission is picked up. This can allow you to monitor just the frequencies that are important on a specific job or in a certain area (those of any combination of city, county, state or federal agencies).

Here are the major features to look for in a programmable scanner:

*AC and DC power. This allows you to use the scanner both at home or in a vehicle.

*16 or more channels, to insure that you can monitor even the large number of frequencies in and around a city.

*Search capability. With this you can search portions of the radio band, seeking out frequencies not listed in the directories.

*Should be able to pick up the following bands:
30 to 50 MHz (megahertz) — VHF Low Band
144 to 174 MHz — VHF High Band
440 to 512 MHz — UHF Band

Most of the scanners made by Regency and Uniden have all these features and more. Once again, though, make sure your scanner can take either AC or DC power.

Once you get your scanner, take time to listen to it at home. You will want to locate the important frequencies in your target area. In addition to local law enforcement agencies, you can seek appropriate federal agencies (Forest Service, Park Service, BLM, etc.) and the frequencies assigned to the forest products industry (in Oregon and Washington, for example, these can be found at: 158.145, 158.160, 158.175, 158.205, 158.220, 158.235, 158.265, 173.250, 173.300 and

173.350). The federal law enforcement agencies (like the FBI, DEA and BATF) are extremely difficult to monitor. Even if you find their frequencies, they often use sophisticated scramblers, making the messages unintelligible. A source for the frequencies used by federal agencies is *The "Top Secret" Registry of U.S. Government Radio Frequencies,* by Tom Kneitel, available from Loompanics Unlimited, PO Box 1197, Port Townsend, WA 98368.

By listening at home, you will learn to understand much of the jargon you hear and can gradually decipher the radio codes in use. Most common is the "10-code" that assigns meanings to numbers from "ten-one" to "ten-ninety-nine." Study the ten-codes in directories and pay attention to what you are hearing. Often an explanation of the call will be broadcast in plain English *and* in the 10-code. In the Forest Service, because of confusion over the 10-code among users, there is now a tendency toward communications in plain English. The Park Service, on the other hand, continues to use a 10-code, perhaps because of its greater emphasis on law enforcement in its day-to-day operations.

Police agencies may use codes that are based on the numbers assigned to various criminal statutes. For example, a "914" or "nine-fourteen" may refer to statute number 12-914 for, say, armed robbery. The statute books in the reference section of a public library will give you the statute numbers. Also, by listening to police radio calls and making notes, and comparing your notes to newspaper accounts of crime incidents, you can help to further break the codes.

Another informative type of scanning to try at home is listening in to the detective frequencies that carry surveillances. These channels are most active when detectives are usually at work, between 8 AM and 5 PM, Monday through Friday. You can, of course, hear some surveillances in the night hours. These detective frequencies are not as active as the standard patrol frequencies, so you may want to use your scanner's "lock out" option to eliminate the patrol calls while listening for the detectives.

When searching for police frequencies, make a note of the frequency numbers as you pick them up. The locations you hear broadcast over the air will indicate whether you are listening to a city or county agency.

When learning about the patrol frequencies, concentrate on weekend nights when police are usually busiest.

Once you have developed some proficiency in monitoring police calls, it's time to take your radio out in your car or truck for a little practice and testing on the road. Keep the radio within easy reach, with a cardboard box, paper bag or something similar to conceal the unit. Listening in on police calls from a car is illegal in some areas, and is considered highly suspicious in all areas. By plugging into the cigarette lighter for power, you can quickly unplug and eliminate evidence that you were actually listening to the radio. Still, keep the radio hidden.

Because your scanner reception is vastly improved with a longer antenna, it's nice to use the external antenna jack to attach a more substantial antenna. Again, in the interest of secrecy, the best antenna type is a disguised type that looks like a normal car antenna. These were invented years ago to protect mobile CB owners from thieves. You can buy a combination CB/AM/FM antenna at a radio shop.

Another valuable type of scanner is the handheld type suitable for use by a team on the ground or by a lone monkeywrencher. These are about the size of a walkie-talkie and have most of the features of the larger units. Their major weak point is the short "rubber duckie" type of antenna that is standard on them. Whenever possible, buy and use a longer and more effective antenna.

FIELD NOTES

*If police or agency calls are being monitored by the driver of a team's vehicle, it will be necessary to notify the rest of the team immediately by radio if it seems likely that the authorities are en route to the area. (See earlier section on radios and communications equipment.) A note of caution is in order here: If you are using mobile vehicle units, make sure that you don't run down the battery of your vehicle, if you have to park for any length of time. Experiment ahead of time to find out how long you can listen to the police radio and your own CB system before the battery is run down to the point where your vehicle won't start. If necessary, the driver may have to drive around for 15 minutes or so to recharge the battery.

It may be preferable to rig up an auxiliary battery for your radio system. The auxiliary battery should be wired in such a way that it never draws on your vehicle's main battery. An RV and trailer supply house can provide you with all the information and equipment, and even installation if desired (though for security reasons you should do your own installation). The auxiliary battery must be mounted in a ventilated area. Also, make sure that you use a deep cycle storage battery rather than the usual car battery. Sears makes an excellent RV/ marine battery.

*Your pre-operational checks should include replacing weak batteries or re-charging your nicads. *Always make sure that your batteries are wiped clean of fingerprints.*

*As with all your radio equipment, test your police band radio or scanner under field conditions before taking it on an actual operation.

EYES OF NIGHT

Flashlights

Night operations may be helped by a variety of mechanical aids. Perhaps the most basic is the flashlight. Small, pen-type flashlights can be easily carried and used when working on equipment, locks, etc. Larger flashlights can also be used and may be easier to manipulate with gloved hands. The lens should be covered with a couple of layers of electrical tape, leaving only a narrow slit to emit light. Best among the larger flashlights are the green plastic military types with the lens at a right angle to the body. The bases of these flashlights unscrew to reveal a spare bulb and two special lenses that can be mounted over the standard clear lens by unscrewing the "O" ring and popping them in. The translucent white lens converts the visible beam of light to a white spot suitable for signaling. The red lens allows the user to illuminate an object without ruining his/her night vision.

Standard Optics

Binoculars and spotting scopes can be of some help at night, especially for observing a well-lit area. Maximum effectiveness requires at least a 50mm objective lens (the lens closest to the object you are viewing) for optimal light gathering qualities. There are special binoculars designed for night use, which may be available from some of the better military surplus houses.

Infrared Spotting Scope

This device dates back to World War II. It consists of a battery-powered spot light that emits infrared light (invisible to the unaided eye), and, mounted directly below, an image converter tube that allows the user to clearly see what the spotlight is illuminating.

One advantage of this system is that it allows you to see into shadows and other dark areas, since you are illuminating them with the spotlight. It is also the cheapest night vision system, although in this case, "cheap" is relative. It is available from suppliers who advertise in "survival" magazines, at prices ranging from about $600 to $1400. Edmund Scientific Corporation (101 E. Gloucester Pike, Barrington, N. J. 08007) has a unit selling for $1195. There are disadvantages to this system as well: The range is limited to what the spotlight can effectively illuminate, which is rarely more than 200 to 300 feet. The unit is also somewhat bulky, and the user must have an effective strap or harness system to prevent dropping and banging it while keeping one's hands free for climbing or other activities.

Starlight Scope

This Vietnam-era development uses a battery powered scope to amplify existing light from moon, stars, rotting forest vegetation and ambient city light. Avoid first generation units, as later designs have an "anti-blooming" device that shuts the unit down if light levels suddenly get high enough to damage the costly image intensification tube.

Advantages: Can be used beyond the range of infrared scopes since the device is "passive" and does not rely on projecting a beam of light onto the area or object to be observed. In addition, there are security advantages with this type of system. With a starlight scope you can readily detect the presence of an infrared device, since the scope converts the otherwise invisible infrared light to visible light. Conversely, neither the infrared nor starlight scope can detect another starlight scope, since it emits no radiation of any type.

Disadvantages: Extremely high cost. Suppliers, like those mentioned above, will charge anywhere from three to twelve thousand dollars for units that vary from relatively compact hand-held scopes to goggle-type units that strap on to one's head. Expect to pay at least four thousand for a good unit. Starlight scopes must have *some* light present in order to be effective. On a moonless, overcast night in the desert, a starlight scope may be useless. Even on a clear night, a starlight scope may be ineffective under certain conditions, as, for example, when the observer is on a hill looking down into a dark valley.

There is also some question as to the legality of these systems. Nevertheless, they are advertised in the survival magazines.

Bionic Ear

While not a visual device, this piece of equipment could be useful to the lookout on dark nights while listening for the footfall of a night watchman. The "bionic ear" is little more than an amplified microphone that plays back through a set of headphones. There is a small parabolic dish that attaches to the mike for higher gain (usually available as an option for a small added cost). These devices are widely advertised in hunting magazines. Total cost is about $110 to $130.

COUNTER-SECURITY

As the incidence and effectiveness of monkeywrenching increases. targets will be "hardened" with the addition of various security measures. A basic knowledge of how to defeat these security additions is therefore important to a successful campaign of ecotage.

Locks

Because of their low cost, various types of padlocks are used to secure gates, equipment sheds and heavy equipment. A lot of earthmoving equipment is designed to allow the owner to put padlocks on all the standard access points like fuel tank and radiator caps, oil dipstick, transmission and oilpan filler tubes, etc. In addition, many machines have metal doors that can lock away access to the cab or engine compartment. There are two methods for defeating locks: jamming or forcing.

JAMMING: Any glue that dries hard within a couple of hours is suitable for jamming locks. The "liquid metal" type is usually quite good. Whatever glue you use, it can be forced into the keyway by one of two methods as seen in illustration 9.1. The syringe-type applicator (A) is very handy, but due to higher unit cost, should only be used where a few locks are to be jammed. The large tubes can be modified by drilling a small hole in the cap (B) to direct a narrow stream of glue into the lock. These are best when a lot of locks are to be jammed. A single earthmover can have six to ten padlocks securing all parts of it.

FORCING: A battery-powered electric drill with a new 1/8 inch high speed drill bit can be used to force open most locks as seen in illustration 9.1. Most keyed locks are pin-tumbler types whose basic operating principle can be seen in (C). When a key is inserted, it pushes up on spring-loaded pins of various lengths. When the tops of these pins are in perfect alignment with the "shear line," the entire "plug" in which the key is inserted can be turned and the lock opened. In most locks, all of these parts are made of brass to prevent corrosion, and its relative softness makes drilling easy. As you can see in (D), the drill is used to destroy the pins along the shear line. You should be careful not to drill too deeply into the lock since this can damage the locking bar deep inside making it impossible to open. Drill in only to the depth of the keyway (3/4-inch in most padlocks). A "drill stop" found with the power tools in a hardware store can be used to pre-set this depth and prevent drilling too deep.

Inserting a pin, like a nail, will keep the damaged remains of the top pins above the shear line. Otherwise they will drop down and prevent the lock from opening. You may need to put the drill bit in a couple of times to chew up any pin fragments that might interfere with opening.

Finally, insert a narrow-bladed screwdriver (F) into the keyway and turn it to open the lock. Before using this method in the field, buy a cheap padlock or two and practice at home.

Combination Locks

You may also encounter the combination-type padlock as seen in 9.2. To "jam" these, it is often easiest to pry off the dial face. Although this can be accomplished with one screwdriver, it is made easier by first inserting a narrow-bladed screwdriver behind the dial face (A). After it is pried up sufficiently, you can insert a second, heavier screwdriver (B) to finish the job. Without a dial face, the lock owner will not be able to open the lock without forcing it.

These locks can often be opened with the same drill and bit described previously. Note how the notch in the shackle (D) is locked in place by a spring-loaded bolt (E). By drilling a hole in the back of the lock case directly over the bolt (F), you can insert a small nail and push the bolt back out of the notch in the shackle (G) and the lock will open.

Some expensive high security combination padlocks are designed to

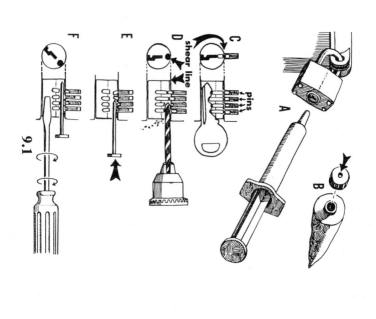

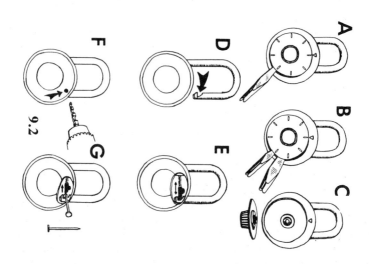

prevent prying the dial face off, and have two locking bolts, one on each side of the shackle. These can still be jammed by drilling a hole in the back of the casing and forcing glue inside.

Fences

Garages and parking areas for heavy equipment, and offices are often protected by fenced yards or compounds. The most common type of fence is made of chain link "fabric" with openings of 2 inches or less to make climbing difficult. Seven feet is the minimum effective height. Often a "top guard" is added, consisting of an angled brace (or two) holding either barbed wire or the newer barbed tape. These fences can be climbed with the aid of a ladder. If you are going to climb the fence without a ladder, wear tennis shoes for the best grip.

The top guard wire can either be cut, or covered with a scrap of old carpet and climbed over. If you choose to cut it, use good bolt cutters. The newest type of barbed tape is reinforced with a steel cable core that wire cutters cannot cut, but bolt cutters slice right through.

It is also a simple matter to cut through the chain link fabric, and a hole sufficiently large to pass through can be made in less than half a minute. Never buy cheap bolt cutters to do this, for they will eventually let you down. Remember that any cutting, unless hidden in a low or concealed spot of a rarely patrolled fence will reveal your presence the next morning. By cutting only at the bottom (just enough to allow you to crawl under) you can minimize this problem. Also, you can carry a few scraps of wire to tie the fence fabric back to a semblance of its former condition, perhaps delaying discovery.

The gates on these fenced compounds can usually be quickly forced open with a 6-foot pry bar. And in an emergency, a car or pickup truck can easily drive through either a gate, or directly through the chain link fabric itself, sustaining little more than a few paint scratches.

Lighting

The presence of security lighting often reveals the location of a sensitive target. Its effectiveness at providing security in bad weather is minimal. Try to time your hit accordingly.

If necessary, these lights can be knocked out, even if mounted high on a pole or the side of a building. An air rifle firing BB's can break an exposed bulb. It is best to avoid using air rifles firing either .177 or .22 caliber pellets, even though these are more effective, because these soft lead pellets pick up distinctive rifling marks as they pass through the barrel and can often be matched back to a specific gun.

A slingshot is probably best for knocking out lights, but it requires practice to develop the necessary accuracy (see section on **Slingshots**). Also, some security lights are protected by a piece of plexiglas to deflect low-velocity projectiles.

Closed-Circuit Television

Before penetrating any fence, develop the habit of checking for CCTV surveillance. These cameras are mounted high on poles or the sides of buildings to prevent tampering, and may be concealed by a round or box-like weatherproof covering. The effectiveness of CCTV surveillance is severely limited by bad weather. Also, right-angle corners of fences might create a blind spot through which you can quickly move. Study the layout carefully. To prevent blind spots at corners, some fences are made in a way which avoids the 90-degree turn and uses three 30-degree bends.

Alarms

Although many types of alarm sensors are visible from the outside of a structure (like the metal foil on windows), some are not readily detected. The surest way to check for presence of an alarm is to force entry. This may trip lights, bells or sirens. If it does not, there may still be a silent alarm system in place designed to summon guards or police without alerting the intruder. These can be detected by forcing entry and hiding a safe distance away to see if someone arrives to check out the target. Most responses occur within a half hour, and usually in substantially less time.

Of course if your hit is to be quick, like breaking windows to toss in paint bags, the presence of an alarm will not deter you since you'll be long gone before someone arrives.

Before climbing or cutting fences, check to see that they are not wired to an alarm system. Any heavy wire or conduit attached to the fence from four to five feet above the ground (as seen in illus. 9.3A) could indicate an alarm system designed to detect both climbing and cutting. If you look further, you will find sensors attached at intervals (see B, C & D).

These can be circumvented by digging under the fence, but you must be careful not to bump the fence. Another way to neutralize this type of system is to trigger numerous false alarms by shaking the fence and quickly leaving the area. Enough false alarms might bring about the shutdown of the system. Since high winds can trigger these alarms, windy nights are the best times to do this. Numerous false alarms on a windy night can cause immediate shutdown, allowing you to enter later that same night.

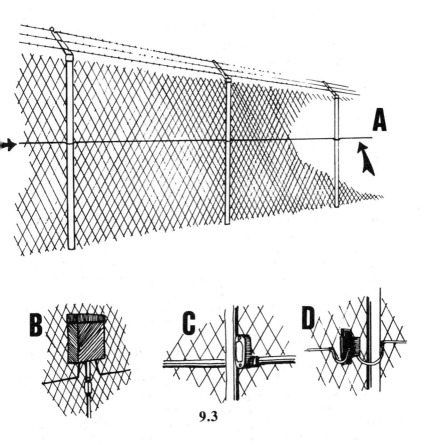

9.3

Guards

Most security guards work for little better than minimum wage, and bring little enthusiasm to the job with them. A lot of them are pensioners seeking extra income, and retired cops. A surprising number are ex-cons and wackos who want to carry guns but are too unstable to be hired by police agencies. You never know what types you'll encounter, so always be cautious if you suspect they might be in the area.

Keep in mind that this is a boring occupation, and the long hours tend to dull the senses. The guards who manage to stay awake often do so with the aid of television, radio or magazines, all of which greatly hinder their effectiveness.

Some guards remain relatively stationary, guarding a specific building or heavy equipment parking lot. Others patrol irregularly, often using pickup trucks at remote sites. All have a tendency to hang out near well-lit areas or in the nearby shadows. Sometimes making a complete circuit of a target will reveal the silhouette of a guard's truck parked with a view of the target.

Always be patient when looking for security guards. The slightest sound or glow of a cigarette will often tip you off to their presence. If you have not been able to locate any guards, but are still unsure, use your flashlight or make some loud noise to see if you can draw them out. Make sure you have a concealed escape route handy.

If a guard is sitting too close to your target, you may want to consider using lights and noise to decoy him away. This is highly suitable if your hit is to be a smash-and-run type. Remember to close your eyes in those brief moments when using a flashlight as a decoy or bait, to prevent loss of night vision.

Among the tools that are useful in your check for guards is a flashlight equipped with a red lens, or covered with electrical tape so that it emits only a pinhole of light. With these you can have some illumination that will not alert a guard. Another useful piece of equipment is a good pair of binoculars. For maximum light-gathering at night, they should have fully coated optics and an objective lens of at least 50 millimeters.

If, despite your precautions, you are surprised by a security guard or other self-appointed guardian of the mindless machine, your best option is immediate flight. When running at night, keep one or both arms fully extended in front of you to prevent being slapped in the face by a tree limb or worse. A heavy jacket provides good protection from unseen obstacles. This writer once ran full tilt into a barbed wire fence that was invisible on a moonless night. The fence bowed almost to the ground, then sprang back up, leaving me standing a bit surprised, but none the worse for wear thanks to the heavy army-surplus jacket I was wearing.

Finally, there is an inexpensive, battery-powered device that can be worn on a cord around your neck and can make it difficult for a pursuer to follow you in the night. A compact strobe light, as is used as a flash attachment for 35mm cameras, can, when pointed at a pursuer on a dark night, cause him to lose his night vision. You, of course, should keep your eyes closed when flashing the unit. Many types are available, so shop around. You are looking for one that is easily operated manually (by a small pushbutton) and can be used while wearing gloves.

Guard Dogs

In recent years, guard dogs have become a popular way of securing fenced areas in and around urban centers. Because of this, any fenced compound should be checked for the possible presence of these dogs.

Guard dogs are usually males, weighing 70 pounds or more, and of a working breed, German Shepherds and Dobermans being the favorites. Because of the recent boom in the guard dog business, quality has suffered. It is estimated that fewer than one in four German Shepherds is really suitable for this type of work. And since many clients base their choice on cost alone, they often get an inferior guard dog.

Guard dogs are often delivered to the site in the evening, and picked up in the morning. Surveillance can reveal the comings and goings of these vehicles. Also, many times a sign will be posted at a gate warning of the presence of guard dogs. In large fenced areas, guard dogs will work in pairs, the weaker dog taking his cue from the stronger.

Another way to check for guard dogs is to lure them into view. Well-trained dogs will not approach the fence, but will hang back or report to a specific place, or "station," to wait for the potential intruder to get well inside the fenced area. Despite this, they can usually be lured into view as a way to check for their presence. A "silent" dog whistle, available at all pet stores (illus. 9.4) is one way to check. Simply shaking the fence, or throwing rocks inside the fenced compound, simulating the sounds of an intruder, can bring a guard dog into view.

If the target protected by the dog is worth the effort, there are several ways to neutralize them. They are based on luring the dog to a selected area along the fence. Although these dogs are usually trained to stay back from the fence, and are further trained not to pick up food baits (called "poison-proofing"), the boredom of their job often makes them amenable to luring. Meat baits delivered regularly to a certain area will establish a pattern of visits by the dog. Or, "house-breaking" spray, bought at pet stores, can be sprayed on a section of the fence. This imitation urine can make a dog curious, and cause him to mark his scent posts regularly. And of course, there is the classic bitch in heat which has proven the downfall of many a protection dog.

Following are some methods for neutralizing a dog that can be successfully lured close to the fence:

9.4

NOOSE POLE — The noose poles described in the **Trapping** section can be used to snare an unwary guard dog. Since many of these dogs are trained by "agitation," frequently by waving a rag or burlap sack in their face, you should try to provoke them into grabbing a burlap sack offered on the end of a pole as seen in illustration 9.5a. Once you have begun a tug-of-war with the dog, slip the noose over his neck and tighten (9.5b). Finally, pull the dog up to the fence, and secure him there with a sturdy piece of wire or a heavy-duty leash clip (9.5c).

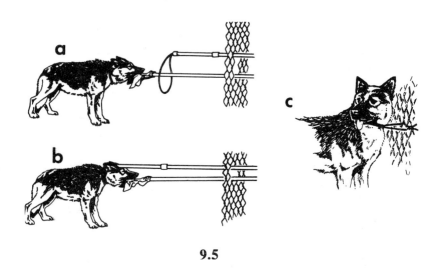

9.5

HIDDEN TRAPS — Standard leg-hold traps can be chained to the fence and slid inside. Once covered with a cloth, they will not be immediately visible to the dog. Use only the Victor "soft catch" type (illus. 9.6a) or a standard trap with added cloth padding on the jaws (9.6b). Kick the fence and make a lot of noise to agitate the dog, then lead him down to the section of the fence where the traps lay. Once the dog has been caught, leave the area immediately. He will settle down and wait to be released in the morning. The padding on the traps will prevent injury. Penetrate the compound at a different point and remain out of view of the dog when working.

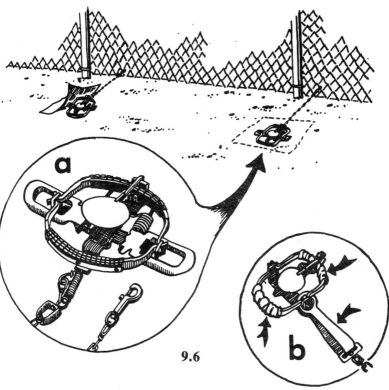

9.6

TRANQUILIZERS — Dogs that will accept meat baits can be slipped tranquilizers early in the evening, allowing you time for the drug to take effect. Adding a little garlic to a meat bait can make it even more attractive to most dogs.

The most effective tranquilizers for oral administration are the CNS depressants derived from Phenothiazine or Promazine. These include:

Propiopromazine HCL (Tranvet)
Triflupromazine HCL (Vetame)
Acetylpromazine (Acepromazine)
Chlorpromazine (Thorazine)
Valium

These are all rated "relatively nontoxic." Clinical dosages for sedative effect would be less than 100 mg for a large dog. Actual field use would require more, up to 600 mg. The effects will be noticed within

15 minutes of ingestion and include ataxia (loss of coordination) in the hindquarters, drooping eyelids, and eventually, lying down. Fullest effect can take from 30 to 60 minutes.

Tranquilized dogs are best snared and then secured by means of a chain and heavy clip. Light weight snaps and nylon webbing are not sufficient to hold a large dog.

The aforementioned drugs are available by prescription only. You will need to have a sympathetic vet, or you may try to get some tranquilizers from a vet by explaining that you are driving a friend's large dog cross country for them, but that the dog needs sedatives before he'll ride in a car. *(Note: thorazine and valium are, of course, prescribed for humans, so they may be obtainable from other sources than veterinarians.)*

FORCE METHOD — Using this technique, an intruder dresses and arms himself to meet the dog head on, if necessary, and frighten him off. A variety of gear and weapons can make this possible. Variations of this method have been used in police raids where criminal suspects own vicious dogs.

Special Ladder — In illustration 9.7 there is a specially built ladder with widely spaced rungs that a dog cannot climb. This is an aid to escape, should that become necessary.

Protection Sleeve — Homemade protection sleeves are made of a thick inside layer of soft cloth and a durable exterior of heavy canvas or old car tire (see illus. 9.8). The sleeve is held out to the attacking dog, who will grab it and then become more vulnerable to blows or the effects of specialized weapons.

Full Protection Suits — Used to train guard and police dogs, these padded suits cover the body from neck to ankle. They can be purchased for several hundred dollars from veterinary and dog training supply houses (like Animal City, PO Box 1076, La Mesa, CA 92041). These are best worn with heavy boots, and a few trainers recommend a motorcycle helmet. They do provide excellent protection from attacking dogs, especially when combined with a protection sleeve that the dog can

9.7

9.8

pull off.

Stun Guns — Where legal, the electronic stun gun can be purchased over-the-counter at pawn shops and some gun shops. The best models discharge over 40,000 volts at an amperage so low that they can be safely used (or so the manufacturers say) on someone wearing a pacemaker. They have a tremendous immobilizing capacity, and are best applied to a dog's nose after he has taken hold of the protection sleeve. *(Editor's note: At the present time, these "stun guns" are being sold legally in Arkansas, and probably in several other states as well.)*

Pepper Sprays — These are far more effective on dogs than tear gas (which is illegal in most states, anyway). The type the postal service uses is available through W.S. Darley & Co., 2000 Anson Drive, Melrose Park, IL 60160. Another brand will soon be available through Bushwacker Backpack and Supply Co., PO Box 4721, Missoula, MT 59806. These sprays contain the active ingredient of red pepper, and are the subject of research for "bear repellents." *Note: to be effective on a dog, the spray must be directed at the eyes. It does no permanent damage.*

If attacked by a guard dog, observe the following procedures: Do not run unless you have a short way to go to safety and a good head start. Dogs can run very fast.

Offer your padded sleeve to the dog. Once he grabs it, use your pepper spray, stun gun, or your booted foot and a club to strike him on the nose, in the throat, or in the abdomen (just below the rib cage).

Shout "NO!!" as loudly as you can as the dog approaches — he may automatically respond to this command by hesitating or stopping. If he stops, command him to "SIT!"

Retreat to safety when possible. Do so at a half-turn so you can keep the protective sleeve between you and the dog.

Most dogs will cease their attack if the victim stands perfectly still for a time varying from a few seconds to a minute. Some have escaped by slipping out of the sleeve and letting the dog have it.

As a last resort, remember that a car or truck can be driven through a chain link fence or gate to rescue someone attacked by a dog.

PURSUIT AND EVASION

Any combination of error and bad luck may find you being pursued by police, security guards or even by a suspicious citizen. Under such circumstances, the best thing you can do is to avoid panic. Your planning should have considered the possibility of pursuit, so you should have some idea of the best place to which to escape. If you must run at night, keep your head down and your arms extended ahead of you to block tree branches or to break your fall. Lift your knees high to step over small obstacles that might otherwise trip you. Stop running as soon as possible and listen for the sounds of pursuit. At night you can sometimes hide and allow pursuers to run past you in the dark. (Do not attempt this ploy if your pursuers are using dogs. For this eventuality, see the section on **Tracking Dogs.**) Whatever you do, don't lead your pursuers directly to where your driver is supposed to pick you up.

Pursuers following your footprints will have a difficult if not impossible task at night. Trackers working cross country at night will be moving slowly enough to allow you to outdistance them. Generally you will want to stay in open areas to allow quick and quiet movement, and need not worry about leaving footprints if being pursued at night.

When moving by day, use roads or hard-packed trails when you can. Stepping on rocks or clumps of grass will leave fewer tracks. Walking on the outside edge of your foot will do the same. Learning to follow tracks yourself will be the best way to learn how to avoid leaving any. (See *The Tracker*, by Tom Brown, Jr.)

Vehicular Pursuit

You may find yourself being pursued when in your vehicle. Again, your pursuer may be a police officer, a private security guard, or a suspicious or irate citizen. Some of these pursuers may be more skilled and/or dangerous than others, but all can be safely eluded by the driver who keeps cool and plans his/her moves.

It is important to remember that a high-speed chase can endanger innocent people, not to mention yourself. This is morally indefensible. Fortunately, simply outrunning the opposition is rarely as successful as outmaneuvering and outthinking it.

We were once actually pursued by an enraged citizen on some dark country roads. Unfortunately our trusty steed, an ancient automobile, could not go over fifty miles an hour. Our pursuer came howling down on us like a banshee and was fast closing the gap. Since we were unable to outrun him, our survival depended solely on our wits (two halves make a whole). Since our advanced planning had included a study of all the roads within miles of the target, we knew that just over the next rise were several small intersecting side roads. We had to think fast, since the opposition was within thirty seconds of closing with us. As we topped out on the slight rise in the road, we were briefly out of sight of our pursuer. In those precious few seconds, we jammed on the brakes and whipped off onto a side road. We then cut the headlights and coasted along slowly in the dark, using the parking brake to stop since this would avoid signaling our location with a flashy display of brake lights. (See **Vehicle Modifications** earlier in this book.)

Our pursuer roared past moments later, in hot pursuit of a car that had been well ahead of us on the same road. Once clear, we turned our lights back on and left the area by the back roads.

This tactic can also be used in urban areas, especially if your pursuer never gets close enough to see what your vehicle looks like. A driver can whip into a parking lot or even into the driveway of a house, shut off the lights and engine, and allow the pursuer to pass. Once it's safe, quietly leave the area in the opposite direction.

The trick of this and other types of evasion is getting out of sight of your pursuer. This can be accomplished by jinking and turning in and out of sidestreets and alleys. We have used this type of evasive maneuvering more than once to evade police cruisers in downtown business areas.

Those who try to rely on speed alone to outrun police often find that they can't outrun the radios that are used to set up roadblocks and alert interceptors.

In rural areas, forest and range roads may provide concealment. If you think you have thrown your pursuer off the track, this may be a good time to rid yourself of any incriminating evidence. But don't just drive to the end of the road and then walk off into the forest or desert to bury the goods. A moderately experienced tracker can detect what you've done after a brief examination. Instead, stop at some random point along the road, preferably at a spot where rocks, hard ground or a thick bed of pine needles might obscure your footprints. Make sure that nothing you dispose of could carry your fingerprints. Burn all papers, maps, etc. (Obviously, if you think a pursuer is still somewhere in the vicinity, starting a fire may be the *last* thing you want to do). After disposing of the incriminating material, leave the area and play dumb if questioned.

It might not be a bad idea to always carry some camping gear in your vehicle. If forced to hide out on a remote backroad, you can set up camp and pretend to be camping should any police inquire. If you are forced to take this approach, pay attention to details of your alibi. For example, don't say that you've been camping for a week if you have only one or two fire's worth of ashes in your firepit.

If you are not discovered, get out your highway or forest map and plot the shortest, safest route out of the county (and possibly the state). Avoid driving through the county seat or other main towns, if possible, as this is where you are most likely to encounter a roving sheriff's deputy. Under dire circumstances, you may want to arrange for only the driver to leave the area, and have a second vehicle, unknown to the police, come later to pick up the rest of the team at a pre-selected rendezvous site.

Self Defense

One of the most serious dangers faced by monkeywrenchers is the very real possibility of being assaulted by security guards (or more likely, by miners, ranchers, loggers and other assorted yahoos) should the ecoteur be unfortunate enough to be apprehended in the midst of an operation. Should you come unexpectedly face-to-face with a real or self-appointed guardian of the mindless machine, under circumstances in which no amount of talking is likely to persuade anyone of your innocence, the best policy is to turn and run. (Of course, if you're staring down the barrels of a 12-gauge double at five paces, running might be the *last* thing you should do.) Most of the people on the other side are dreadfully out of shape, and any good monkeywrencher should count it a matter of professional pride to be in top cardiovascular fitness. Being able to run fast, and for several miles *can* save your sweet ass.

There is a readily available tool which can greatly deter a pursuer, should you unexpectedly encounter someone at close range, and which has the definite advantage of not causing any permanent injury. This is a small, hand-held, battery-powered strobe light (normally used for taking flash photos). Select a unit that will flash at a very rapid rate. Note: This unit should be purchased unobtrusively. Perhaps the best place to purchase it would be through a large discount house or catalog showroom.

A short strap or cord will allow you to hang the strobe unit around your neck or secure it to your wrist for ready deployment. If the trigger button of the strobe is exposed and easily depressed, use a thick, hard adhesive to build up, layer by layer, a protective ring around it. The ring should allow your gloved finger to reach the button, yet should protect the button from accidental discharge (as, for example, might happen should you be forced to lay down on top of the unit).

The strobe unit can be used on daring daylight raids to distract and temporarily blind prospective witnesses, but is most effective at night. Practice with the unit before taking it on operations. The last thing you want to have happen with this unit is to trip it accidentally and reveal your presence.

When using the strobe at night, flash it several times at the guard or other individual who steps around the corner or pops up from behind a bulldozer to surprise you both. *Remember,* close your own eyes when activating the flash, or you will lose your own night vision. Hold the light out at arm's length out to the side. After a few flashes, turn away and *run like hell.*

If your flash unit can be set to repeatedly flash automatically, it can be left behind to distract pursuers. Lay the unit on the ground or roll it to the side before running. Don't do this unless you're sure that there are no fingerprints on the unit or on the batteries inside.

Do not attempt to use the flash unit if you are looking down the business end of a gun barrel. A sudden move on your part might cause a nervous guard to pull the trigger in panic.

Other devices may be of benefit in deterring pursuit. Some individuals suggest the use of tear gas sprays. While these devices may be effective under certain circumstances, and will not cause permanent injury, their mere possession is a *felony* in many states, and their use by a monkey-wrencher would probably be construed as an assault. If one nevertheless decides a spray device is useful, be advised that the large units designed for use by law enforcement personnel are the only reliable ones, and that the small purse and keychain size devices may be ineffective. Some have suggested tear gas sprays be carried only for use against dogs, but even in this case you would be violating the statutes against possession, and pepper sprays are more effective.

All in all, the best self defense is to be prepared, and to avoid sudden surprises. A carefully prepared escape plan (including alternate times and locations for meeting with other team members or drivers), and a pair of good, strong legs will do more for insuring your continued freedom than any other factor.

Cross-Country Evasion

Occasionally, problems of transportation or terrain may necessitate long cross-country travel in the course of a mission. As with the more conventional short-range mission (where foot travel is limited to a mile or two at most), the emphasis should be on spending the minimum amount of time necessary on the ground. To speed up your travel, you should consider the possibility of using cross-country skis in winter, and "mountain bikes" in other seasons. Hiking can of course be hastened by using back roads or foot trails. All of these methods carry an increased danger, since you may come onto searchers too suddenly to take evasive action. Because of this, it is often best to stash your tools in a spot where they can be easily located and recovered at a later date. Also, it is important to change your footwear, since searchers may have photos or diagrams of footprints to match up to the footgear of suspects. In the event you are stopped for questioning and searched, your "mission" shoes should be concealed inside a pack, and should be further concealed inside a bag. This may prevent a searching officer from being able to claim he was searching you for a weapon (as they can legally do) and just stumbled upon the shoes. In a real pinch, you can claim to have found the shoes discarded alongside the trail. You tried them on for a fit, and decided to keep them.

The legal latitude given police to search backpacks is not clearly defined, but court rulings have made it clear that a tent is not considered a dwelling, and no warrant is required to search it. The same probably applies to backpacks. Regardless, you should always state clearly that you do not consent to a search, although you should never attempt to physically interfere with one.

There are two types of search a monkeywrencher might encounter:

Conventional Search

Here the officer responding to a call or complaint searches the area quickly to see if any suspects are present. The police canine unit consisting of an officer and a trained police dog are highly effective at this. The responding officer and others may also cruise adjacent roads looking for suspicious activity, parked cars, or cars cruising slowly through the area.

The best way to avoid this type of search is to leave the target area immediately after the mission. At the time of the pick-up or shortly thereafter, all tools and incriminating items are to be stored in the trunk, camper shell or similar location where they cannot be readily discovered by an unscrupulous officer inventing "probable cause" to search your vehicle. As always, you should have a good story for being in the area (even it it's something simple like "just out partying"). The story must be extremely short and simple. All members of the team must know it. Even on a roadside stop, officers sometimes split up the suspects and question them separately to look for differences in their stories. Keep your story short and simple and you won't slip up. If pressed, repeat the same answers over and over.

Intensive Search

An intensive search may be mounted if the authorities believe that the crime is serious enough to warrant it, and that the suspects might still be in the area. There are a number of search methods which might be employed:

AERIAL SEARCH — Both helicopters and light planes can be used in conjunction with the search methods described below. Search aircraft are not very effective at finding you if you observe basic precautions. If you hear or see an aircraft, conceal yourself immediately until you can determine its purpose by observation. Do *not* look directly at the aircraft if it is close. An upturned face is often very visible, especially against a dark background. Since movement also increases detectibility, remain still.

The best way to hide from aircraft is to remain in shadows. On bright, sunlit days, the harsh contrast between light and shadow make it extremely difficult for searchers to see into shadowed areas. The reverse is also true, and the airborne searcher is considerably more effective on cloudy or overcast days, and during the brief daylight time before sunrise and after sunset.

Lying down can expose more surface to the eyes of an observer flying overhead, so its usually better to crouch or sit down. Don't panic if a search aircraft passes directly overhead. Most aircraft have a blind spot directly beneath them.

Lying under a camouflage tarp (or white sheet on snow-covered ground) can render you essentially invisible to spotters in an aircraft. Beware of your visible tracks leading such airborne searchers to you under such camouflaged cover.

CORDON —In this situation, authorities may set up roadblocks to check cars leaving an area (this method is usually employed when the suspects are thought to be armed). By extension, authorities might apply this method to the backcountry by posting officers or rangers at trailheads leading out of the area in which the suspects are thought to be. The way to deal with this problem is to avoid using major trails, especially when getting within a mile or so of a road or trailhead. If you are "clean," you might try to bluff your way through, although even if the authorities let you pass, you should recognize that they will probably make a record of your presence.

SCRATCH SEARCH —In this method, small teams of searchers check only the most likely spots. Major trails, cabins and the like are obvious choices. Search planning is usually based on the principle that the person for whom they are searching will move downhill. Avoid this type of search by staying away from obvious landmarks, campgrounds, major springs, old cabins, mines and caves.

SURVEY SEARCH — This type of search is designed to cover large areas quickly with aircraft, jeep patrols and horseback patrols. Officers may be in uniform, but bear in mind that they are just as likely to be in plainclothes, attempting to look like ranchers, hunters, fishermen and the like. Staying off major trails and roads will help one to avoid this type of search. Be careful that you are not observed *from* a road. If you must cross a road, do so at a low spot or at a bend where you can not be observed from any great distance. While crossing the road, move slowly, erasing your tracks carefully behind you (see **Tracking Search** below). Remember that searchers might stop on a high point and use binoculars to scan the surrounding terrain.

SATURATION SEARCH — This is a highly intensive search method which usually involves moving a line of searchers back and forth through an area. This method is not commonly used because it requires a lot of people. It *is* sometimes used to search the immediate crime scene for physical evidence. Keeping your tools in pouches and on lanyards prevents accidental loss and possible recovery by police during such a search.

TRACKING SEARCH — This method uses both human and dog trackers. Capable human trackers are rare. Still, some sheriff's departments and search-and-rescue outfits do have semi-experienced trackers on call. The best way to avoid a tracker is through speed and changes in direction. It's difficult enough for a tracker to keep up with, much less overtake, someone walking at a normal pace. The tracker usually hopes to catch up with the poorly-conditioned subject who is taking a break or camping overnight. Also, trackers often attempt to determine the general direction of movement and radio ahead for other teams to intercept the suspect along the trail or at road crossings.

Practice walking in ways that leave minimal tracks. You will learn that stepping on rocks, gravelly areas and small clumps of grass makes tracks difficult to spot. On soft soils, walk slowly, putting your entire sole down at once and lifting it in the same way. Most tracks leave distinct impressions when the weight is concentrated on the small surface area of toes or heel. Forget about walking backwards to deceive a tracker, as this only fools a rank amateur.

In areas where you cannot avoid leaving tracks, like the soft dirt in a road, erase your tracks as you go. Do not erase them with wide, sweeping actions, since this makes your trail all the more obvious. Carefully use your hand to brush out your tracks one at a time.

If you will be moving cross-country for some length of time (say, eight hours or more) be careful not to leave too clear a trail nearest the target. The beginning of your trail will be used to indicate the direction in which searchers will concentrate their efforts. If possible, leave the target at right angles, or in the direction opposite to the one in which you eventually intend to travel. Circle back later, avoiding major trails that might be checked in the immediate area.

TRACKING DOGS — Tracking dogs are probably more likely to be used in an intensive search than are human trackers. While a well-trained tracking dog can be a difficult adversary, they too have differing levels of ability. As with human trackers, the best principle with dogs is to move fast and outdistance the pursuit. Tracking dogs have three basic abilities:

1) They can follow scent on the ground, both fresh human scent (in the first few hours, usually) and the scent of crushed vegetation and disturbed soil (which lingers much longer).

2) They can follow scent trails in the air. Airborne scent lingers on calm days, and settles in low spots like ditches.

3) Tracking dogs can distinguish the scent left by different individuals. For example, a tool dropped at the scene can be matched to a specific individual in a line-up. For this reason (and others) we try not to leave tools and such at the scene.

Most dogs can follow a trail that is less than 24 hours old (the record is over 100 hours). Here are a few methods which will make things difficult for a tracking dog:

*Leave the target area by moving through a spot that is likely to be "contaminated" by the first people to arrive at work in the morning.

When other scent trails are laid on top of yours, the dog often doesn't know which scent trail to follow.

*Be careful not to drop any articles like clothing or tools. If you must get rid of incriminating items, toss them far off your trail, preferably into thick brush, deep water or off the top of a cliff.

*Walk on roads (if safe) where the smells left by passing cars will both disperse and mask your scent trail.

*Travel in exposed, windy areas (if safe), where the scent will be dispersed by the wind.

*Walk in areas that will get direct sunlight. Direct sun kills the bacteria that produce scent. Tracking dogs have been known to track people by skipping from one shady area to another, the sunlight having destroyed the scent in between.

*Dry sand and gravel have little bacteria to enhance the scent trail. Conversely, rich humus and thick vegetation provide ideal conditions for the tracking dog.

*The back trail can be contaminated with red pepper and pepper sprays (such as the postal service uses), and gasoline. Dust is also bad for the dog's nose, causing fatigue. The French Resistance reportedly used to scatter cocaine to foil tracking dogs (presumably it deadened their sense of smell) but this method is probably too expensive for anyone except movie stars and rock musicians.

*Walk on the upwind side of cactus and rough ground that can injure the dog's feet and slow it down. In summer, walk through fields of seed-bearing grass (like foxtail) that will cling to your clothing. They will work into a dog's paws and possibly force the handler to abandon the trail.

*Change directions at a sharp angle, ideally an acute angle back in the direction from which you came. Change directions on sections of easy trail or downhill stretches where the dog's speed and momentum will cause it to overshoot the turn. Though the dog will likely find the turn, the handler may lose some confidence in the dog. If possible, change directions by walking with the wind. In this way, the wind will not carry your airborne scent back to your old trail.

*Before changing directions, walk about in a small area, crossing and crisscrossing your trail. Imagine the confused look on the dog handler's face as the dog dashes to and fro. The dog may be following your trail, but the handler may think the dog has lost the trail and is casting about for a fresh scent. Repeat this procedure each time you change direction. Eventually, the average handler will assume the dog has lost the trail and may terminate the search.

ARREST

If, despite all of your precautions, you nevertheless happen to fall into the hands of the police, try to remain calm and collected. What you say at this point may well make the difference between your being freed or being indicted for a criminal offense and possibly convicted and later imprisoned.

The basic principle to observe when dealing with police is to be polite. An angry cop will go out of his way to make life difficult for you. However, being polite does not mean that you necessarily have to acquiesce in everything that the cop wants. Don't be intimidated by the uniform and gun. Never (if you still have any say about it) consent to a search of your person or vehicle. When asked, politely but firmly say "no."

Most police are well aware of how intimidating their presence can be. They know that putting someone in handcuffs or driving them "downtown" is sometimes all that it takes to make a suspect cooperate fully in incriminating himself/herself. The shock of arrest, isolation from friends and family, and well practiced questioning are all designed to force the suspect's cooperation, confession and the implication of others.

If you are arrested, do not talk to police until you have talked with your lawyer. You will be read your "Miranda" rights only if police officers wish to question you. Do not be lulled into casual conversation since this is a standard method for lowering a suspect's defenses and causing a slip of the tongue. Your only safe answer to questioning is to politely tell the police that you have nothing to say until you have talked to a lawyer. Then say nothing, *not even small talk*. This measure alone may spare you from later conviction.

Don't believe the cops if they say it's too late at night to get a lawyer. You can call one or else have one appointed when the courts open in the morning.

Watch out for the "nice" cop who wishes you would cooperate for your own good. His partner will often come on with the "tough guy" approach to make the "nice" cop seem friendlier still. Another classic ploy is to tell you that "we know everything, anyway." If the police really knew everything, they wouldn't waste time asking you questions. Sometimes the police will reveal a few bits of information and tell you that they are only trying to fill in "a few minor details."

Perhaps the most common ploy is to tell you that it will all go easier for you if you cooperate. In reality, your cooperation will only make it easier for them to convict *you*. Never forget that the interrogating officer is a trained professional, in his own element, and that you are out of yours. If you try to talk your way out of trouble, you will probably only make it worse. Say *nothing* until you've seen a lawyer.

Even should you slip up and reveal something damaging to the police, you are under no obligation to continue talking or answering questions. In such an instance, when you come to your senses, stop talking immediately.

Before undertaking serious monkeywrenching, it might be advisable to read up on a few pertinent points of law. A book well worth reading is *The Outlaw's Bible,* by E. X. Boozhie (Available from Circle A Publishers, 8608 E. Hubbell, Scottsdale, AZ 85257 — $12.95 postpaid). It tells you how a few extra precautions may maximize the protection of your "constitutional rights," something most people take for granted until it is too late.

MEDIA RELATIONS

Although the secrecy so essential to monkeywrenching generally dictates against contacting outsiders about clandestine activities, it may on occasion become necessary to communicate with governmental bodies, target industries or the media. Keep in mind that all of these contacts will be reported to the police, who will run down every lead in their efforts to identify and arrest you. At any face-to-face meeting with media representatives, there may be plainclothes police officers masquerading as reporters. Any written messages, even the envelopes they come in, will be chemically treated in the crime lab to reveal fingerprints. Any handwriting samples will be carefully filed and compared with samples of every suspect's handwriting. Telephone calls may be tape recorded, and valuable voiceprint evidence may be obtained this way. *All* telephone calls to police agencies are routinely tape-recorded.

When dealing with the press or other media, never assume that they are interested in impartially presenting the facts to the reading or viewing public. Some news people will gladly turn you in to the police. Others, whose code of professional conduct will not allow active cooperation with the police, will nevertheless not hesitate to fabricate lies, distort truths and seek out anyone who will provide a derogatory quote about your actions, if that will make a more sensational story. The truly impartial reporter/newscaster is unfortunately rather rare, and must be treated with care. (Nonetheless, there certainly are friendly, supportive or professionally ethical reporters.) *Never* lie to the press. You should also be careful never to give out information to the press which might reveal your identity, numbers or intended actions. If asked revealing questions, politely explain that you cannot answer that question. When in doubt, leave it out.

The four basic forms of contact with the press and others, in descending order of security, are: communiques, telephone contacts, photographs and personal interviews.

Communiques

Never write a communique by hand. Anything you may do to disguise your handwriting can be nullified by an experienced handwriting analyst. It is much safer to use a typewriter (preferably a rented one), or better still, the classic method of cutting words out of the newspaper and pasting them up on a sheet of paper to make your message. Don't make the mistake of leaving the chopped-up newspaper in plain view or throwing it in the trash where police can easily (and legally) retrieve it. Take it out somewhere and burn it.

If you choose to use a rental typewriter, there are a number of places where they are available. Libraries may be the best place, as you may be able to work in a carrel which provides a bit of privacy. Some of the more sophisticated printing/photocopying establishments may also have rental typewriters. If you have to type in a public place, be sure to "bury" your message inside an innocent-looking text, in case someone looks over your shoulder. You can later cut out the text, paste it together, and photocopy it under more secure conditions.

Do not deliver the original. You may have accidentally touched the paper and left fingerprints that can be revealed through chemical fuming in the laboratory. Another drawback is that a typewritten original (and possibly even a clear copy) can be linked to the exact typewriter that produced it. (It is particularly important not to deliver the original if you use the classic method of cutting words out of a newspaper and pasting them on a sheet to make your message.)

To increase the level of security for your written communiques, photocopy the original and deliver only the copies. Use only a photocopy machine whose location or amount of use makes it unlikely that someone will accidentally observe what you're doing. If you are copying something incriminating and someone walks up before you are through, calmly stand so as to block their view, or else gather up your materials and leave. You can always come back later. Copying machines are common, and are now found in libraries, post offices and supermarkets, so finding a suitable one should be no problem. *Note: Don't use a copying machine where you are known, one near your residence or place of employment, or repeatedly use the same copying machine. While it is not yet a commonly known fact, it is sometimes possible to trace a copy to the exact machine which produced it, due to irregularities in the glass, etc. We have further heard that copy machines may leave some other kind of built-in identifying characteristic on photocopies that can be traced to the specific machine.*

When copying a communique, run off several copies. When you are finished, pick up the copies by handling only the outside sheets. Slip them in a folder or large envelope, and later (with gloves on) destroy the outside copies you touched and never handle with naked hands the copies you intend to send. *Do not forget to pick up your original* before leaving the copy machine. If you fail to do this, somebody is likely to get quite a surprise!

The importance of taking precautions to avoid leaving fingerprints on both message and envelope cannot be overstressed. Recently a gang

ECODEFENSE

of arsonists in Boston were caught because *part* of a single fingerprint was uncovered by the crime lab on the *inside* (gummed portion) of a postage stamp on an envelope used to send a bragging message to the authorities.

If the copy machine that you are using has an adjustment for lightness and darkness, set it as light as possible while still allowing the message to be readable. This is especially helpful in disguising the origin of a typewritten original. It also may be useful to make a copy, photocopy that copy and then photocopy *that* copy to make a poorly reproduced copy that will mask the identifying marks of the typewriter used.

Delivering a communique can be dangerous, and should be well planned in advance. If your message could be construed as threatening in any way, you should avoid the use of the U.S. Mail, as this may needlessly violate Federal law. However, if you are simply sending a matter-of-fact statement of some action that has already occurred, you are probably not incurring any additional legal penalty. Certainly, using the mail simplifies delivery of a communique.

If you choose *not* to use the mail, there are a number of ways of delivering your message. You might tape your message to a door or bulldozer. Again, be careful to wear gloves and leave no prints on paper or tape. For delivery to the press, you might leave your communique in a remote location, such as in a phone book in a phone booth, taped to the bottom of a garbage can, or in any number of locations. Once away from the area, you can call the newsroom at the newspaper or TV station and briefly tell the person who answers where your message can be found. Ask them to repeat your directions. Don't forget that any communique which you deliver to the press will be photocopied by them before being passed on to the police.

If you choose to mail your communique, make sure that the envelope, as well as its contents, have no fingerprints or other distinctive identifying characteristics. You might type the address ahead of time on a sheet of paper with a rented typewriter. Later, xerox the address sheet as described above as a precaution against leaving fingerprints. When you are ready to send your communique, you can cut out the address and glue it on an envelope you have pulled from the middle of a package of envelopes, wearing gloves during this process. (Wearing gloves while using the rental typewriter would eliminate the necessity of using glue, but if someone were to observe you so attired they might become suspicious.) Once you have your envelope addressed and sealed, ready for mailing *(be careful with the postage stamps — fingerprints!)*, place it inside another envelope for carrying until you are able to mail it. Always use a sponge to moisten stamps or envelope flaps — saliva can be identified as to blood type. When you are ready for mailing, take the inner envelope out (wearing gloves, of course) and drop it unobtrusively in a mail box far from your usual haunts. If you are operating in a rural area or small town, you should mail communiques from some nearby large city, so as not to tip off your location.

Telephone Contacts

All telephone contacts must be kept to a minimum, whether with press or others. Phone calls may be tape-recorded (even though you may request press not to do so, you can never be completely confident that they will honor your request). Phone calls can also be traced, should the authorities be listening. In the past tracing calls took at least several minutes, but the technology for this is improving. Some big-city police departments are installing computerized systems which have the potential to trace calls almost instantaneously (911 systems, for example).

For your own security when using the telephone, *only* use pay phones, and even then make your call as brief as possible. For added security, call the reporter/newscaster and instruct them to go to a specified pay phone, where you will call them within a specified time. Then call them from yet another pay phone. Get to the point right away and get off the phone.

Personal Interviews

A direct meeting with reporters is one of the most dangerous contacts a monkeywrencher can make. However, such an interview can be highly advantageous in getting your message across. The notorious ecoteur "The Fox" was once interviewed by Chicago's popular columnist Mike Ryoko with considerable advantageous publicity resulting.

If you do decide to take the risk of a direct meeting with media personnel, take certain precautions. First, direct the reporter (or other media person) to a phone booth to await further instructions. Then have him/her go to yet another phone for *more* directions. In the meantime, have someone observe the reporter to make sure that he/she is not being followed, knowingly or unknowingly, by undercover police. Do not attempt to follow the reporter in your car, because if the police do have him/her under surveillance, their trained eyes will probably pick you out. If you think it is safe, finally direct the reporter to a remote rural location which gives you multiple avenues of escape. Hold the interview at sunset since the oncoming night will conceal your withdrawal from the area. Always wear mask and gloves to protect your identity. Don't even let your hair show, as this will tell an observant reporter more about you than is necessary. Make sure that you have someone concealed nearby to provide you with backup security. Never allow more than one newsperson at an interview.

Sometimes it is possible to arrange a spur of the moment interview at night. Make sure that you are familiar with the terrain in the event that something goes wrong and you must escape into the darkness. If TV lights or camera flash is used, save them until the end of the interview as they will likely draw unwanted attention.

Photographs

Photographs of actions, delivered to the press, can be an excellent method of gaining media attention. Since photos can also convey information to the police, make sure that there is nothing in the picture that can be traced to you. It is probably wiser not to have people in such a photo, but if you do, everyone must be well-disguised and lack distinctive clothing. Anything else in the photo must be of common manufacture and widely available.

If you do not have your own secure darkroom facilities for processing and printing, it is recommended that you stick to Polaroid-type film only. Never entrust film from illegal actions to commercial labs. Many people have been busted for a variety of offenses after being turned in by a photo lab's quality control inspector or some "friendly" drugstore clerk. *Destroy* extra photos and negatives, and resist the temptation to start a scrapbook. Photos constitute some of the most incriminating evidence imaginable. In England, saboteurs who attacked the grave/shrine of foxhunter John Peel were undone by a random license plate check that led to a search warrant that turned up a mere one-half of a negative that the photographer was unable to destroy in time. This scrap of evidence led to further investigation which ultimately put the saboteurs in prison.

NO EVIDENCE

After any act of ecotage, it is essential that there be no evidence —
in your possession or at the site of the action — which could link you
to the "crime." The basic principles for eliminating all evidence which
might lead to your arrest are:

1) Don't leave anything at the site that can be connected with you.

2) Don't take anything away with you that can be connected with
the site.

More specific suggestions include the following:

Wear coveralls or common work clothes. Should a button or another
fragment from practical clothing of this type be lost on the site, it
would be unlikely to arouse suspicion. Use common work gloves, such
as cheap cotton ones.

Minimize what you wear and take with you onto the site. The less
you carry with you, the less likely you are to drop something which
might later be used as evidence.

Remove fingerprints from everything on your person before you enter
the site — even such internal parts as flashlight lens, bulb, and batteries;
radio batteries; and the insides of cases and tool boxes. Authorities will
fingerprint any possible piece of evidence they find, in every conceivable
place you could leave a fingerprint.

Don't leave footprints. Wear common work boots or shoes. Cover
them with a cloth bag or wrap to blank-out the sole. Cotton duck
canvas and burlap work well for this, and are easily disposed of.

Don't leave tire tracks. Used a common brand, size, and style of
tire. Avoid damp or muddy ground. Generally, if you stay on compacted
roads that site workers use, tire tracks shouldn't be much problem. If
you must drive where tracks will be conspicuous, sweep with a branch
or broom; or drag a large branch tied in such a way that it can be
released quickly while driving. This last technique is often ineffective
on wet ground.

Use top-quality tools. Tools that break cause injury and leave evidence.
Use common US brands such as Proto, Thorsen, Challenger, Utica,
Bonney, Wright, Snap-On, New Britain, SK, Diamond, Ridgid, H.K.
Porter, Channellock, Craftsman, etc. Avoid tools made in Taiwan or
Hong Kong.

Dress-up the working surfaces of tools like wrenches and bolt-cutters
which leave distinctive marks with a stone or file after use. Better yet,

remove the broken bolts, nuts, chain link pieces, and other fragments of metal which you have cut; discard them off site.

Anything written should be either innocuous or coded. It's safest never to write anything related to the action.

Use deliberate "false evidence" with great care, if at all. If no real evidence is left behind, the scattering of false evidence is a waste of time. It can also backfire and/or get innocent persons in trouble.

Remove dirt, grease, oil, paint, etc. from tools and clothes as soon as possible. Use an ultraviolet light to check for special marker dyes. If you suspect a special marker dye, dispose of the article. Clean tools of plating chips or paint chips before and after the action. (Remember that if you worked on your green car yesterday with the same wrench, and if you leave the green paint on the bulldozer or have yellow bulldozer paint on your wrench, it may be incriminating.)

Think. The length of your step is evidence. Your blood is evidence. Watch for infrared cameras or any strange electronic equipment. Don't photo-document your action (surprisingly, some people do!), and never tell anyone who doesn't need to know.

Avoid creating suspicion in the first place. Act normal. Use clothing and equipment that have other legitimate uses. Don't hide anything that wouldn't be hidden under normal circumstances. Use big tool boxes that can be used to hide things in a "legitimate" manner. Prepare your story/alibi in advance.

FIELD NOTES

* Medicine for monkeywrenchers: Ecoteurs have fallen into ditches, scraped knuckles on heavy equipment, cut themselves on glass, and otherwise suffered numerous minor injuries. Usually there is so much adrenaline pumping through your system ,that you are scarcely aware of the injury. You must make it a point to examine the wound at the first safe opportunity. A penlight flashlight can be carefully used for the examination. Each member of the team should carry a dark, clean bandanna to use as a bandage.

* Disposing of tools: *Never* bury tools used in ecotage on your own land or that owned by friends or associates. Police agencies are experienced in the use of metal detectors to uncover buried caches. Metal detectors çan be thrown off, nevertheless, by burying metal tools in old landfills that have other metal present or by scattering nails and scrap metal through the soil where you do bury your "monkeywrenches."

* Water: Monkeywrenching can be hot, dry work. Keep a water jug in your vehicle. If you carry a canteen on your person, remember that a partially full canteen can make a loud sloshing noise. If you're traveling at night under strict security precautions, you should drink all of the water in your canteen or pour out the remainder when you first drink in order to keep it from sloshing and revealing your position.

*Psychology: Learn to play your hunches and be aware of subtle feelings. Life in the underground sharpens the senses to the point where you can develop a protective "sixth sense" that defies rational explanation. Dreams and "feelings" with no basis in fact or observation have saved many an outlaw or monkeywrencher from arrest. Nevertheless, under no circumstances should you allow this to become a substitute for proper planning and preparation. On the other extreme, make sure that neither you nor your associates slips into paranoia. If fears and pressures seem to be mounting, take a vacation.

Another type of behavior for which to be on alert, particularly among experienced operatives, is euphoria. This energetic, go-getting, "nothing-can-stop-me-now" attitude almost inevitably follows periods of depression. The pattern will be acted out by even the most highly motivated individuals after prolonged exposure to danger. First comes a slow, creeping depression when the individual loses enthusiasm and begins to question his or her basic motivation. It begins to seem as though nothing will ever change for the better, regardless of what one may do. After a few days or weeks, the mind snaps out of this way of thinking but then overcompensates by making the individual feel invincible. This is euphoria. Locked in its heady grip, experienced monkeywrenchers have been known to charge forward without taking even elementary security precautions. This is a dangerous state of mind, and team leaders, in their coordinating role, must remain on the alert for it (even in themselves!). The solitary Earth defender must carefully evaluate her or his own moods. A break or vacation will help to restore proper balance.

*Keep in mind that police, Forest Service and other government agencies, and industrial security specialists will study this book in the hope of developing countermeasures. Be thoughtful and inventive. Do not leave this book lying around your home or car in plain view.

* If you have suggestive bumperstickers on your car, you can cover them with masking tape and duct tape while "on the job" or visiting unfriendly towns like Escalante, Utah. Cover your sticker with masking tape first, then cover the masking tape with duct tape. The masking tape will protect your bumpersticker from being peeled off or torn when the duct tape is pulled off. When your need for maintaining a low profile is over, simply peel off the duct tape and there is your bumpersticker proclaiming its message to the world.

*Regardless of what you are doing, or where you are operating, re-member that your abilities are cumulative and only acquired through experience. The prospective monkeywrencher should read and re-read pertinent sections of this volume before attempting an actual operation. It is then recommended that one start with simple tasks and easy targets, and only gradually work one's way up to major monkeywrenching.

*Power tools, chainsaws and oxy-acetylene or propane torches all bear serial numbers (sometimes not readily apparent). A tool such as these dropped at the scene of a hit can be traced from the manufacturer to the retailer who sold it. There must be no paper trail linking you to the tool purchase.

*In all of your monkeywrenching endeavors, do not be afraid to constantly experiment, improvise and practice your techniques. Monkey-wrenching is a highly creative field in the fight to preserve wild country. Use your imagination!

*When driving in rough country or on jeep trails, try not to leave evidence in passing. If you scrape a rock, the paint chips you leave can be compared to the FBI's National Automotive Paint File to determine the year and make of your vehicle. Also, grease smears rubbed off on the high-centers of such roads can sometimes be linked to the remaining crud on the undercarriage of your vehicle. Whenever you leave such a sign, stop to brush it away.

*Get a black, dark green or camouflage fanny pack and fill it with basic survival gear (space blanket, matches, candle, candy, pocket knife, first aid kit, small flashlight, etc). Strap it around your waist as soon as you leave your vehicle for operations such as tree-spiking in the woods. Do not remove it. In case you are confronted by Forest Service law enforcement agents or deputies, you can high-tail it through the woods to escape and be sure that you have the minimum survival requirements on your person to get back to safety even if you have to spend several days in the backcountry.

HELP!

ECODEFENSE: A Field Guide to Monkeywrenching is a continuing project. Revised editions will be published every 12 to 18 months. We hope to include additional material and techniques, revised and improved material, new field notes, and additional illustrations and photographs.

We encourage users of this manual to send us their field-tested suggestions for improving the information contained in **ECODEFENSE** as well as new material.

We *do not* want to know your name or address and your correspondence will be burned after we extract the information. It will be good practice to use the guidelines for contacting the media contained in the **Security** chapter for communication with us as well.

We also would appreciate clippings about monkeywrenching in any form. Please indicate the date and name of the newspaper on any clippings you send us.

Please send all material to:

Ned Ludd Books
POB 5871
Tucson, AZ 85703